Voices from the Great War Women's Land Army

Voices from the Great War Women's Land Army

Helen Frost

Pen & Sword
MILITARY
AN IMPRINT OF PEN & SWORD BOOKS LTD.
YORKSHIRE - PHILADELPHIA

First published in Great Britain in 2024 by
Pen & Sword Military
An imprint of
Pen & Sword Books Ltd
Yorkshire - Philadelphia

Copyright © Helen Frost, 2024

ISBN 978 1 03610 783 3

The right of Helen Frost to be identified as the Author of this work has been asserted by her in accordance with the Copyright, Designs and Patents Act 1988.

A CIP catalogue record for this book is available from the British Library.

All rights reserved. No part of this book may be reproduced or transmitted in any form or by any means, electronic or mechanical, including photocopying, recording or by any information storage and retrieval system, without permission from the Publisher in writing.

Typeset in INDIA by IMPEC eSolutions
Printed and bound in England by CPI (UK) Ltd.

Pen & Sword Books Ltd. incorporates the Imprints of Pen & Sword Archaeology, Atlas, Aviation, Battleground, Discovery, Family History, History, Maritime, Military, Naval, Politics, Railways, Select, Transport, True Crime, Fiction, Frontline Books, Leo Cooper, Praetorian Press, Seaforth Publishing, Wharncliffe and White Owl.

For a complete list of Pen & Sword titles please contact

PEN & SWORD BOOKS LIMITED
47 Church Street, Barnsley, South Yorkshire, S70 2AS, England
E-mail: enquiries@pen-and-sword.co.uk
Website: www.pen-and-sword.co.uk

or

PEN AND SWORD BOOKS
1950 Lawrence Rd, Havertown, PA 19083, USA
E-mail: uspen-and-sword@casematepublishers.com
Website: www.penandswordbooks.com

Contents

Acknowledgements		vi
Preface		vii
Introduction		x
Chapter 1	Adequate replacements	1
Chapter 2	The awakened women	12
Chapter 3	Pluck and patriotism	20
Chapter 4	Strength in unity	37
Chapter 5	Infra dig!	44
Chapter 6	The picturesque garb	54
Chapter 7	Billets from hell	63
Chapter 8	Wasp stings and weary heads!	79
Chapter 9	Quirks, oddities and curiosities!	93
Chapter 10	Unshakeable camaraderie	100
Chapter 11	Farmerettes and friends	125
Chapter 12	Royal approval	130
Chapter 13	An epidemic of marriages!	135
Chapter 14	Misbehaving Misses!	139
Chapter 15	Respect and recognition	158
Chapter 16	Self-sacrificing service: The Land Girl Roll of Honour.	192
Chapter 17	Demobbed and beyond: Carry on. Hold on. Look on.	211
Epilogue		215
Bibliography		217
Notes		220
Index		232

Acknowledgements

I am immensely grateful to Great War historian and author Richard Van Emden for his sound advice and continued support throughout the seven years I have spent writing this book. Thank you Richard.

My sincerest thanks goes to the Archivist of St Hilda's College, Oxford, Oliver Mahony who made it possible for me to visit St Hilda's College for my research. Oliver has been so helpful, assisting me by sourcing relevant archival material and allowing me to use photographs from certain collections held in the archives at St Hilda's in this book.

In particular, I would like to thank the Archives Officer and Archivist at Bristol Archives who went out of their way to assist me with my research.

To those loved ones that have lived and breathed Great War Land Girls every day for more years than I can remember. An enormous thank you. You know who you are! Also to dear friends that have offered encouragement and gone out of their way to help me.

Then there is the tiny village of Brockhall. To me, this place has always had a magical feel to it, even when I was very young. It still feels the same to me today whenever I go there. To discover that students from St Hilda's became Land Girls there for a month during their summer vacation in 1916 made it feel as if writing this book was perhaps meant to be!

My final thank you is to the Land Girls of the Great War who inspire me in some way every day.

You lived not in vain!

Preface

For well over a decade, I have researched the remarkable and very personal stories of landswomen that proudly and voluntarily served their country by joining various land organisations during the early years of the war or by becoming a member of the Women's Land Army in early 1917. Women were drawn to such work first and foremost by the call for emergency help but there were also those who perhaps possessed a curious fascination, (hitherto unrealised) about working on the land.

These women selflessly left behind all that was familiar to them, often without hesitation. They came from the length and breadth of the country, from villages, towns and cities and from every walk of life in order to join the new army of women, serving as 'soldiers of the King' in one of the three sections: Agriculture, The Forage Corps, (the foundations of which were established in 1915 under the auspices of the Army Service Corps) and Forestry and Timber Cutting.

The resolve and determination shown by these women as they admirably served their country during the Great War years was, for the most part, exemplary and in strict accordance with the rules stipulated in the L.A.A.S, (Land Army Agricultural Section) Women's Land Army handbook and yet, despite their selfless service, many stories still remain untold.

The journeys that they made both as individuals and collectively in what was seen at the time as an unorthodox organisation are worthy of detailed scrutiny because they are so unique. Their recollections are a constant source of inspiration; never failing to surprise and affect with their ingenuity, resolve and resourcefulness. Land Girls had a twinkly, irresistible, ever-present sense of humour and an appetite for fun. They possessed an unflinching ability to always look on the bright side no matter what.

I hope that through this book the attitudes and approaches that they showed to their work when faced with such adversity inspire others too more than a century later.

Since the cessation of the First World War, these landswomen and Land Girls have rarely had the spotlight shone upon them and yet their contribution to the war effort was significant. Mention should rightfully be made of the women that worked tirelessly on the land for the same outcomes in countries all over the world.

In 1919, Meriel Talbot, Director of the Women's Branch of the Board of Agriculture and Fisheries stressed how important it would be after demobilisation to continue to remember the contribution that had already been made and that was still to be made by Land Girls who went on to join the National Association of Landswomen when it was formed in January 1920.

The passing of more than a century tells us that sadly this is exactly what happened; their existence as a bona fide organisation in their own right is given a fleeting mention at best and at worst, overlooked and unjustly forgotten.

Not only do the individual stories and enthralling minutiae of their daily lives deserve to be brought to life again but the fervour and energy that encompassed these 'new' women does too. Their stoical nature and dauntless work ethic also deserves to be acknowledged.

Life in any land organisation was by no means an easy or glamorous option and was the least well-paid of all the auxiliary services. This however did not deter many thousands of women of all ages from giving land work a try. Women needed to show resilience and determination in order to prove their worth to farmers; farmers that all too frequently sneered and sniped at the mere thought of having Land Girls on their farms.

These tenacious character traits proved to be a secret weapon in the fight against engrained, societal prejudices, predominantly from men but also from women too. By and large, these prejudices were abraded as the war ground relentlessly on. There simply was no other alternative.

Landswomen, Land Girls, Land Lasses, the Land Ladies, Britain's Iron Maidens and the War Brownies are just a few of the terms used to describe this influential yet modest, (in number as well as character) official, civilian army of women. But, whatever they were called, one thing holds true - these women of all ages left their friends and family behind to fulfil what they felt was their obligation and duty to volunteer for National Service and over time, they proved their worth.

Steady, professional occupations were vacated in order to satisfy the national necessity to serve. Married, unmarried, inexperienced, experienced, naive, worldly-wise, educated, unlearned, wealthy women, privileged women, poorer women, countrywomen and town women all worked towards one common aim as they mixed together in fields, forests and forage depots during the unprecedented years that spanned 1914-1919.

Land Girls as individuals still have a very loud voice. What they have left behind, (whether found in archives, newspapers, on war memorials, on film reels, in personal accounts or on photographs) tells of the pressing need that some felt, quite profoundly to make sure that a record of their service was being left behind. Their own, candid, personal and solid testimony of 'I was there.' Interwoven with my overriding desire to tell the stories of these fascinating women is the deep affection and connection I have always personally felt for the land and countryside. I am drawn to the rich, regional variations in farming and to the village folklore so lovingly and faithfully passed down through countless generations; old traditions, customs and practices, (that reflect a time now long gone) that have all but died out and yet once formed such pivotal moments in the calendar year for everyone that worked on and for those so inextricably linked to the land.

These 'crux' moments united villages, whether it was via long-held customs or via faith - by way of timely church services such as Plough Sunday, Rogation Sunday, Lammastide and Harvest Festival. These services celebrated the fruits of intense spells of effort, labour and the fertility of the land itself, (by way of blessing the soil, seed and of course, the plough).

These services were a constant cyclical reminder to each and every person of the fragility of the preparations required for harvest; the success of which relied upon the right kind of weather at the right times and of course the right amount of labour too.

Farming folklore fashioned an innumerable, glorious-sounding glossary of regional vocabulary all its own and some sayings are still in use today, (although much less commonly and even less so, passed on nowadays). All of these rich veins of agricultural heritage lead ultimately to one point; that being the enormous respect felt for every man, woman and schoolchild that worked so very hard during the Great War to increase food production in some way - no matter how big or small their contribution was.

This of course is especially true for the women who got their hands and themselves dirty for the first time in their lives, becoming in the intervening decades, the unremembered of the Great War.

They were the women that behaved quietly.

Introduction: Mud, filth and clouds!

Without question, Land Girls have left behind many intriguing and humorous stories. A Land Girl's daily life was far from mundane. She came into contact with farmers, bailiffs and foremen every day and interacted with local people both at work and socially too. What was her attitude towards the tasks she was given? What problems did she face in her new life? What was she like as an individual?

The women who joined the Women's Land Army during the Great War were drawn to it from all different backgrounds, from all over Britain to work on the land, in woodland, forests or forage depots. Whatever they opted to do, they each played their part to help stave off the ever-present, persistent threat of food shortages and starvation; a situation that had been exacerbated by underinvestment in farming during the late 19th century and early 20th century along with the successful German U-boat campaign which targeted merchant ships.

Women were recruited from all walks of life and didn't perhaps fully appreciate what they were signing up for. If they were returning to work in the countryside having left it for employment or educational purposes, they would still have been well acquainted with 'the way things were done' and would still know the local farmers in their area. Many would not have forgotten how uninviting working on the land was either!

It was perhaps therefore rather admirable that the call of the land was one they still felt duty-bound to answer; a gut feeling that only somebody deeply connected to the landscape and seasons could even attempt to explain to others not accustomed to the life.

Regardless of the drawbacks and pitfalls, women felt the pull of the land very deeply. It was almost as if it took on human characteristics; it spoke to the women, they heard its voice and they listened to it. It was as if a spell had somehow been cast over them; the effect of which endured, often for the whole of their lives.[1]

Joining a land organisation was life-changing. It would have meant leaving behind stable urban lives and well-paid, secure jobs with good prospects or a more privileged way of life in order to 'do your bit' and opt for a life which comprised of relentless, monotonous manual work instead.

Recognition is much deserved for each woman who made the courageous decision to switch careers. After all, many young women opted for land work, frequently against the wishes of their strict, Edwardian parents, who were horrified at the choice of National Service their daughter had made. For those girls trapped in the drudgery of domestic service, they in effect, took a step down the social ladder to work on the land but reaped the rewards of being able to literally escape and swap an indoor life for an outdoor one.

It is impossible to realise the true extent of the apprehension they must have felt as they moved into the unknown, rather bizarre world of agriculture, forestry or forage. This new world was taken on against the strict constraints of a society which had firmly entrenched ideas of what a woman should 'be' and 'be allowed to do.'

Land Girls needed to be patient or at the very least, learn to be so, especially when learning about the complexities of the land. Patient when trying to understand and unravel the seemingly impenetrable personalities of some country folk or the intricacies of village life and the relationships deeply embedded within in each one. Patience with the weather and the animals they worked so closely with and ultimately, patience with each other as everybody was learning so many new and different things all at the same time.

All the more necessary therefore to not only champion but value and delight in their quiet, unassuming stories of grit and determination. The shifting sands of time mean that so many quirky, unusual facets of their short years of service, whether spent officially in the Women's Land Army or in other land organisations during the Great War have all-but vanished from the public psyche.

Unflinching camaraderie enabled them to navigate a way through the personal family losses experienced by so many Land Girls, who, separated from their families found solace in their peers. What were their opinions and concerns with regard to what was happening around them at the time? What about the Land Girls that went off the rails? How were their misdemeanours dealt with by the Women's Land Army as a respected and upstanding organisation? What happened to Land Girls who fell ill? How were they looked after? Did Land Girls have any bad accidents or sustain serious injuries? How was their devotion to service and gallantry acknowledged and recognised? Did any Land Girls die whilst serving their country? How are they remembered today?

The very sight of seeing women in their standard issue uniforms, carrying out such a variety of dirty jobs might have been a difficult concept for many to fathom or accept in the early days of the organisation's existence, but, regardless of everything, these women did the dirty work that would otherwise have seen languishing, unproductive farms depleted of their younger, male workforce.

They instead quietly got on with it and more than proved themselves as they served their beleaguered nation. They did so much more than roll their collective sleeves up. They thrived on the challenge! Their unique world is explored along with their spirit, inventiveness and taste for fun which fizzes off the page!

Land Girls have unquestionably left behind a distinctive, exceptional and enthralling legacy.

Chapter 1

Adequate replacements

During the Great War years, the daughters of Britain were asked to work with a will and a purpose never before seen. Areas like market gardening saw an influx of women come forward to form a new workforce, (more often than not in the early part of the war as beneficiaries of wealthy patrons or sponsors). Many had joined land organisations from the onset of the Great War in order to serve their nation.

Organisations such as the Women's Farm and Garden Union, the National Political League, the Women's Defence Relief Corps, the Women's Legion, the Women's National Land Service Corps and the National Land Council were up and running well before the Women's Land Army was officially established. They worked hard to get women to volunteer for work on the land from all classes. The realisation was beginning to dawn that food production and the supply of it from overseas was going to become a huge problem if the conflict continued to grind ceaselessly on hence the need to act speedily and plan accordingly.

Their collective ranks never realised high enough numbers to make a massive impact hence why a unified, regulated and coordinated army of women was required in the early months of 1917. Existing members of the WNLSC however were enrolled immediately into the Women's Land Army without having to go through its selection system thus saving precious time. Other recruits had to pass through its enrolment process which, when completed officially, involved providing three references, attending an interview and passing a medical before being provided with the appropriate training.

Having passed the medical and had her references accepted, any new arrival at the newly set up training centres that sprang up around the country would have found herself working in the grounds of the training establishment itself or its immediate environs under the supervision of an instructress, (complete with an assistant).

Here, the work she did, (depending on the individual) may have been graduated with regard to its physical demands so as to allow the woman to build up her strength and hardiness over time. This of course minimised the risk of injury and lowered the chances of new recruits dropping out.

After six weeks of training, the Land Girl was then placed on a farm in the locality or a market garden. It then became the responsibility of the farmer to continue any further training should it be necessary.

Girls of high school age were also taking advantage of schemes run by local War Agricultural Committees whereby they undertook training at a designated centre, after which they were placed on farms or on flax camps.

Lists appeared in newspapers that advertised venues and times for meetings and lectures provided details on the many ways that women could work on the land. The response and subsequent take-up needed to be rapid indeed if the target of ploughing an additional one million acres, (set by the Board of Agriculture) was to be met.

Not all accounts however were positive regarding women workers. Harmful headlines appeared that stated women from the towns were failures on the land. The situation was made worse by the fact that the viewpoints had emanated from county War Agricultural Committees. Sweeping generalisations such as this did little to enthuse farmers that may have been considering employing the new female workers. Also, it was a real blow to the morale of women who were doing well who had come to work on the land from towns and cities.

It was infuriating for those women who were gaining hard-earned respect as it poured fuel onto the fire of the 'old school' farmers. For those that found the thought of employing women workers on their farms as quite hideous, there were also those that viewed the women's efforts as a fad that would soon pass!

For some women, it was a temporary switch but for others it was a decision that had far-reaching, long term effects. In some of the remotest corners of the land, the urgency to take on Land Girls was not as keenly felt as it was in other parts of the country hence these flippant viewpoints lingered in the more untouched, rural backwaters.

Whatever was said, whether favourable or unfavourable, these strangers to the land often left behind established careers as varied as artists, typists and actresses. For others, it was a departure from a pampered and stifled life, devoid of any ambition or wage. Some escaped the drudgery of domestic service and saw joining a land-based organisation as the escape they had only dreamt of.

Most women progressed well in agriculture, forestry or forage, more often than not, excelling in certain aspects, however, 4-6 weeks of training would not produce a polished, well-rounded expert. That was beside the point. The point was that for the women leaving training centres they were at least prepared to some degree for what lay ahead. Inevitably, there was always fall-out and many women didn't succeed as their character proved too lightweight, frivolous or 'flighty' to stick at the grind that stretched before them.

Women brought a melting pot of issues with them. Adolescent girls had mental and physical changes to cope with and manage which was not easy, especially when they were placed in unfamiliar places with strangers; all too often much older men. Acceptance from not just male workers but other female co-workers sadly proved to be one of the greatest hurdles that women had to surmount.

Over time, this hard-earned respect was advantageous as the men would begin to impart ways that were both time and labour-saving. Strong bonds were forged over time and great respect established for those that had spent their whole lives understanding the idiosyncrasies of the land. Often, quiet kindnesses were discreetly carried out by the men that worked alongside the newcomers. Land Girls noted that corrections were sometimes silently made to their work. Mistakes had been rectified without fuss. Something that had inadvertently been forgotten was tactfully pointed out along with encouraging feedback that didn't lay the blame solely at the feet of the Land Girl.

If women struggled with tasks, men would often pitch in and assist without drawing attention to the immediate problem. Long after their service, Land Girls still remembered how these silent acts of thoughtfulness had eased especially hard days and gone a long way to helping them feel part of what was an experienced male workforce. Crucially, they remembered being treated equally.[1]

The magnetism of the land never left the souls of many women who had fought hard initially to resist it. Those that had struggled to fathom it at first wrestled with the hold it eventually came to have on them!

Aside from learning the required skills, what also mattered is that the women possessed character. Grit kept women going when all else failed and women simply had to possess mental mettle in order to endure the tedium of agricultural work.

One 19 year old girl, born and raised in London went to do her training on a large farm. By the end of her three months, not only had she learnt the skills required but she was 'Head Cowman' and moreover, she trained other women to be able to carry out the same work. Proving the doubters wrong was the best way of showing your worth.

Any united female labour force that overtly challenged the social order of the day struggled to get the opportunities it deserved in the early part of the war. Only when the Women's Land Army was officially formed was there finally evidence of a more structured, bonafide emergency organisation; one which finally saw numbers from other land organisations amalgamated into its ranks and trained if necessary into a properly regulated, civilian army of women landworkers.

Women opted for one of three distinct branches. A commitment of either six or 12 months was required depending on which was chosen. There were of course problems with placing women but this was almost inevitable due to prolonged resistance from a) farmers b) male workers that remained in agriculture due to exemption and also c) the request for soldier labour that farmers frequently chose to opt for if it was still available.

Archaic farming machinery had also slowed down the wheels of Britain's agricultural machine – a machine that ran on the narrowest of margins. Over time, mechanisation saved time and improved the acreage of crops being sown. More hours were worked over 7 days which was groundbreaking in itself as working on a Sunday was not commonplace.

Land Girls were provided with basic mechanical instruction and maintenance so that they could ably fix problems if required. Initial prejudice from an engineer at the Harper Adams College in Shropshire was quickly mollified when he saw at first-hand how well the Land Girls worked – so much so that two of the women were retained as instructresses! Three stripes were awarded to a 17 year old girl at a rally in Carmarthen who, unaided had ploughed 25 acres of her father's farmland. Each red chevron or 'stripe' denoted 6 months of work of no less than 1440 hours. This was an astonishing feat for any recruit let alone for one so young.

The new uniformed women were indeed a curious spectacle as they ploughed fields with the new-fangled, cutting-edge, motor tractor ploughs.

The 'old school' ploughmen were often heard commenting that the eight furrows that were turned over each journey up and down the field would not have been of a high enough standard for a ploughing competition.[2]

Harking back to what had been was no use. There was no time to plough prize-winning furrows acre after acre now. The new ploughs did the work of 16 horses and eight ploughs. The age of the super-ploughwoman had commenced!

The Women's Land Army could at times be a rather complex organisation and grey areas abounded. 'Leave' was one such area. 'Dismissal' was another. The rules as laid out in the L.A.A.S Handbook clearly state that should a farmer want to dismiss one of the L.A.A.S, he was required to consult the Women's Agricultural Committee and give the Land Girl a full week of notice.[3]

Where this system worked, it provided a reasonable window of time for the appropriate wheels to be put in motion to ideally, swiftly re-place the unemployed Land Girl thus minimising the level of disruption and upheaval to the girl herself. However, many were not afforded the luxury of a week's notice and without any warning were unceremoniously told that they were no longer required, (often because male labour had suddenly become available).

In early November 1919, (just a few weeks before demobilisation) two Land Girls had taken some leave for a few days. They were shocked to learn that due to male labour becoming available, there would not be any field work for them on their return.

Through no fault of their own, they were cast aside without any due consideration as to where they would stay or gain new employment having been paid 15 shillings.[4]

15 shillings was only one week's maintenance and rather unjustly, they had been released and subsequently discharged without the required notice. Women who were placed in this difficult position faced the prospect of being out of work potentially for a considerable amount of time. They desperately wanted to work but the rules and regulations of the Women's Land Army, although put in place to provide security for those wearing its uniform often

had the opposite effect and left Land Girls high and dry, with few belongings, miles from home or a suitable depot.[5]

The system had clearly failed these two girls and any appeal would probably have been futile. Moving on to pastures new would have been their only option. This upheaval created unnecessary worry and the inconvenience of having to relocate and potentially find new billets.

Instances like this also did little to improve the delicate relationships that often existed between Land Girls, farmers and HQ. Women's Land Army personnel had to intervene and liaise with farmers and Land Girls when circumstances deemed it necessary to do so.

A free railway pass was granted to a Land Girl every six months on the condition that her work had been satisfactory throughout her time in employment. The employer however had to actually grant the leave. Leave was not always given to Land Girls as regularly as was stipulated in the rules.

The Women's Land Army was never an organisation to shy away from being the first to do something and it held the largest one-day agricultural competition in Hertfordshire during the hot summer of 1917. Approximately 300 young women from all walks of life competed against each other in all manner of events, having travelled from a dozen counties.

Due to the competition taking place during one of the crucial harvest months, counties that would otherwise have sent participants held their women back. The judges and spectators were hardened, staunch male farmers from Hertfordshire and Essex who came to witness for themselves the new women at work. They didn't hold back with their criticism but the laughs that they had intended to expend on the women were soon switched to words of praise having seen first-hand just how capable they actually were.[6]

A Land Girl described what it was like to take part in a demonstration which was held at Mr Rew's farm at Heavitree, just outside Exeter on Thursday, September 11th 1919. Mr Rew was one of the judges!

"I had to catch the 7.22 train to be in time, (the test commenced just after 10). Arriving at Exeter at 8.30, I presented myself at the office. Outside, I met some girls on the same errand as myself, but who had gone through their milking test the day before and spent the night in the YWCA. We girls boarded a tram which took us to Heavitree and a walk of about 1½ miles brought us to the farm on which the test was to be held. First came horse-work, which consisted of grooming and harnessing, putting the horse in the cart, taking it around through gateways and posts erected for the purpose, backing our carts into their places and letting out our horses, taking them back to the stables and unharnessing them. Then came questions as to why horses were groomed and the object of the various parts of the harness etc. The milking test over and various questions asked about cows, we were also free to catch our trains and now I am patiently waiting to hear the results and can only hope I am not an absolute failure."[7]

This account provides an invaluable insight into the structure of a demonstration. After each test, an experienced farmer thoroughly checked that there was a solid underpinning of agricultural knowledge by asking the Land Girls questions.

Women that set up smallholdings with sums of their own money knew that they had to readily accept all kinds of advice and study the ways of the soil in order to begin to understand what farmers had wisely learnt over centuries. By negotiating with others, perhaps even swapping items or by accepting the loan of pieces of equipment from their new neighbours, Land Girls gained knowledge and confidence. Over time, they became less afraid of making decisions and learned to accept both success and failure.

Looking after goats, chickens and ducks meant acquiring further skills. The milk, meat and eggs that the animals and poultry provided were an invaluable source of vitamins and supplemented the ration. They may even have been sold or shared out.

Jobs such as renovating old outbuildings so that they took on a functional use again or bringing an untended orchard back to life were incredibly satisfying, plus, over time it produced an additional and welcome harvest. Any surplus food could be preserved by bottling or made into jams and marmalades.

The land could not be rushed. It needed to be taken care of, understood and respected. By working together, outlooks would have been broadened, attitudes changed and a mutual respect steadily gained. Engrained, stereotypical perceptions and expectations often eroded over time but initially women felt the watchful, vigilant, defiant gaze of the farmer as he attempted to weigh up their worth. The benefits of having members of this new female workforce on their farms soon became apparent and in the end, they proved to be invaluable to farmers; a factor which previously, for many had been unthinkable.[8]

Miss Wilkinson was a Land Girl who had at first ignored and then resisted the pull to return to the land having worked in a department at a munitions factory in London. In January 1919, she recalled how difficult it had been for her friend to secure land work before the establishment of the Women's Land Army.

After much searching, her friend found work and after a few days, the farmer said that he would consider taking Miss Wilkinson on too. She speaks highly of the farmer, expressing admiration that he had in effect, gone against the negative hearsay that was circulating amongst his peers at the time about how troublesome taking women on would be; that they would cause him many problems and that it would all be a waste of time.

Throughout the land at War Agricultural Committee meetings, the merits of women workers were discussed by men. Mention was made of the effectiveness of mobile gangs that had stepped in to replace soldier labour. In January 1919, it was reported that a gang of twelve women had been tasked with planting work for about two months. The result of their collective effort was simply staggering. 50-60 acres had been planted in a short space of time. They had worked far more efficiently than the gang of soldiers used previously. It was made known that female labour would be preferred to that of soldier labour if a choice was given in future.[9]

Miss Bennett was a registrar based in Cornwall. In late 1917, early 1918 she regularly cycled long distances around the countryside gathering information on applicant numbers and local opinion from the many village registrars dotted around the county. She remarked on how the Cornish farmers said that doing this was a complete waste of time.

Some farmers rejected the offer of help from L.A.A.S women whereas others supported mobile gangs of women workers. When asked about mobile gangs, farmers stated that they needed to be raised quickly in towns and transported to the farms that required them. Cornish farmers however did not appear to require additional soldier or Land Girl labour beyond their own regular 'hands' and this was duly noted. It was genuinely felt that there was reluctance in some areas to make any real or concerted effort to utilise the additional labour that was now available. This of course went against what the government required from its farmers.[10]

Village registrars ranged from rectors to schoolmistresses and their task was not easy. The daily resistance they faced from villagers and farmers must have been demoralising and frustrating. Sourcing suitable housing was a constant problem. Shortages of cottages are often mentioned.

Travelling registrars had to get used to inclement weather. In her diary entry for Wednesday, February 20th 1919, Miss Bennett's work was curtailed because of having to turn back due to being soaked! Many days were spent looking up women who had applied for the Women's Land Army but ironically were not able to be placed!

Land work by its very nature could be sporadic and this posed a genuine dilemma for women. For women that needed to earn a regular wage to provide for themselves and their family, seasonal work simply wasn't lucrative enough. Many women opted to grow food on their own allotments instead which provided a more steady income and a readily available source of food.

A newspaper in 1917, early 1918 reported that a landswoman and two small boys had produced incredible yields of fruit and vegetables on a smallholding in Wimborne, Dorset. The variety of produce grown and harvested comprised of artichokes, asparagus, beetroot, broad beans, cabbages, carrots, cucumbers, lettuces, marrows, parsnips, peas, potatoes, runner beans, tomatoes, apples and rhubarb![11]

Women cultivated new areas of land that hitherto had stood idle and against all odds sowed crops and grew huge amounts of produce, much to the amazement of farmers who had advised against it. It was reported that there were:

> "Gloomy mutterings from all the neighbouring farmers that all the crops would be doomed to failure on newly-turned land."[12]

Crops were thoughtfully selected and sown. Manure was used to supplement the nutrients in the soil as was every other available fertiliser utilised to maximise crop yield. Additional crops of mangolds, potatoes, oats and wheat were the priceless results.

Victories such as the one achieved by the all-female staff working on Great Bidlake Farm near Exeter would have been especially sweet considering that the farm itself and its 145 acres of pasture and marshland was taken over by the Defence of The Realm Act, (DORA) on October 26th 1917. By sheer hard work, the farm became hugely productive once again.

Women were no strangers to using machinery and once established on a farm they often began to trial new Syracuse ploughs, (as opposed to the older Huxtable one-way ploughs) which allowed for much more land to be ploughed up per day. Farmers noticed how immaculate the machinery was, how well implements were maintained by the women and how organised they were. When they arrived however on November 2nd 1917 there was:

> "No single tool, implement or building available, nor any authority to purchase except by the lengthy way of requisitioning, nor any petty cash fund available."[13]

Although some farmers were quoted as being bewitched by the sight of Land Girls, many remained unconvinced. One farmer who was in attendance at a farmers meeting during the summer of 1916 ruthlessly declared to the speaker that women were of no use, had never been any use and would never be of any use! The irony of this story is that the farmer had been married three times! Sadly for those women who came forward to serve in land organisations, these were the obstructive and upsetting opinions that still prevailed in some circles.[14]

Further derogatory accounts of Land Girls continued to circulate. Some women were clearly not suited for land work. Two were openly ridiculed at a tribunal which took place in the village of Potterspury in Northamptonshire. The farmer was applying for three men at the tribunal: a ploughman, a shepherd and a carter, (all three jobs could of course have been ably carried out by women). The farmer was asked about the ladies and spoke about how they had given up after only a few days of working on the land having quickly tired of the grind; preferring to return to their books. He commented on how their attire of rings, spats and wristwatches had caused much amusement.[15]

Soldier labour was not always the best replacement workforce as the men were often unskilled or unsuited to work on the land. Farmers in many cases thought that their own local workforce could not be bettered. Skilled agricultural men who had signed up to fight had without question left gaping holes that required skilled replacements - a void which the Land Army had of course attempted to partially fill and surmount. These shortages were felt right across the country, in particular at pivotal times in the farming calendar.

Novel yet practical solutions were trialled by the War Agricultural Committee, (under the direction of the Board of Trade) and put into practice, such as the formation of cycling gangs comprised of Land Girls. Women in these transient gangs would be under the authority and supervision of a trained leader.

It was envisaged that where this enterprise was sanctioned, gangs of 12 workers would cycle within a five mile radius of the selected town to work. This idea was a two-pronged attack as it attempted to firstly reverse the effect that the exodus of men had had with a flexible, trained female workforce. Secondly, it attempted to avoid the recurrent headache faced by Welfare Officers to secure adequate, habitable billets for the Land Girls as women were billeted together, usually in village halls, huts or tents.

A figure printed in the Penrith Observer in January 1918 showed that over 90% of women had been satisfactorily trained and placed by the Women's Land Army or other landworker organisations by that time. Land organisations were clearly prepared to demonstrate radical forward-thinking when trying to solve the pressing labour shortages. Efforts however, although well-intentioned were not always consistent throughout the country hence any aims of colossal success always remained limited. It was no use getting women successfully through the system of training farms only to find that when it came to the crunch, they struggled to stick the daily grind of working on the land or remained unplaced!

Despite all of its teething troubles and failings, when and where the system ran smoothly, a Land Girl was a welcome addition to a workforce as she brought a new dynamic and outlook to anywhere she was placed.

Chapter 2

The awakened women

The Great War years offered women of all classes the opportunity to temporarily break free from the strict constraints and limitations imposed upon them during the Edwardian era. Social shackles were shattered and for some, their lives for the first time were unchaperoned. Emancipation was tantalisingly close and yet this unprecedented, golden opportunity to break loose proved to be a step that many women were still hesitant or reluctant to take!

For women that shunned the idea of signing up for any war service, unless they lived in a bubble that was devoid of any outside influences whereby they didn't actually perceive the public mood, they simply could not fail to notice how women were expected to do some form of national service for their country.

By turning their backs on the many thousands of other women who were already doing important war work, these 'targeted' women still appeared to distance themselves from the call simply because of their wealthier circumstances.

Reporters during the summer of 1916 did not mince their words when it came to asserting their exasperation - aimed fairly and squarely at the well-heeled shirkers. Time and time again they stressed the necessity for women to come forward to work. Such were the spoilt lifestyles of some women, they remained, (often deliberately) oblivious to the fact that they were languishing. Somehow, such females needed to be roused into action where victory was gained by way of achievement and showing patriotism for one's country.[1]

Words had to be eaten to an extent because women from all classes did indeed roll up their sleeves. Many finally joined various land organisations having had their consciences well and truly pricked. For those women who swapped their comfortable lives for work on the land, the ensuing months saw them swiftly gain knowledge in all manner of subjects. The land had been an alien world to them prior to joining but the Great War afforded so many women of all ages the scope to try something radically different.[2]

France and Germany had utilised additional female labour from as early as January 1915. Schoolchildren were also playing their part in their tens of thousands in other countries and in Britain for the national effort so why were some women still resisting the call? Farm work and working in the fresh air every day would prove beneficial in so many ways. A slogan on a recruitment banner summed up the mood felt at the time.

"A day on the land is worth two in the house."[3]

Lots of women may genuinely have considered joining a land organisation but stalled because they felt they would not have been very good at the work and also a life on the land simply did not appeal to them. Others dismissed it more or less immediately.

Lack of life experience was a drawback for many women. They were not always worldly wise having had scarce interaction socially with any others outside of their own circle. The Women's Land Army was also beguiling to some women; those of which would undoubtedly have had a real shock once the reality of working on the land hit them.

Working in a forage depot was equally challenging. Women wore masks and fine mesh veils over their faces in order to minimise the amount of dust inhaled whilst working with the hay. It was a relentless and dirty job!

Inevitably there were tasks that were beyond the limits of the physical strength of women - wheat sacks weighed 18 stone each! Tasks allocated to women had to be realistically achievable but not given as an easy option. Elderly farm labourers were also unable to perform some of the really heavy tasks that they had completed with relative ease during their youth. Hence, a balance needed to be sensitively struck.

Fortunately, there always seemed to be a farmer that was willing to take the most tenacious girl on to do piece work. There was also the additional problem of no official kit issue in the early days so old clothes had to be altered and modified accordingly.

The women that took up the challenge to serve their country in the years leading up to the official formation of the organisation rightly deserve a particular kind of recognition as the whole process of securing work and being accepted was met with even more reluctance and scepticism during that time.

The national push and incentive to serve was markedly less palpable then and individuals who wanted to work on the land really were heading for unchartered waters. One would-be Land Girl hired her own pony and trap to travel from farm to farm in order to enquire about employment such was her resoluteness to serve her country.

What was therefore seen as more of an experiment in 1915 had evolved into a fully formed, coordinated and regulated Army by early 1917. There were often huge contrasts in the volume of work being carried out across the country during the war years; women worked successfully and productively in the Lowlands of Scotland however shortages of labour were commonplace in the Home Counties and parts of Yorkshire.

In 1915, there was also frustration at the lack of urgency being shown by the government with regard to collaborating with other organisations to get women working on the land. Merely trying to coax them to come forward both delayed and hampered the progression that was required. In particular, the call for dairy workers and milkers fell on deaf ears.

Gaps that had been left by men leaving to serve had an impact on every stage of food production; from the raw materials that arrived at the ports that then required distribution, through to the sowing, tending and harvesting of crops ready for hungry mouths to eat in the months to come.

Mr Rowland Prothero, President of the Board of Agriculture stipulated such requisites at a meeting at the Royal Albert Hall in March 1917.

Women who came forward from wealthier backgrounds were often experienced horsewomen. Hunting was often a pastime for them. There were opportunities to complete their war service in a sphere of work where any equine experience would prove to be most advantageous.

Such women travelled from all over the country to take up roles in Remount Depots which in-turn released men for service. Women also volunteered to take delivery of horses from railway stations and terminals such as King's Cross. Horses arrived in poor condition and lacked fitness. It was the responsibility of the women to rectify this and make sure that the horses were suitably convalesced and made ready to be reissued back to troops in the future. Usually, 100 horses were the normal intake for these depots and the women looked after all aspects of the horses care.

How each individual coped with the problems, both mental and physical that arose during their training and also from ensuing placements is impossible to fully comprehend but many women would have felt terribly homesick. It was reported that some Land Girls, whilst hard at work on the south coast of England, could occasionally hear the sound of the guns being carried on the south-easterly wind from over the channel. This sad reminder must surely have made them feel as if their own personal sacrifices were almost insignificant when compared to what was happening elsewhere to their family and friends overseas. That said, it would have spurred them on to do everything they could to ensure that any eventual harvest was plentiful.[4]

Shifts also began to occur in other areas of employment during the Great War. Posts for female domestic servants became vacant in much greater numbers as girls grabbed new opportunities with alacrity!

This of course left vacancies in the staff of country houses up and down the land. The prospect of earning at least £2 a week working in munitions was just too tempting to let pass by.

By the summer of 1916, the unrelenting U-boat threat coupled with the lack of soldier labour highlighted the lengthening shadows of dearth which were biting ever more deeply into civilian life. Continuing losses in the merchant naval fleet meant that food was not arriving in the country in plentiful enough supplies.

Aside from the monumental task ahead for the organisations that were attempting to place additional landworkers on the land, there was widespread resentment aimed at women who wore any unfamiliar costume.

Letters were sent to daily newspapers from outraged readers declaring that the uniform being worn by Land Girls, (legitimately issued by the government for National Service) that comprised of breeches, gaiters or puttees should be viewed as immoral and obscene.

One farmer commented on a 'batch' of ladies, (who numbered about six) turning up at his farm wearing fine shoes, volunteering to assist with pitching dung. Glancing at their shoes, he immediately recognised that they were fine women.

Although sceptical, he told them that if they were that intent on pitching and spreading manure then he could certainly oblige with more work than they could ever complete! Having changed their fine shoes for boots and puttees, the women set to work. The farmer who had at least 30 years of experience was astonished at their efficiency and standard of work.[5]

He also discovered that one of the women had a title and a double-barrelled name suggestive of a society or aristocratic background. For those farmers that did not fight the tide, they would still have foreseen many potential hurdles arising just as readily as those that refused to budge with their outdated opinions - but by entrusting the women, most need never have feared.

For some men, seeing women in their mould-breaking uniforms remained perplexing. They failed to grasp what the true purpose of the organisation was and were flippant with their comments.

> "Men came up to ask whether married women were admitted into the Land Army as they wished their wives to join - one being 'Fair sick of his old woman' and another feeling he would be the better for a rest from his."[6]

Local people however were often eager to catch a glimpse of Land Girls in order to show them their support.

> "Everyone connected to the work and the general public have been exceedingly kind to us and as we ride along the streets on the top of the thresher, people wave to us and cheer. Last week one lady stood in her dining-room and waved a table napkin until we were out of sight."[7]

Land Girls often made up a significant part of proceedings during charitable fundraising events. The Farmers Red Cross Day took place in Yeovil in December 1917. The event was unique in the sense that it witnessed the first large gathering of women landworkers in the West of England. Local people commented that the procession highlighted the dramatic changes being made throughout the country. No longer were certain jobs exclusively in the male domain. The old way of doing things had been supplanted by a new, female, emergency labour force.[8]

Local people looked after the Land Girls by supplying them with calorific cocoa and buns to keep them going!

For lots of women, this new, independent life determined their future path for good. Many married countrymen and after the war, raised families.

Any landswoman that dared to question long-established, accepted farming practices would have made herself unpopular right from the word go however Land Girls immediately recognised that some farms were not anywhere near as productive as they could be.

If only farmers would just be receptive to a few changes! Pent-up exasperation and the inability to feel able to ask spiky questions, for fear of causing trouble would have inevitably stirred up resentment. If she dared to, the outcome could have been detrimental and her work life made intolerable. Fronting it out was likely to be the best option.

It is important to bear in mind that many farmers had been promised that some men would be returned to the land in time for the gathering of the harvest but due to the continuing war, it quickly became apparent that this was not going to be possible. Women were appealed to time and time again. Come forward. Work together. Succeed together.

Working as part of a mobile gang suited some women much better and they thrived being able to work on different farms. The work was much more sociable and could involve threshing, picking potatoes or a myriad of other jobs that relied heavily on intense periods of work at specific times of the year. As a result, there was a greater sense of togetherness. This kind of work suited restless women because if you did not like a particular place or particular people, it was never very long before you moved on.

Each Land Girl was an individual and had unique traits to her personality. Each and every one would have brought a new energy and dynamic to a farm. Their work proved invaluable to farmers, not merely as just an extra pair of hands but also a nice presence to have around. A humorous tip was imparted by a Land Girl going under the pseudonym Sunny Jim.

> "Don't be afraid of being taught by 'ye ancient farm hand.' They generally know the right way to do things and if they don't, it's best to let them think they do."[9]

Shared knowledge saw many women become experts in certain aspects of farm work in a relatively short time, especially in animal husbandry.

Champion goat-breeders and prizes won for breeding bulls were not unheard of! One young Land Girl, Blanche Ingram joined the Women's Land Army along with her cousin and they both worked with livestock on a farm on the south coast.

The farmer that employed Blanche had an additional interest in rearing goats, something which seems to have appealed to Blanche. In a very short spell of time, she was rearing prize-winning animals herself! Blanche's daughter recalled how her mother had proudly passed down to her the stories of success that her newly-acquired expertise had brought her!

The versatility of women was highlighted in January 1919 at a meeting of Leicestershire Women's Agricultural Council, Ashby-de-la-Zouch District Committee. The village of Heather in Leicestershire, (population 700) had seen women take the place of men in certain roles:

1 trained Land Army girl.
1 employed at Swepstone Dairy Factory.
6 in the Measham Colliery Bank.
3 working at Heather brickyard.
1 working in munitions.
1 post girl.
2 shop assistants.
2 partly employed at Heather Post Office.
1 portress at Heather Railway Station, (she is a grandmother and has done the work of a man since March 1916).
29 women have been employed in potato lifting.
20 of them are now employed in cutting off turnips.
2 are following the threshing machine. Others help when required.[10]

There was of course always the additional worry of whether their old job would still be waiting for them when the war came to an end.

During their working lives, women would have received letters that contained news of all kinds, including details of personal loss. They helped each other through the highs and lows of life, trying to constantly lift each other's spirits and maintain a good sense of humour.

"All through these operations our brothers and friends fighting in France are never forgotten and as one walks up and down the field, strains of various war songs come floating down."[11]

What better motivation could there possibly have been for these women to continue serving their country?

Chapter 3

Pluck and patriotism

For those women that were too apprehensive to come forward or lacked the ambition or daring to make the brave step towards enrolment, they were urged to look at those already working in the Women's Land Army and see their spirit and pluck as the example to follow.[1]

Joining any land organisation exposed women of all ages and backgrounds to new and varied social and employment opportunities. A new life beckoned in the countryside and depending on the choice of the individual, a placement hopefully ensued in agriculture, forestry work or producing forage. This meant learning the required skills quickly, often with very little training. Women soon become adept in areas such as thatching, hedging and livestock rearing.

The jobs that Land Girls readily turned their hands to is simply staggering. The jobs that they were asked to undertake was just as staggering. They ranged from the mundane, necessary, routine tasks to highly-skilled jobs that in peacetime, would have taken years to become accomplished in.

Not only did they have to learn to understand the land but cosset it too in an immensely intimate way. It was as if they were conversing directly with the land itself. The knowledge imparted by farmers, countrymen and women, (who themselves, embodied generations of experience) was readily taken on board and swiftly applied by the recruits. Land Girls wanted to excel and prove the doubters wrong.

Depending on the attitude you approached work on the land with, it could be viewed as an exciting adventure. Riding horses three abreast as the binder began to do battle with the harvest fields would have been an exhilarating experience for many.

They would have felt the national urgency and a sense of pride at being part of a process that was attempting to alleviate it but women simply could not have foreseen the odd deviations they would make in their lives.

Farmers on market squares all over the country deliberated the worth of this new labour force. Over time they acknowledged that women were in fact steady workers who, once trained were thorough in their farming practice.

Stories that informed the public about the feats of Land Girls were initially reported with a sense of disbelief. Reporters witnessed their capabilities and versatility at public demonstrations or by visiting farms directly. Many were clearly flabbergasted at what they had witnessed. One described how a Staffordshire Land Girl had driven 30 head of cattle to the market and sold the whole lot for £900 singlehandedly all without any male assistance!

This Land Girl would have been one of very few women in that particular environment at the time, so to succeed on such a scale must have felt very gratifying.

Women did appear to possess a natural aptitude for rearing and caring for livestock. They displayed a genuine interest in learning about and providing the best husbandry possible for their beasts and for the other animals and poultry in their care.

Female characteristics, (as they were judged then) were seen by farmers as crucial factors for success in this particular aspect of agricultural work. Animals appeared to respond favourably to a gentler approach and Land Girls even took the farm bull for a daily walk! Farmers commented that men often lacked the patience required to cope with uncooperative or weaker animals.

Seeing women toil away in the new uniform might have been quite confrontational for some men as they appeared to be filling not only the masculine gaps left vacant in agriculture, forestry and timber but also the roles that were traditionally inherited or handed down through the male generations.

Land Girls frequently established gratifying and rewarding working relationships. By gently coaxing and encouraging the women, both elderly and younger farm labourers nurtured their interest and inexperience; patiently setting them straight with a kind, reassuring word before continuing with their own work. Land Girls commented frequently on men's attitudes saying that on many occasions, they were so kind and respectful it became rather embarrassing. Any swearing or rudeness appeared to take a back seat and as a result, the general tone of the farmyard was elevated![2]

When farm bailiffs and foremen uttered words, everyone acted upon them. They rarely gave any praise but on the very odd occasion that they did, their words made a real impact. Day to day, Land Girls soon realised that silence from a foreman generally meant that they were doing their work satisfactorily.[3]

There were good and bad examples of leadership and direction. One Scottish farm bailiff gave the Land Girls a chance to show their ability. They were given sole-charge of a harvest wagon on steep hillsides. It would have been all too easy to allocate the tricky tasks to the experienced men as opposed to the new, inexperienced female members of the workforce. Trust had to be placed in the women but it took time to gain and this proved difficult to do if Land Girls relinquished posts early.

This particular issue posed a real problem for farmers and the Land Army organisers as the task always fell on them to replace such labour.

> "One of the most frequent causes of complaint made against our Land Army by the farmer is, that many of the girls do not at all realise the importance of remaining in their posts and that they are often inclined to give them up for very trivial reasons."[4]

This comment reinforces not only the necessity but also the benefits of remaining in one place of work. By working for a year or preferably two at any allocated placement, Land Girls were able to really get to know the routine of an individual farm and establish a good working relationship with the farmer and his workforce.

If a Land Girl moved around frequently, her wage was unlikely to rise. If however she remained at a farm for a long time, she would more likely have been recognised for her loyalty with a rise in her wages, a Good Service Badge or Long Service Award.

Sympathy of course can be felt for the farmers. Their frustration was totally justified, especially when valuable weeks or months had been, in effect lost because of having to invest time and effort, (either the farmer's own or someone else's) to train women to carry out certain tasks. Patiently teaching and encouraging a new recruit in the difficult first few months of service only to lose her soon after could seriously mar any future liaisons between the farmer and the Women's Land Army. A reliable workforce was imperative as eleven hour days were not unheard of and hours varied according to each particular season. During the particularly frenetic harvest months, work even continued by moonlight if the weather ahead looked doubtful.[5]

Situations naturally arose where women had no choice but to move on. The reasons that necessitated their departure could number many but one Land Girl recounts having to leave her position with her friend due to the death of the tenant farmer, having worked on his farm for a year. It certainly was not a given that a new tenant or owner would still want to employ Land Girls!

Women that worked on the land before the Women's Land Army had been set up would have received next-to-no support in securing a seamless transition to a new place of work. It was usually left to the individual to sort out what their next course of action was going to be.

Many women saw the interim period of time between postings as an opportunity to catch up with family and friends, take a well-earned holiday or spend some of their hard-earnt savings! For those women in depots their training continued whilst others took part in demonstrations.

Judges at a thatching demonstration, held on a farm in Framlingham in Suffolk in May 1919 commented on the quality of the Land Girls' work. Out of 8 entries, 7 were Suffolk Land Girls and the other girl was only 14 years old. Their work was of such a high standard that at the prize-giving, two additional prizes had to be awarded. The young girl came a respectable fourth!

Demand for Land Girl labour on farms did not lessen after the Great War had ended. Applications actually increased from farmers. Some of the requests submitted were futile because demand far outstripped supply. Trained women however went from strength to strength and one atypical example of where a Land Army woman was selected for a highly paid position was reported on in late June 1919.

This particular successful applicant had taken on the £140 a year position of Milk Recorder.[6]

For those men that were too old for military service, conscientious objectors, (who were often unsuited for agricultural work) or men who had a reserved occupation, having to work with uniformed Land Girls who looked and spoke differently to them would have been quite bewildering at first. No doubt they were watched very closely!

Not only did Land Girls have to cope with the endless work that the yearly cycle determined but also the stress that came with the job; stress that often pervaded into their personal lives. They knew they had to be flexible and realised that they could be transferred to a different section if required. Freeing up men was part and parcel of their service. In November 1917 at the government's request, 17 Land Girls were permanently transferred and 10 temporarily 'lent' to the Forage Department in order to release men for service. The roles that women took on in the Forage Section were strenuous and numbered many from weighing, baling and stacking hay to thatching hayricks and taking horses and wagons from farms to railway stations.[7]

Accepting without question what you were told to do with quiet forbearance reflects the kind of qualities required in order to keep on task day in and day out. Hardiness and unwavering support for each other must have eased the grind of long, endless days. If women were inexperienced, they were not always given whole days of work. In order for a Land Girl to work alone for a whole day, she would need to have acquired the relevant skills and knowledge.

Jobs like forking and breaking up what seemed like mountainous heaps of manure did nothing to lift the flagging spirits of a Land Girl who may have felt low in mood. This is where working with other labourers who had a keen sense of humour and perhaps a mischievous twinkle in their eye would surely have brightened up proceedings!

The interminable length of days, (whatever the season) spent doing mind-numbing tasks on farms took some time to adjust to and tolerate. It was therefore imperative that Land Girls got a good night's sleep.

Depending on their age, women had husbands, sons or brothers serving at the same time they were doing their own National Service but everyone would have had friends serving. Thoughts of their loved ones would never have been far away from their minds as they toiled. Breaks and the hour for lunch would provide welcome relief for aching knees, backs or sore feet! The dinner hour also allowed Land Girls to catch up on news. All too often, it flew by!

Breaking the monotony in any permissible way was imperative if morale was to be maintained. Land Girls often recited short poems and liked to sing well-known tunes and much like soldiers, they enjoyed adapting poems.

Robert Burns' 1782 poem, 'Comin' Thro' the Rye' was subject to Land Girl inventiveness. An adapted version was submitted to The Landswoman magazine.

> Comin thro' the rye!,
> Gin a body meet a body
> Comin thro' the rye,
> Can a body plough or dig?
> Let a body try!
> Every lassie gaily tripping,
> Ready hand and eye,
> Raking, hoeing, laughing, singing,
> Comin thro' the rye.
>
> Should you ask them how they do it,
> Each would wink an eye,
> Take their rake and tell you smiling,
> Come and have a try!
> Turn the soil and dig and weed it,
> Sow it by and by,
> Every girl can serve her country,
> All among the rye.[8]

This need to keep upbeat whilst working meant that the fields would regularly come alive to the sound of singing and whistling. The ploughboys were no exception; Land Girls often commented on how they heard whistling emanating from some distant part of a field through the mist.[9]

It seems fair to assume that women who joined the Women's Land Army would not have foreseen becoming road menders but that is exactly what a group of them became in February 1919. Wearing their distinctive uniforms, a group of 12 Land Girls were photographed together enjoying a well-earned break and a hot drink, sitting on what appears to be some of the road-mending equipment in Merrow, a small village 2½ miles out of Guildford.

The weather was wet and cold and snow lay on the ground. Rather unbelievably and no doubt to the absolute amazement of local people, these women had been employed by the Guildford authorities, (the Rural District Council) as a novel experiment to maintain and repair neglected country roads; the outcome of which was a success. It was a truly ambitious idea that was applauded for its bold, progressive implementation. Their working days were long and physical, starting at 7am and finishing at 5pm with an average weekly wage of £1 2s 6d. Work was overseen by a Council Foreman and a Women's Land Army Forewoman. The Land Girls' work was of such a high standard, it was hoped that they could be kept on after the initial phase of work had been completed.[10]

The success of this venture generated great publicity for the Women's Land Army. It showed that recruits could turn their hand to pretty much anything that was asked of them in times of war including more unusual tasks not linked to land work. It proved that excellent working relationships could be established with the Women's Land Army and local councils to achieve a common goal.

Land Girls were also deployed to King's Cross railway station in London in early October 1919. They had volunteered to look after horses that came in and out of the station. The efficiency and professional manner in which they went about their duties was observed by other tradespeople who also worked at the station.[11]

Once Land Girls signed on the dotted line, they had to be prepared to go wherever they were needed. These less obvious work locations highlight the importance of realising this before committing to service. Landswomen would not ordinarily have worked in such locations during peacetime.

Wages were often a contentious issue for those serving in the Land Army. Often, the women's wage barely covered even the most basic costs of living. After deductions for billets, food and uniform expenses there was little, (if anything) left over for socialising or treats. It was the worst paid of all the auxiliary services. Angry parents submitted letters to newspapers complaining about the low wage. The life of a Land Girl wasn't glamorous in any way but it did afford some who joined a genuine escape from their humdrum lives and a chance to be entrepreneurial.

In 1919, a Cornish landowner temporarily gave 10 acres of his estate to enable two Land Girls to establish a smallholding. They kept cows, pigs and poultry and grew vegetables and a crop of violets to be sold at market.

Violets were hugely popular with Edwardian ladies who wore them in sprays and corsages. They were grown commercially during the First World War in counties like Devon and Cornwall and were sent by express train to be sold at Covent Garden. Boots the chemist had sold violet perfume since 1910 and the delicate flower was also a favourite of Queen Mary, who had them regularly sent to her on her birthday.

There was a further side to the violet as the flower is associated with sorrow and death. They also carry the double meaning of faithfulness and modesty; qualities that were especially important to husbands, wives and sweethearts separated by war.

The cultivation of such a flower was frowned upon by some county agricultural committees who felt that the growing of such a fanciful flower should be sidelined in preference of life-sustaining crops such as potatoes during times of national need. This however was not made compulsory until after 1918 when a notice was served. It stated that potatoes and other vegetables should take preference over growing violets, especially under fruit trees.[12]

It does however show that despite opposition, tenants (up until it was made compulsory not to) had a shrewd eye on where additional income could be generated whether it was morally right or not. These two Land Girls seized the moment with regard to the marketability of this delicate flower, making extra money by tapping into its mass appeal.

As demobilisation loomed, organisations such as the Women's National Land Service Corps knew that time was of the essence in order to 'catch' trained and skilled Land Girls who were deliberating leaving the organisation in order to return to their old jobs. New ideas and incentives to keep such women interested in working on the land sprang forth in the form of informative articles or advertisements in newspapers. In January 1919, it was stated that the WNLSC was attempting to raise funds, (£10,000) to set up a smallholding cooperative which would allow Land Girls to continue the work they had carried out during the war after demobilisation.[13]

Many women jumped at the chance to continue working in this way but there was the inevitable fall-off of women who couldn't wait to return to civilian life again.

Many agricultural jobs were tedious, none more so than the task that greeted the Land Girls who had been sent to work, (together with village women) in an area of Kent to try and prevent a significant loss in crop yield due to an invasion of weeds, which was a common problem across the country. Weeds were a genuine threat and as much as half of any crop could potentially be lost if they were able to take hold.

Losses of this scale would have been disastrous considering the current situation in the country which had seen worsening food shortages and nationwide rationing of certain foods by April 1918. This problem demonstrates how bodies of women were deployed quickly to where they were needed. It also shows how efficiently the wheels of the Women's Land Army could turn, if required in order to avert a crisis.

A persistent thorn in the side of the Women's Land Army was the issue of trained women remaining unemployed despite so much work needing to be done. If a woman was highly skilled in a particular area such as tractor driving then she would not generally be out of work. Land work however was all too often weather dependant and seasonal fluctuations in the amount of labour required meant that for many, employment was often sporadic.

Due to the critical nature of the world food situation, seasonal work always took priority over the many other jobs agriculture demanded be done and was carried out under the instruction of the farmers. Women who were in the National Land Council worked under the supervision of trained leaders doing a gamut of jobs such as picking stones from fruit fields, cutting cabbages and hoeing to seasonal work such as fruit-picking. Out of their 15 shilling weekly wage, 10 shillings was usually deducted for board. Seasonal work realised a higher wage namely due to the work being paid at 'piece rates.'

Time was never wasted and specialist courses that trained women in hedgelaying were set up in many counties. Girls who were in depots, (accommodation where Land Girls spent a minimal amount of time, ranging from 2 to 4 weeks free of charge if they became unemployed through no fault their own) were put to good use. One example of this saw each girl attend a series of 12 lessons; the instructor being provided from the County Council. They practised on the hedges of neighbouring farms until the completion of the course. Skilled hedgers and ditchers were always in demand so it made sense to utilise any spare labour.

For those women who had to switch from field work to nursery work, the transition often came as a shock, especially if they had to work in stifling greenhouses during the summer months. Where fruit crops had failed, (as in 1918) transferable labour was crucial to force certain foods that were in demand such as cucumbers and tomatoes. During the colder months, cleaning out the hothouses meant coming into contact with all kinds of creatures that perhaps pre-war they would have been petrified of. Turning flax was also a particularly awful job and Land Girls recall the horror at seeing the wet flax bedecked with large tangles of pink, fat worms![14]

Flax growing and harvesting eventually produced linen which was used for aeroplane wings and other army canvas products.

Working with livestock meant that Land Girls faced both unfamiliar and unpredictable animals that before the war they would never have come into such close contact with, let alone been in charge of. The level of knowledge required and husbandry needed to look after animals properly like pigs, cattle and sheep not only meant studying books and pamphlets provided by the Women's Land Army but by also absorbing the wisdom of years of experience passed on by farmers, their wives and village workers too. However, by imparting their newly-gained knowledge and skills, Land Girls also demonstrated many new methods and practices to farmers that they had learnt from the recently-established training centres. They had little choice but to take challenging jobs on too, such as breaking in animals such as heifers and young horses.[15]

This clearly was a dangerous task. In the first instance women would need to be taught the necessary skills to competently and safely break heifers in. It was a task that saw Land Girls frequently sustain bruises or injuries; the scars of which they bore forever.

Land Girls placed with nurserymen and fruit growers were taught how to implement the more intricate techniques associated with fruit-growing, such as grafting fruit trees and how to correctly spray trees to prevent infestations from insects.

The ability to learn quickly and then capably execute their newly-acquired skills ensured that women gained a good reputation locally. Over time, they were given full responsibility to grow various crops as well as to cut and harvest them. This could mean that on farms comprising of 500 acres, (now devoid of male labour) women, (who were members of organisations such as the National Land Council) would sow, grow and pick a variety of fruit and vegetable crops and also produce flowers.[16]

For the 50 or so Land Girls that were lucky enough to be billeted at St Augustine's College, (used as a Women's Land Army training centre) in Canterbury, Kent, their daily routine was far removed from that of other Land Girls. They slept in ancient monastic cells and ate breakfast in the 13th century dining hall! This was a world away from the women who had to set their own fire and struggled to ever get warm in a drafty cottage after a hard day toiling in all weathers! The St Augustine's Land Girls were referred to rather humorously as inmates and they started their day at 5.30am when reveille was sounded with military precision. Land Girls recall the sound of their morning bugle call reverberating around the cloisters signalling the need to spring into action! Their routine was regimented and organised down to the last minute. Fifteen minutes was allowed for breakfast, after which the girls set off for their day's work with their ration baskets. For the Land Girls that were billeted at St Augustine's, their placement appeared to have been a happy and contented one, in spite of the hard, manual toil.

They commented on how men and women worked side by side and that the exhausting nature of the work was regularly alleviated by lots of laughter and singing. Farmers quickly got used to the new female workforce and soon felt proud of the efforts made by them and of the results they achieved. They were often heard discussing their Land Girls to other farmers in the district at the market; of how reliable they were and how they never complained if they were asked to work extra hours.[17]

Newspapers reported to curious readers the precise details of what a Land Girl's day was like at St Augustine's. Depending on the weather, 6pm saw the return of the women, who unlike many were able to change out of their uniforms and enjoy a bath. This was luxurious compared to the primitive conditions endured by some Land Girls! By 6.30pm, supper was served in the ancient dining hall amidst chatter and laughter. 7pm saw the Land Girls packing up their rations for the next day. Everyone had to be ready for the 8pm roll call, (with the exception of those who had applied for a weekly pass which allowed the holder to stay out until 9pm). Roll call was carried out outside if the weather allowed or in the shelter of the cloisters if it was wet. The long and hectic day continued with Compline which took place in the chapel and finally bed was at 9pm with the call for lights out coming at 9.30pm.

This demanding routine took some sticking but Land Girls were versatile and adapted well - not only to the variations in weather but to the many different types of jobs they were required to do. They donned all manner of clothing, improvised or otherwise to protect themselves from the prolonged wet spells of weather; wearing clogs and using sacks to wrap themselves up was not unheard of. Physical labour carried out over many hours meant that by the close of the day, Land Girls had always worked up a hearty appetite! They enjoyed relaxing in the evening in their billet or hostel - many women still had enough energy to play a game, sing songs, go swimming or learn to dance.[18]

16 hour days were commonplace during peak times such as harvest. Overtime was offered but it was not a choice, it was a necessity! If Land Girls worked in a pair, they could split the day into stints of 3-4 hours, taking it in turns to cut the crop, then swap tasks.

The countryside came alive in June and July to the sounds of rattling reapers. The crop needed to be raked once the sun had dried it, then swept, cocked and raked again. Every part was physical right up to loading the wagons and even this task was accomplished in a specific way too.

Spreading manure was a job that most Land Girls disliked intensely but nonetheless encountered at some point during their service. In coastal regions, manure was hard-to-come-by but one ingenious, back-breaking method of adding fertiliser and nutrients to the soil was to gather seaweed from the beach and transport it up to the fields. In early 1919 a newspaper reported that a Land Girl had done exactly that during the previous four months. By using a donkey to carry sacks of seaweed up from the beach, (which was 300 feet below the half an acre of cliff land she had to prepare for cultivation) she was able to grow and harvest over three tons of potatoes. This highlights the enormous efforts Land Girls were prepared to go to in order to grow crops.[19]

By utilising a plentiful, readily available, natural material for such a beneficial purpose on an exposed, otherwise unproductive, barren piece of land, it was transformed into a useful, hugely productive area - much to the surprise of local men who had deemed it nigh on impossible to achieve such a feat!

It certainly was not uncommon for Land Girls to tackle jobs that men had flatly refused to do therefore any gains or successes that were achieved on this basis, no matter how great or small must have felt very sweet indeed to them!

The competitive and meticulous mindset of the seasonal workers was noted by employers who felt that women often put work before wages! The only criticism that was made about flax workers, based at a camp in the West Riding came from a farmer who said that the girls were too meticulous when pulling flax and it wasn't necessary to be so. The women were clearly conscientious but there was a drawback to working so methodically. It slowed progress down. They clearly took the comment on board because they set a record on only their third day, pulling an acre of flax in just one day!

In the years that preceded the outbreak of the First World War, farming had seen much neglect and underinvestment. Barns and other farm buildings were dilapidated, crumbling away and unfit for use. They were unhygienic to work in and were often used for storing old, rusty farm machinery. Land Girls got to work in shippons (an archaic word for a cattle shed). They cleaned them out and whitewashed the walls so that they were made fit for purpose again. With the passing of the Defence of the Realm Act in 1914, (DORA) it meant that many buildings reverted back to their original purpose or were given a new lease of life.

Cleanliness was an aspect of a Land Girl's work that was regularly commented on by observers and old hands alike. The differences in how they approached their work were glaringly obvious. They were organised and methodical. Dirty jobs that hitherto were rarely done or never done were now a necessity if a farm was to function both hygienically and effectively. Land Girls led the way in showing others how to do things properly; any slovenly ways or bad practice was soon exposed. For the first time in a long time, cows were washed and utensils and other equipment kept scrupulously clean. Gone were the days where dirty hands were dipped in the milk pails![20]

This championing of Land Girls' working methods in no way set out to demean the work of men who had decades of experience on farms - it merely demonstrated that the new techniques, when implemented were game changers.

Old ways of doing things still prevailed and the Land Girls that worked in mobile gangs pulled up acres of potatoes on their hands and knees or were bent double, picking for hours at a time. In some parts of the country, they had filled the gaps of the seasonal Irish labourers who had, in previous years, assisted with the gathering of the crucial potato harvest. For those that lived in the countryside, harvest was a unique time of year. Everyone was involved in it or impacted by it.

Villagers of all ages joined forces with soldier labour and also with other women who were not only members of the Women's Land Army but other land organisations too.

When work was at its peak, food and drink was taken to the workers in the fields twice daily. Lunchtime picnics saw everyone down tools for a well-deserved rest out of the hot summer sun. During the harvest months, food and drink was included in the wage. Wages were paid for the whole month and were near double that of a normal month.

Time moved in a very different way during the harvest months. The passing of time was kept track of and governed by the sunrise and sunset! There are many stories of Land Girls working under the light of the moon during the harvest months. How people were paid and how everyone worked completely altered for that short window of time. Land Girls spoke fondly about this unique time of year despite being exhausted by its demands. The harvest was so physically demanding that it required everyone involved in it to work together as a team. Working as part of a team clearly made an impact on Land Girls. Despite the enormity of their workload, they enjoyed the feeling of togetherness as they worked in the fields; a feeling that only harvest could create.[21]

Problems caused by rats, moles and rabbits prompted the emergence of a government initiative in 1917 whereby Land Girls were trained in pest control. They were supplied with nets and ferrets in order to try and reduce the risk of crops being damaged by pests. A simple yet vital mission was theirs to implement. Net and destroy! Yet again, women came up against prejudice, not only from the farming fraternity but from society, who felt that it was unacceptable for a woman to perform such work.

Professions such as farriers and blacksmiths saw an upsurge in training and demand. Horses needed to be shod and tools made and repaired too. Farriery was a designated section of the Women's Land Army and at recruitment rallies, women could be seen holding banners aloft with the word 'Farriery' on them. Photographs of female farriers also began to appear in the national press. It seemed that the sky really was the limit for aspirational women.

Newspaper headlines often made reference to famous poems such as "The Village Blacksmith" by Henry Wadsworth Longfellow, (first published in 1840).

The poem vividly depicts a strong, male blacksmith. The physical strength required to carry out his craft is captured in verse as well as the sights and sounds of the forge itself. The Great War triggered drastic change and what were once perceived as male only roles now had to be carried out by women. The poem highlighted these changes.

Food shortages bit ever-harder as the war dragged on. The Food Controller adopted preventative measures in case of future vegetable shortages and sought to employ women in vegetable drying factories. No food was ever deliberately wasted and at county level, fruit and vegetable collecting societies were formed in order for any surplus food to be distributed or disposed of appropriately.

Pulping stations were established, frequently set up in buildings whose usual purpose was far removed from that of its war service. One was run from a Kentish hop kiln. Stone fruits like plums were processed in vast amounts of up to 60 tonnes daily. The plum pulp was bottled and preserved instead of going to waste.

All viable land was either ploughed up or prepared for crops to be sown on. This even applied to golf courses! Many courses lost acres in order for land to become available for ploughing and to enable potatoes to be sown. Requests were made which asked for permission to allow cattle to graze on the links!

Needless delay was caused by politicians who failed to initially acknowledge the true scale and severity of the burgeoning food problem or how unprepared agriculture was as an industry to respond to the worsening crisis. Multiple problems arose and months of poor decision-making had, albeit at different times, eventually reached the same conclusion - that the nation had fallen way behind in putting a plan into action; one that prepared the way for a nation-saving harvest which was only a few months on in the calendar.

Voluntary rationing was not likely to be sufficient. In early 1917, the dark clouds of compulsory rationing now loomed large on the horizon. 15 weeks of work needed to be crammed into 6 if the land was to be readied in time for a harvest. The crucial yields would ward off the ghastly spectre of starvation. The word famine began to appear in newspaper articles such were the grave forecasts for the harvest of 1917.

In order to try and make up for the agricultural dallying, it was proposed that motor tractor ploughing should be carried out at night in order to catch up with the lag. Headlights fuelled by acetylene would be fixed to the ploughs in order for this marathon task to be carried out. Land Girls would have been amongst the volunteers called upon to fill any gaps in the required workforce.

And so the nation got its head down and ploughed through the day and through the night, through every Saturday and even every Sunday. This was the case for six weeks until it could be said with certainty that the desired plan had indeed been put in place; a plan that would see realised, (in due course and weather permitting) an abundant harvest.[22]

Tractors, (or miniature tanks as they were known) that had bright lights to illuminate fields in remote areas away from heavily populated towns or cities were not deemed a risk should any enemy aircraft approach. This however was not the case in the Eastern counties of the country, where the risk of air raids was significantly higher.

Seven Sundays were all that remained. The consequences of not achieving this monumental target were unthinkable. It was imperative that sowing was completed by April 15th. Sunday was the day that many people attended church or was a day of rest to enjoy being with family and friends. Even the sacred day was not safe from the clutches of war. The growing seriousness of the food problem saw something being asked of members of the clergy that pre-war would have been quite unthinkable. The Food Production Department asked clergy from different denominations to encourage those that usually attended church on a Sunday morning to work on the land instead. A service could still be attended on Sunday evening after work had ceased for the day.[23]

This would still have been a very difficult decision to wrangle with in spite of the seriousness of the situation. People of all ages attended church regularly at this time and would have seen this request, (despite being perfectly practicable) as sacrilege and against their faith beliefs. The situation was however unprecedented and faith alone was not going to feed the nation. Hard though it would have been, the bitter pill regarding Sunday work would need to be swallowed.

The Great War turned things topsy-turvy and for the first time, locations like Covent Garden Market in London were invaded by Land Girls; the spectacle of which had never been seen before. It was reported that traders looked on with genuine admiration at the way the Land Girls conducted themselves; how they wended their way through the busy London streets adjacent to the market with skill and ingenuity and how speedily and efficiently they unloaded their horse-drawn vans which were full of goods.[24]

Land Girls had clearly gained respect from the established and permanent traders at the market. They were scrutinised wherever they went but it did not seem to perturb them. Sticking at it was always at the forefront of their minds.

And, with the exception of a few, that is exactly what they did!

Chapter 4

Strength in unity

The Women's Land Army aimed to attract and recruit educated and society women. Lightweight lifestyles were indeed forsaken but women also joined from the complete opposite end of the social spectrum too. For the first time, aristocratic women and domestic servants worked and socialised alongside one another.

It is impossible to measure the true extent of how these social distinctions affected their social interactions or ability to adapt or work unitedly together. Everyone had to share the same humble dwellings and billets; snobbery therefore could never be seen to find a foothold.

The argument against educated women working on the land was that it was viewed as a waste of their intellect. If women were allowed to continue with their studies, it would surely have a much wider, valuable impact on the nation in time. If they continued to be actively encouraged to go and take up land work or war work of some kind, this brief window of opportunity would see their studies interrupted and their chance to excel squandered. Many thought it quite preposterous to give even the merest consideration to losing this wealth of talent from the privileged classes for any longer than the summer vacation. A case was also made for highly skilled women. Women that worked at The Potteries in Staffordshire left their jobs behind to serve their country by working on the land.

Spare a thought for village women who may have heard these views about educated women coming to work on the land. They must have felt full of trepidation, perhaps fearful. When any contingent did arrive they would have been viewed with suspicion and with regard to fitting in, well that was often for them to do! Perceptions of country people were often ill-judged and could have been just as harmful and divisive.

By assuming that village women alone would solve the nation's food problem it showed what ignorant and selfish viewpoints were circulating.

Summer work was seen as a more acceptable, character-building, life-affirming break for the university girls; a chance to experience another world far removed from their own. However, could any prolonged removal from their studies run the risk of them mentally stagnating?

War precipitated many uncomfortable and unprecedented changes. Everybody from every walk of life made a concerted effort to absorb these radical new ways, reluctantly or otherwise.

Women had always worked on the land, assisting in the daily running of farms. Farmers wives during the Great War were not necessarily seen as farmers in their own right – even on the death of their husband. Whether pre-war or as a result of the war, widows who were permitted to take on the sole responsibility of their late husband's farm faced persistent prejudice due to societal restrictions and other constraints imposed on them.

This of course varied from county to county but it certainly was not unusual for women to have to send a male worker to market instead of going themselves. It was regarded as demeaning for a woman to go. Such was the curious swirl of 'what was acceptable' or 'beneath someone' it must have been a somewhat bewildering working environment.

Many young village girls chose to stay at home and work on the land alongside ex-munition workers, society girls, university students, domestic servants and other part and whole-time land workers who were all being placed by various land organisations.

English Author, Ella Hepworth Dixon provided an interesting perspective on the situation in agriculture in April 1915. Her views would have given rise to intense debate as she felt that in order for the land to be readied for harvest, any female workers, (if it were possible) would need to be sturdy girls from the middle classes. Those women born to labourers she deemed would not be fit enough to come forward for such demanding work due to weakness and anaemia.[1]

Some farmers appeared to corroborate this view, also preferring to take on suitable town girls as opposed to country girls. They felt that such girls brought a spirited attitude and dynamic with them to land work that was lacking in those already accustomed to it.

It could be argued that countrywomen would easily triumph over the more delicate, overindulged, middle and upper-middle class women of the time! For girls that were used to tennis parties, afternoon tea and who wore dainty, feminine attire, a rude awakening was in store. Being hired in a cattle market was as far removed as it was possible to be from the surroundings that some women were accustomed to and yet there they stood, willingly, signing up for 18 shillings a week.

Unusual career switches necessitated by war were commonplace. Hairdressers became adept with the plough and an author was photographed taking a bull out for its daily stroll. Artists, actresses and the daughters of respected professions such as doctors and solicitors began to sign on the dotted line!

Such transitions were viewed as rather astonishing; that it was actually possible for women to turn their hand to something so far removed from their usual professions met with an unerring fascination. Newspaper headlines regularly proclaimed these wartime miracles.

College and university women would not have been able to interact with villagers in the same way they did with their peers and vice versa. Invaluable knowledge and pearls of wisdom from countrymen and women would have been exchanged as well as perhaps some poetry or lines from a play too!

Common ground somehow had to be established in order for the bridging of classes to begin. As time wore on, what a girl did, where she studied, if she had any education counted for nothing. It simply wasn't about that. Qualities such as loyalty, kindness, honesty, humour, patience, politeness, humility, persistence and resolve would have won the day and made the hard days easier to endure.

Any unlikely friendships that were formed saw class barriers dissolve and any preconceived ideas would have slowly dissipated. Working on the land meant that women discovered the very best and the very worst of their character traits and those of others' too.

Regardless of their background, trained women should have been of great benefit to the farmer despite the fact that they did not possess a natural aptitude for many of the tasks they were being asked to carry out. Expertise took time to gain and learning new skills required others to show a certain level of patience and tolerance. The reward of which was a more proficient and productive employee. Before the Women's Land Army was established, the amount of training women received showed inconsistencies, especially when taken on a county to county, stand-alone basis.

Innovative experiments were trialled which resulted in women from the East End of London being sent to work in Radlett in Hertfordshire during the summer of 1915. They worked under the supervision of two trained women from Studley College in Warwickshire. For the 30 strong all female workforce who were employed to plant orchards, the intense physical work of having to dig trenches, (to allow for drainage in order to prepare the 34 acres of land for fruit trees) saw their health dramatically improve.[2]

Often, women from towns and cities could not easily settle to country life or even develop a fondness for it. Newspapers in October 1916 reported that girls from London had failed in their attempts to stick at work on the land.[3]

Whilst this headline told the truth about those women it specifically referred to, it in effect, unfairly tarred all women from London who had come to work on the land with the same brush. If the other women who came from the East End of London to work at Radlett in Hertfordshire are used as an example, they carried out excellent, competent work. It must have been very upsetting to see such detrimental headlines.

The statement emanated from the Wiltshire War Agricultural Committee, who closed down their training school on the back of, (but perhaps not entirely due to) the Londoners' failings. There were initial successes at the training school but these did not transfer to the farms when the women finally were placed.

All women to a degree struggled with the monotony of farming work. It was a case of how much that struggle affected them and if they felt they could continue to cope with it long term. Holding fast to a Land Army motto "Stick it if it kills" was not always easy!

Fierce anti-slacker articles continued to appear unabated in the national newspapers and ruthlessly berated the behaviour of women who continued to enjoy empty days whilst the rest of the nation faced growing uncertainty. Nothing was held back and the press tore away at their consciences through unashamed browbeating. Many women, born into great privilege still stubbornly resisted the call and felt it was beneath them to work in any of the spheres of work that were still very much open to them.

Emphasis was placed on making the additional benefits of land work appealing. Working outside brought to the mind, body and soul stimulation that could not be gained elsewhere. The strict diet that some society ladies had to adhere to in order to maintain a certain weight, (or risk not being able to fit into the fashions of the day) would be forfeited for calorie-burning agricultural jobs, but only if forks on the dining table were replaced by forks in the fields!

Land work had a profound effect on women's figures. They developed muscle and gained weight as a result of eating hearty breakfasts, (that is of course if they were fortunate enough to have them). Some women described eating fish, eggs, bacon, grilled tomatoes, a bunch of watercress and on several occasions, even a steak! This was in stark contrast to the pale, delicate, slightly built women that had left families and friends behind in order to join land organisations. It wasn't long before they were unable to fit into old clothes or tie up their corsets, such was the change in their figures.[4]

Women generally lost the extra weight they had gained on completion of their service as the extra calories required and consumed were no longer needed.

In the image and weight-conscious world that society women circulated in, it would be deemed necessary for them to conform again on completion of their service - so the once bonny Land Girl, preferred by many quickly became unrecognisable again; that is if she chose to return to such a lifestyle!

Whilst working on the land would never have been a career choice for a lot of women, there may have been a glimmer of curiosity in their eyes having been actually offered the chance to carry it out. A feeling of "What if?" must have tempted many. There were a large of number women who had neither profession or employment across the length and breadth of the nation. Such overindulged women could fill gaps in the labour workforce but they had to be roused into action. They had to be made to feel that volunteering for war work was no longer something they could escape from.

Would conscription have to be considered if general appeals to serve their nation continued to fall on deaf ears? Working women had already answered the call and gone to train and work in the various industries of war that were completely alien to what they had known prior. Why shouldn't the rest do the same? Hiding places were getting harder to find, as were the excuses!

The fashionable London 'set' did not recognise the ladies that had made the decision to leave it. One Land Girl, having returned for a brief holiday between jobs became aware that she was not noticed in quite the same way as she had been prior to working on the land. Her face was now suntanned and her complexion much altered by the wind and rain. London was clearly not familiar with the gait usually adopted by a ploughman![5]

Women were divided into two classes: those that wear khaki and those that don't. Hostile, prickly language attempted to make the shirkers transform themselves from parasitic weaklings into patriots. For the sake of balance, as soon as it was possible, thousands of wealthy women did jump at the opportunity to escape the stifling lifestyles they had been born into or had been afforded by marriage. It really was the time to expend yourself for the sake of your country.[6]

Women who volunteered to harvest flax during the war would not have been sighted anywhere near fields of flax otherwise and yet the magnetism of duty lured university and college girls away from their summer holidays and into the fields. There was no place for snootiness or snobbery to take hold. Everyone had to get on and get the job done efficiently and to the best of their ability.

Many village women left the countryside to work for higher wages in towns and cities and the lack of a readily available, replacement workforce saw an outcome that was both pressing and concerning for organisations to try and facilitate a speedy solution to.

Flax was in much greater demand during the Great War as it had a multitude of uses. Not only did flax yield linseed oil once processed, it was also used for biplane fuselages and wing coverings and satisfied the insatiable demand for linen cloth products for the army. The acreage of land being turned over to flax as a result increased considerably, hence an influx of workers were required to sow, tend, harvest and process the crop. Other sources of labour were Boy Scouts, Girl Guides, schoolchildren and village women of all ages.

Workforces often travelled hundreds of miles to become trained in order to be able to take newly-acquired skills back home with them and train other women to do the same, pivotal war work in their own locality. In July 1918 it was reported that women had travelled from Scotland to Somerset to begin six weeks of training to become leaders of flax-pulling gangs. Once trained, these 150 women would return to train others to do the same.[7]

The attitude of the girls was to be applauded as they made it abundantly clear that they didn't mind uprooting themselves hundreds of miles if it assisted the war effort.

Thanks to the resolve shown by these diverse groups of women, the nation's shortage of certain materials and food supplies was thwarted and they became the farmers salvation. Hitherto commonplace events held during the summer such as garden parties with traditional strawberries and cream were now replaced by work carried out with hoes and scythes!

The message had got through.

Chapter 5

Infra dig!

A huge culture shock awaited those from academic backgrounds who were plucked from their studies and hobbies headlong into the realms of agriculture. The urgency and necessity to undertake war work far outweighed any societal, supercilious grievances felt about working alongside someone who may have been considered 'infra dig' or in plain terms - beneath you!

Through these forced experiences, snobbish perceptions needed to alter. It would have been refreshing, if not a little perplexing for villagers to meet women whose world was academia. The varsity women may have taught them things they could only have dreamt of having spent weeks or months working closely together; the village women likewise. Some interests would transcend class and result in unlikely friendships.

Study for the academics was halted, much to the horror of some who felt that this lengthy break from study would be more than just a mere disruption. Could their intellect be more permanently deadened by working on the land?

For those that still went ahead with the decision to spend their summer vacation or longer periods of time on the land, war service meant foregoing a pleasant and comfortable college hall lifestyle. They had to accept ways that were far removed from their own and took great care not to cause offence. Despite thwarted ambitions, there would have been excitement at the new challenges that lay ahead plus a swirl of teenage hormones thrown in for good measure!

Instructive pamphlets were produced by Women's Agricultural Councils and given out to the university women. They included descriptions of how to carry out agricultural practices and duties. It was unfairly and incorrectly assumed that the information might be beyond their comprehension whereas they were in fact grateful for the guidance.

The national scheme run by the Board of Trade trained such women. Fruit picking made up the lion's share of the work in counties synonymous for their seasonal bounties such as Gloucester, Hereford, Kent and Worcester. Applications were also received from farmers in Cambridgeshire, Scotland and many other areas of the country. The demand for varsity gangs far outweighed what the actual supply could satisfy, especially during the summer of 1916.

Contingents of students from King's College, London worked at a flax camp in Somerset. Women travelled from Bedford College to work on the land as well as students from several other Oxbridge colleges: Girton and Newnham, (Cambridge) and students from Lady Margaret, Somerville and St Hilda's Hall, (Oxford). They formed 'emergency gangs' or 'relays' and assisted with seasonal farm work.

War work was a fundamental part of female students' lives. Newnham students worked on smallholdings in Norfolk during part of their summer holiday and Somerville students planted their playing fields with potatoes to assist with food production.

In 1916, students from St Hilda's Hall, Oxford undertook a variety of temporary vacational work in schools, farms, canteens, munition works and assisted with the processing of prisoner of war parcels at Kensington Palace. They were also employed in permanent positions such as: Teacher of Latin, English, History, Scripture and Maths, Paymistress, doing statistical work for an experimental station for agriculture, Assistant Welfare Supervisor in a munitions works, working in the National Insurance Audit Office and in the Enquiries Department for the Red Cross, (wounded and missing). The roles clearly utilised their intellect. Some women taught during term time and gave up their long summer vacation to work in agriculture.

Young women from Lady Margaret Hall, Oxford, (the first college to give women an Oxford education, founded in 1878) held posts as under gardeners, worked on farms and tended allotments for soldiers' wives. Many worked in organisations set up in the early part of the war such as the Women's Volunteer Reserve.

By April 1915 the scheme that trained and placed academic women was up and running, (albeit on a much smaller scale and heavily reliant on wealthy patrons). The university women that came forward for farm work were generally extremely fit and resilient. Their approach to tasks was methodical and disciplined. If they experienced setbacks, a lightness of spirit saw them carry on unperturbed - unlike some of the other women they worked alongside.[1]

By April 1916, the Cambridge University School of Agriculture, (who worked with the Women's National Land Service Corps) had trained and produced its first squad of 15 agricultural recruits from Girton College. They worked on the University Farm and lodged at Girton College. These women trained to become forewomen, who, once trained went into villages to lead and guide village volunteers.

Girton girls were physically fit as they participated in various college sports such as hockey. Another advantage was that many of them hailed from East Anglia and therefore had some knowledge of the agrarian nature of the area. Two Girton girls that travelled to Kent to work in the hop gardens were based near to an oast house and slept under canvass at night.

Organisations trained the women for a period of between three and six weeks on farms that had been lent for the specific purpose by landowners. Eight of the 15 Girton College girls had already been placed by the end of their training.

For the women who made up the emergency gangs they required little, if any training as the work was unskilled seasonal work such as flax plucking, hop-picking, fruit-picking, dropping potatoes and other harvest work. It was undertaken between the months of July through to September and October.

All of these harvests depended on the unpredictable British weather and it was not unheard of for delicate harvests of fruits such as strawberries to be held back for a month due to cold weather. Once the time was just right, soft fruits like cherries and plums needed to be picked carefully and prepared for sale or other uses. Nothing would have been wasted and bottling fruit was extremely popular. The hay, corn and hop harvests comprised of a more carefully steered programme of work.

Farmers were so impressed by their work ethic and of the results achieved by taking such gangs onto their farms that in April 1916 they frequently requested that the same workers be sent back to them the following year.

It was reported in May 1916 that 1000 women from the Universities of Oxford, Cambridge and London would be working on the land. St Hilda's students also continued to put plays on for convalescing wounded soldiers in a hospital, (previously the Examination School) and also assisted in medical settings. For eight other St Hilda's students, they became Land Girls during the summer of 1916. One of two working parties or 'relays' as they were referred to, volunteered to spend their long summer vacation doing agricultural work. St Hilda's Hall report for 1915/1916 mentions that:

> "A large proportion of the students undertook agricultural work on an estate in Northamptonshire or did picking in a hop garden in Herefordshire for a month in the vacation and received invitations to come again next year."[2]

The working party that travelled to Suckley, Worcestershire in 1916 to pick hops even saw their arrival heralded in the local newspaper! The public appeared to have an unremitting fascination with the educated hop pickers!

These students worked outside during the warmest months of the year. Intense heat, (as well as intense cold) invariably created a range of problems for Land Girls such as sunburn, bites and stings, allergies and blisters. High temperatures would have made working long hours in exposed fields devoid of shade a real trial. Having to work with irritable horses constantly aggravated by flies wouldn't have felt like much of a holiday. Consequently, Land Girls often said that they preferred working in the cold.

The rigours of land work and the often substandard accommodation that went hand in hand with the life of a Land Girl was viewed by many at the time as 'beneath' or 'not of a good enough standard' for a woman of the middle to upper classes to reside in.

The 40 or so hop-picking students were allocated a huge barn which formed their spartan sleeping room. Tents were also located around the oast houses that were used to dry the hops. There was very little in the way of comfort. The girls' beds comprised of chaff-filled mattresses. These were elevated on platforms made of wood that were located on each side of the building.[3]

Washing facilities were just as basic with a pump in an outbuilding, (washing with cold water at 5am was an unpleasant task that tested the mettle of many a Land Girl - even during the summer). A mess-room was located in a repurposed cowshed![4]

The young women followed rules not dissimilar to those of a military camp and led a truly outdoor life. The large doors to the barn in which they slept were kept open throughout the night and the girls were able to stare out at the stars! This dramatic change of lifestyle must have taken some girls a while to adjust to. The odd shadows that their lamps formed across the whitewashed walls at night as they hung from the beams must have initially seemed quite scary! Sleepy girls reached up again to their lamps as dawn broke. Another long, arduous day lay ahead. They had next-to-no privacy but complained little.[5]

Any romanticised depictions of life spent sleeping under the stars would have been in stark contrast to the reality of having to rise at the crack of dawn and partake in the, by now, infamous cold water wash with 39 other girls!

Before the working day started, Land Girls had a multitude of chores to complete. This routine ensured that everything ran like clockwork in the camp with everyone having a role to play. They worked from 7am until 6pm and had a short half an hour break at 8.30am and a lunch hour, usually taken at midday. The girls returned to the camp with ravenous appetites, ready to enjoy a nourishing evening meal and by 9.30pm most were ready for bed.[6]

Accommodation for the St Hilda's contingent, (who were placed in the tiny village of Brockhall in Northamptonshire) appears to have been in a cottage-cum-dairy. They washed their hair outside in the cobbled yard every Sunday under the flow of water being drawn by one of their friends from a pump. Life was just as basic and devoid of any luxuries as it was for the hop-picking contingent!

The female students who worked at Brockhall during the summer of 1916 are listed along with the year that they went to study at St Hilda's.

Margaret Shufeldt, (1913) Lorna Howell, (Geography 1914) Eleanor Verini, (English 1914) Kathleen Gibberd, (1915) Susan Macy, (1915) Katharine Kempthorne, (1914) Ruth Woodthorpe, (1914) M Jones, might refer to Gwen Jones, (1915).

Eleanor Marguerite Verini, although not named directly by Lorna Howell appears on one of the photographs. During an interview on the 10th November 1986, (which survives in St Hilda's College archive) Eleanor briefly mentions her vocational work and how she had enjoyed exploring the countryside. She went on to have a successful career in teaching and was a Headmistress and Principal at several prestigious schools and colleges.

During her vacation at Brockhall, Oxford student turned Land Girl, Lorna Howell took a series of photographs that depicted daily life. This personal album was donated to the archives at St Hilda's in 1952. The photographs provide a precious, rare and personal insight into this brief, somewhat alien period of time in their lives.

They also show the unpleasant, monotonous manual work that the women carried out whilst working alongside seasoned agricultural workers, livestock farmers and soldier co-workers, (stationed at the nearby Barracks at Weedon) who all assisted with the harvest.

The Rector of St Peter and St Paul's, Brockhall wrote about the students in the September 1916 edition of the parish magazine.

> "We have had with us a party of students from St Hilda's Hall, Oxford and we can say that this 2nd relay has shown what women can do for their country and their church."[7]

A revealing and skilfully penned poem written by the St Hilda's Hall students was also published. It humorously details their shared experiences of working on the land. Five out of the six verses were printed in the parish magazine but the complete version appears here.

Farming Song

I.

When'er Britannia goes to war, the men must up and fight,
And women must do the work at home - for that is only right,
Suffragettes must be no more and tennis parties cease
And all our little feminine joys must wait for times of peace!
And Oxford students most of all must do their bit at once,
For Asquith says this war will last for months and months and months!

II.

Now to Northants there came one day eight students seeking work,
And they told the farmers all around no hardship they would shirk;
So the noble Squire who owned the place, he promptly hired five,

And some employment for the rest a farmer did contrive;
And "Oh" they said, "We're longing so to start the work at once!"
(I don't suppose they'll "long" again for months and months and months!)

III.

Now after three weeks on the land their spirits began to sink,
But they struggled bravely on with it for they wanted all the "chink!"
So they scythed and hoed and tossed the hay and even fed the pig,
And all these sort of menial jobs they thought not "infra dig",
For "Oh" they said, "When duty calls, we always go at once!"
("Let's hope she will not call again for months and months and months")

IV.

For one she got a spotty face and one a weary head,
One lived with thistles all day long and dreamt of them in bed;
A wasp stung one upon the nose and one upon the hand
The strawberry jam was made of plum and the butter was "Blue-band."
But "Oh" they said, "We love to live the simple life for once
But we are rather glad it will not last for months and months and months!"

V.

Now Sunday was the only day that brought them any rest
And even then the Rector said he hoped they'd do their best
So they rang the bell and joined the choir and one was going to blow,
But as she came in rather late, the Rector, he said "No."
And as it was the Sabbath morn their hands were clean for once
I don't suppose they'll be clean again for months and months and months.

VI.

The Squire he called them patriots and watched his money go
The farmers praised their willingness but thought them rather slow
The natives thought them very mad in spite of all their brain
And no one ever said to them they hoped they'd come again
And "Oh" they said, "We like to do a month on the land" for once,
But we'd rather work in the Bod or the Rad for months and months and months.[8]

Although the poem can be seen in one respect as light-hearted and tongue-in-cheek, it does chronicle the difficulties that were faced by the group of students who quite clearly were not used to this form of work. Their efforts do not seem to have been universally appreciated by the local people. This was often the case for Land Girls.

Villagers perceived them as slightly mad and did not appear to care if they returned or not! This is in spite of them participating in aspects of village life, such as attending church services, joining the choir, pumping the organ bellows and ringing the bell for services. The Land Girl that arrived late for a church service did herself a disservice as the die-hard members of the congregation would have frowned upon latecomers - especially those that were new to their congregation!

The final verse may have been omitted for good reason as it is conflicting in its message. Although the girls worked rather slowly they still gained the farmer's praise for being willing which says something for their character at least. Many farmers and villagers would still have been completely unaware of the many organisations that were trying to attract, recruit, train and place women on farms. Amongst those already established and recruiting, (albeit in considerably smaller numbers) were the WFGU, (Women's Farm and Garden Union) the WNLSC, (Women's National Land Service Corps) and the L.A.A.S, (Land Army Agricultural Section). There were of course many more.

The final line of the poem demonstrates how the women longed to return to their familiar world. They refer to "The Bod" (The Bodleian Library) and "The Rad" (The Radcliffe Camera). Quite a contrast to thistle-picking in the blazing summer sun!

Customary ailments or hazards of the job are also documented. A spotty face could have been an allergy or even a reaction to long hours spent out in all weathers. It could even have been due to changes in their diet.

Somerville College student and writer, Emilie Rose Macaulay DBE also volunteered for land work in 1916. 'Rose' penned a poem which expressed her thoughts about one of the dirtiest jobs encountered during her time spent working on the land. She called it "Spreading Manure" and its seven stanzas depict the monotony and unpleasant physical nature of the work, often carried out in freezing weather. Parallels are drawn to the harsh conditions endured by Land Girls and those of soldiers serving in the trenches. There is a lot to glean on many levels; a poetic protest perhaps at the social standing of women in society at the time and yet also an unworldliness that fails to accurately acknowledge the exacting horror that men faced second by second in the trenches.

Lorna Howell's photographs show the new binding and reaping machine as well as the traditional farm hay-cart. The girls generally used traditional farming tools such as scythes, pitchforks, hoes and rakes. Specialised thistle-pulling tools were wielded by four 'thistle-dodgers'. Their work was carefully overseen by an experienced labourer or the farmer himself! In some spheres of society, genuine disgust was felt at seeing educated women reduced to pulling thistles!

Despite this opposition, it fell upon the students to perform this extremely unpleasant, potentially harmful, time consuming job. The students turned their hand to various tedious physical tasks such as hoeing fields full of turnips, pitching hay and roping up loads. They refer to the weather and the many mistakes they made. Two of the photographs have amusing annotations written on the back: "A hot day for the turnips" and "Amputation of a turnip."

In addition to farming arable land, the farm at Brockhall also kept and grazed cattle and sheep, (specialising in the Wiltshire Horn breed). Two photographs show these horned sheep being put through a sheep dip.

When the weather was fine, the working day was usually eight hours. The Girton girls certainly kept to this routine and more than likely the St Hilda's girls would have experienced a very similar day. Most women that worked on the land were up at 5am as there were many tasks that needed to be completed before the main part of the day started. Horses needed to be fed and made ready for their work in the fields and cows milked. For those women that fed the other animals on the farm, their working day may have started at around 7am. Meals were almost always taken at set times with breakfast at 8am. Hours of work were generally between 9am and 1pm and in the afternoon, from 2pm to around 4pm. After their evening meal, there was an opportunity to socialise if any energy was still left![9]

Unfortunately, on the 1915 and 1916 intake photographs for St Hilda's, there are no accompanying names to match to Lorna Howell's album of photographs and list of names. Despite this, most of the young women can be identified visually with some degree of certainty when comparing the two sets of photographs.

Harvesting flax was an aspect of war work that brought to the fore the necessity to utilise educated women as a workforce. These shifting mobile gangs comprised of 'the best sort of girls'. This phrase alone embodies the inherent snobbery that was still so prevalent at the time.

Educated women who considered turning their hand to manual labour for the first time must have triggered hot debates and arguments in wealthy households all over the country. Many parents would have opposed the idea of their daughter performing such dirty, heavy work. Strict parents would have taken the moral high ground; attempting to dissuade their shielded offspring from taking such a drastic, unconventional course of action in their life, notwithstanding the fact that it was the correct one at the time.

Thankfully, for the parents of those young women that did dare to venture into the unknown, they soon began to see what the benefits of working on the land were. Not only were their daughter's efforts for the national good but also, every individual that made the decision to volunteer returned much changed and enlightened both mentally and physically.

War changed lives and attitudes.
Working on the land changed lives and attitudes.
Often forever.

Chapter 6

The picturesque garb

Unprecedented times called for unprecedented actions. When the public first got a glimpse of the Land Girl 'soldiers' of the King wearing their new uniforms for the first time, it stunned and shocked onlookers. The uniform was even viewed as immoral and obscene. The thought, let alone sight of women wearing such a masculine looking uniform was enough to make some reach for the smelling salts!

Women wearing breeches, leggings, puttees and long boots challenged the perceptions of what femininity was meant to be in a society that made such definite distinctions. This however did not deter women of all classes from enrolling. The whole span of the social spectrum was represented among its recruits. They all signed up for the same cause, in the same uniform and endured much the same conditions.

The conventions of the day proved hard metaphoric nuts to crack and yet regardless of the opposition, ridicule and prejudice that the Women's Land Army endured initially, they, (a civilian army of women) stood firm and resigned themselves to their cause. Being stared at was something they got used to whether it was out of curiosity, admiration or resentment. In spite of these obstacles, the Land Girls doggedly persisted with an iron resolve to aid food production in what was, by early 1917, an agriculturally-ailing and hungry land still very much at war.

The uniform appeared to hold a strange fascination for spectators that attended rallies and demonstrations; locations where the curious public and farmers could go to study close-up the new 'breed' of women.

Many men were complimentary about the new uniform and embraced the appearance of the Land Girls when they witnessed them en masse, commenting that the women looked soldierly and businesslike.

Several women encountered difficulties obtaining the relevant items of their uniform. This was the case for landworkers who had volunteered in 1916 in Braintree, Essex. Their experience at the hands of the manufacturer had been unsatisfactory and a complaint ensued!

For the women who had to wear these new uniforms every day, they felt strongly about being told to do anything to the contrary, especially after work. One such case was reported on in 1916 where some young women who were training to work on farms travelled into Aberavon in their uniforms having finished work. They had gone against the rules set by the County Women's Field Labour Committee which stipulated that they had to change after work into civilian attire. Their case was supported by Miss Farquharson, (Graduate Organiser of the Women's Land Army) who felt that this was an unfair request, especially when taking into consideration that the women had so little free time to enjoy as it was, having worked a ten hour day.[1]

Although comments vary about the practicalities of the Land Girls' uniform, most women agreed that although the breeches in particular were fairly comfortable to wear whilst working, they were difficult to wash and dry quickly especially during spells of wet, cold weather. Daily newspapers fuelled debates asking how appropriate it actually was for women to be wearing trousers as part of their war service.[2]

Opinion was of course divided but for some elderly ladies who attended a Women's Land Fete during the summer of 1917, the uniform caused something of a stir. This was not altogether surprising when consideration is given to the times they had lived through.

The purpose of the fete was to promote the work of the Women's Land Army which was only a few months into its official existence at that point. Despite looking smart and purposeful in their government approved uniform, the Land Girls came under intense scrutiny from the very elderly ladies that had gathered at the event; the subject of breeches appeared to draw the most criticism.[3]

In spite of the criticism, respectful recognition was aimed at the oldest residents of the village during the land fete, who attended in their traditional yet old-fashioned work smocks. Seeing the old guard standing next to the contemporary Land Girls clad in their leather gaiters, corduroy breeches and slouch hats brought it home to people just how radically the country had been required to discard outdated attitudes and instead consider how useful Land Girls could be if given a fair chance.

A one-act play written in 1918 called "Hannah Comes Round" highlighted the prejudice that Land Girls often experienced. It was set in a Welsh village and the main character was an elderly woman called Hannah. Hannah not only had an aversion to the uniform worn by the Land Girls but to Land Girls per se! That is until she came around to the idea of them and allowed one called Connie, (who worked on a nearby farm) to help her with her garden!

For any successes to be achieved, the assimilation of Land Girls into the rural landscape was imperative. A distinct and rapid shift needed to be made; one that moved right away from the stereotyped imagery of what farmworkers should look like. And yet, the words used to describe them remained, (ever-so-slightly) condescending.

The Cambridge University educated women from Girton College who travelled to work in the hop fields of Kent during the summer of 1916 clearly cut a dash in their various styles of work outfits as they were described as picturesque. In the early years of the Great War, the clothes that landworkers wore varied considerably. Women traditionally wore long skirts in the field, even though breeches, long boots or short boots worn with gaiters were becoming more common. Many different combinations of smocks, overcoats and sacking were however trialled throughout the year to combat the heat or cold![4]

Stout boots were an absolute must for any land worker. Those women that worked on the land knew only too well the need to have sturdy, practical, waterproof and above all, comfortable footwear. Any problems with their feet would of course have hindered their ability to work effectively and thus affected productivity in the longer term.

Boots frequently became the bane of a Land Girl's working life as they were often ill-fitting. Various techniques had to be adopted that attempted to counteract the problem. One girl placed insoles made of cork inside each boot to stop her feet from sliding around in them as she worked.[5]

Boots worn to play hockey or go walking in were not suitable for land work. Boots for land work needed to be specifically designed and manufactured. Due to government controls implemented on the use of heavy leather, footwear that was suitable for arduous agricultural work became harder to come by.

Officials at the Royal Army Clothing Department came up with two boot designs and one shoe design for the women war workers footwear range. The boots were heavy, sturdy and rigid in appearance with two buckles and straps at the top and big hobnails on the soles and a horseshoe iron tip on each heel. The two boot designs were for a high-leg boot, (a field boot) just over 10 inches in height and a more practicable, serviceable ankle field boot.

Both styles of boot were made with the same leather that the army used for their boots and shoes albeit it was lighter in substance. The shorter boot was a more popular design overall. With no straps or buckles to contend with, the risk of any areas of skin or clothing that could potentially rub, blister, chafe or become irritated was minimised when compared to the high-leg boot.

The town of Northampton and county of Northamptonshire can be rightfully proud of its centuries old association with shoemaking and cobbling. Factories such as Bostock's and W. Nichols and Son. Ltd. of Kettering manufactured footwear and Ernest Draper and Co. Ltd. manufactured and sold field boots and clothing to female landworkers. During wartime, these specialised skills were called upon and the town and county produced an estimated 50 million pairs of boots and shoes out of the estimated 70 million that the United Kingdom manufactured as a whole for the Allied armies during the First World War.

Before the official formation of the Women's Land Army, women's apparel varied as they were recruited from different landworker organisations such as the Women's National Land Service Corps or National Land Council to name just two. Members of the National Land Council had to provide their own uniform which comprised of knickers, (a term used then which meant breeches) an overall of red-brown cloth or a similar inexpensive material and a white blouse.

Aside from the picturesque garb, what often distinguished one member of any land organisation from another was the armband worn on the upper left part of the arm. Women's National Land Service Corps members wore a brown canvas armband with the words 'Women's National Land Service Corps' printed on it in a red, elliptical shape. The National Land Council's armband was khaki in colour. On the armband itself was a mauve triangle and a white central disc which bore in black letters the words Land Army. For those women in the Women's Land Army, their armband was made of green felt and had a red crown on it.

A late example of this variation in uniform appeared in a report that detailed events at Barnet Fair in 1919. The girls present appear to have purchased items of uniform privately which, if you could afford to do so was possible, if a little expensive! Some girls wore green riding breeches, velvet caps and boots trimmed with coloured cloth tops. The girls' hats were positioned confidently to one side as they walked around and carried out their own inspection of the horses. Onlookers would naturally have stood and stared as they would not have seen the likes of it before![6]

The public penned letters to national newspapers that championed the very existence of the attire of Britain's Land Girls. They expressed their concern that after the war had ended, the very much-loved, neat and tidy uniform would cease to exist. This it was felt would be a great tragedy as it had proved to be such a practical and surprisingly appealing war 'costume' to many. The new-found health, fitness and glow that land work placed on the cheeks of its recruits lent itself to the fondness that so many people felt towards Land Girls at that time. Praise was heaped on the functionality of the outfit and pleas were made to those that set the fashion trends to move away from long skirts, (which conformed to the ideals still set by society) and instead move towards more mainstream designs that incorporated features made popular by the Land Girl uniforms.[7]

Women that worked on the land in the early part of the war would not have been as identifiable as the later, uniformed members of the Women's Land Army were. The Land Girls were influential and effected change. The practical design of their uniform allowed women to, (when and where it was possible) use cycles to travel to and from work in relative ease especially when compared to the clothing they had worn pre-war. Small adaptations were suggested to make the weighty leggings and breeches and tightly fastened, inflexible gaiters more comfortable to cycle in. These adaptations however often created new problems; gaiters became oversized and women struggled to wear them.[8]

Such was the success of the utilitarian uniform - it was hailed as more than a 'prototype' and forged the way ahead as the go-to clothing of choice for the lady cyclist of the future!

It must have felt almost revolutionary to women that were so used to the constraining conformity of the clothes that society expected them to wear. Billowing, long skirts were impractical to cycle in or undertake field work in and yet that is exactly what women wore in the early years of the Great War. Emphasis continued to be placed on what the uniform should outwardly display so as to maintain an air of elegance and femininity.

There was even talk in the press about radically overhauling the design of women's bikes in order to accommodate the increased interest in women cycling. One report went as far as to state that it reckoned that the stand-alone ladies bicycle design would in time totally vanish from manufacturers catalogues!

The durability and merits of the Land Girl uniform were hailed as a triumphant example of utilitarian design. Its functionality and versatility eventually gained credence; so much so that with the odd tweak and minor alteration, it was rumoured that a variation of it might well become worn universally by women cyclists in peacetime.

Now that educated women were working on the land, manufacturers quickly became aware of a potential, lucrative new opening for clothing manufacture and sales. New, dedicated departments were established in many high-end department stores such as Harvey Nichols and Harrods. They sold variations of the uniform, designing fashionable workwear for wealthier women to purchase. Burberry was the luxury clothing brand chosen to launch the different designs that women, (who could afford to buy them) could wear whilst working on the land. It took place in the Haymarket in London. Land Girls had had the last laugh on London as the fashionable set were now taking notice and buying versions of the uniform that they had been wearing for the past few years![9]

A woman that worked on the land prior to the formation of the Women's Land Army remarked that although long skirts were cumbersome and impractical to wear for land work, there were few alternatives. To wear breeches pre-war would have been unthinkable! As the war progressed, more land organisations were established and breeches became an integral and accepted part of the standard issue uniform - despite fierce opposition from some quarters.[10]

The word 'accepted' highlights just how vexing it was for Great War society to construe the multifarious changes required in order for women to carry out vital war work. This however did not stop women from pushing the parameters of what was acceptable with regard to work dress. Alterations and tweaks to garments were regularly carried out!

In January 1917, a Land Girl took it upon herself to actually design her own uniform. She was clearly an academic as it was reported that she could speak four languages.[11]

The American 'Farmerettes' were not so lucky regarding their uniform as its design had still not been formalised by late 1917. By 1918 however, photographs appeared in British newspapers showing the uniform being worn by members of the Women's Land Army in America. There were marked differences to the uniform worn by the British Women's Land Army. The breeches worn by some American women at that time had a distinct, wide frill around the bottom and resembled bloomers rather than breeches. The hat looked very different too as it had a wide brim, (possibly made of straw) which resembled a sun hat.

There were of course variations and women wore dungarees with their hair cut into a short, practical bob. However, by early 1919 the uniform bore a striking resemblance to that of their British counterparts.

The general public probably assumed that each land worker who had volunteered for National Service would automatically be kitted out with the appropriate uniform and kit for the section they had chosen to work in. This was not always so. Undersupply was a frequent problem.

During the summer of 1918, girls working in the Forage Corps under the command of the Army Service Corps were only being supplied with one pair of boots which, through long hours of arduous labour were being quickly worn down; soon becoming beyond repair. Some girls were even suffering from foot problems and injuries as a direct result of worn out footwear and the insufficient supply of any replacement boots. It was reported at the time that a landlady, (who had Forage Corps workers staying with her) had to provide food over three days for one of the workers. The woman had developed problems with her heels and was unable to work for four days. The Forage Corps had only provided enough rations for a single day![12]

Instead of the government providing adequate replacement boots for them, they were clearly expected to stump up their own hard earned wage to get repairs done themselves. Boots could be purchased privately but they were expensive and were beyond the reach of many workers. Running repairs would mean little money was left over to put by, save or send back home. It was well documented that the wage barely covered even the most basic of items after deductions for billets, rations and other expenses such as laundry and insurance had been made. Other expenses that needed to be budgeted for such as repairs to boots, additional items of clothing, necessities like toiletries and a small amount of money set aside for any social activities was difficult to scrape together. It was the unforeseen expenses that proved to be a stumbling block for many girls as they could not always count on their parents to be able to meet these extra costs. Often, parents were unable to assist due to suffering financial hardship themselves.[13]

At the end of a hard day, a Land Girl was only too pleased to get out of her uniform! Depending on the season, Land Girls finished work in the fields around 4pm. After which, they would take the horses back to the farm, unharness and feed them and any other animals in their care, wash any implements and leave any machinery tidy for the following day. It was then a case of getting out of their uniform, doing any housekeeping chores, having a wash or bath, preparing dinner and enjoying an hour or so of relaxation before retiring to bed, usually around 9.30pm.[14]

The Women's Forestry Corps workers wore a uniform similar to that of the Land Girls but once again, there were many variations. Some women wore green beret-style hats as they worked. In comparison, the uniform of the Forage Corp workers was quite distinctive, comprising of a hat, jersey, dark green breeches, overalls, khaki overcoat, gaiters, black boots and a knapsack. The women wore the insignia 'FC' on their shoulder which was sometimes also worn on the hat. A brass badge was also worn showing the letters 'FC' located within the eight-pointed star of the Royal Army Service Corps.

Praise and respect was hard earnt in farming. Country folk were loathe to waste words but there was immense pride in how each farm was represented and viewed by the outside world. Healthy and unhealthy rivalry existed between farms but one thing is for sure, no respectable farmer, wagoner or Land Girl for that matter worth their salt would allow his cart and horses to be taken into the nearby town without putting on a good show.

Land Girls always wanted to look smart as they represented both an organisation and the farm where they were working. It meant rigorously cleaning their boots, leggings and uniform before they set off. When Land Girls took horses to the village blacksmith to be shod, they polished up the horse brasses, smartened up the tack, washed the horses down, plaited their manes and tails so that they drew admiring glances as they trotted into town.

Ornamental additions, such as bells and brasses would be attached to various pieces of the horses tack for this special trip. So, not only would you be seen but you would be heard approaching too!

Farm employees could be extremely competitive and would always strive to be the best and this outward 'show' demonstrated that standards were still as high as they had been pre-war. It was therefore the responsibility of the driver to ensure that the brasses on the horses shone brighter than anyone else's.[15]

Land Girls also added personal touches to their charges such as coloured ribbons, which adorned the tails of the horses. This all-round effort, with everyone adding their own individual details showed great pride, not only in their work but also in sustaining the positive reputation of where they worked. It must have been both rewarding and reassuring to see newcomers like the Land Girls wholeheartedly engaging with and valuing the importance of rural traditions.

It was vital that they made a memorable and lasting first impression.

Chapter 7

Billets from hell

To billet or not to billet? That was often the question for householders although this was no longer a choice for some by April 1918. New powers had, by this time reportedly been given to the Food Production Department whereby householders who lived in the countryside had to provide accommodation for land workers if it was required.[1]

Originally, women that signed on the dotted line had to serve for the duration of the war, but this was soon changed as it affected recruitment.

Once this change had been made, women signed on the dotted line either for six or 12 months. During the first month of training, no salary was paid but board and lodging was provided and the all-important 'kit' was issued. If a woman chose a six month term then she had to choose between Agriculture or the Forestry and Timber Cutting section, however if the girl chose The Forage Corps, which was part of the Army Service Corps, (this section was part of the regular army) commitment in the first instance was required for 12 months. Therefore, once the promise to serve had been made, Land Girls had to go wherever they were required. Sourcing suitable accommodation was always a challenge!

In late May 1918, WATS, the Women's Agricultural Tractor Service, Barrow Green Tractor School in Surrey already had approximately 30 pupils with 100-200 recruits set to follow. The Tractor Service overall predicted an intake of 3000 women. Newspaper articles at the time stated that the government provided the women who opted to work in the Tractor Service with a range of kit, comprising of the usual standard issue items but in addition: dungarees, (2 pairs) cap, gloves, coat, trousers and a sou'wester. They could join at any age and both single and married women would be accepted.

These women could earn significantly more after their initial training had been completed. Once they were under contract, they received 30 shillings a week and for every acre they ploughed, 1 shilling. As much as 70 shillings could be earnt as the daily average that was ploughed was between 6-8 acres. Usually, between 12 to 15 shillings were deducted for food and billets. Included in the terms was a 2 week holiday to be taken once a year. Any late passes or leave at weekends had to be authorised by the superintendent.[2]

New recruits at Oxted attended lectures in the open-air. The instruction itself was carried out solely by women who taught the mechanical elements required for tractor work. However it was not all work and no play! Any friends of the trainees were welcome to attend any social events that were organised.

As time wore on, 247 training centres sprang up all around the country meaning that Land Girls were billeted in a myriad of ways: caravans, (mainly used as a 'mess') tents, cottages, bothies and barns, village and parish halls, Wesleyan Churches, large country houses, stately homes, old monasteries, schools, huts, hostels, oast houses and even a cricket pavilion! Although the intention to house every Land Girl comfortably was an honourable one, it was not always realised!

'A Land Girl's lot' was down to complete luck. Tents were the easiest solution for housing the temporary, seasonal influx of women made up of mobile gangs and younger girls, (that were under supervision) during the summer holidays. In June 1916, it was reported that a caravan and a tent was the accommodation of a group of teachers and other seasonal workers who were working on the land.[3]

Wherever girls of school age were being brought in to work seasonally on the land to help, the advice was that supervision should be carried out by women who were educated.[4]

Farmers were often wary of outsiders and reluctant to put up Land Girl newcomers on their own farms because they feared trouble.

By 1917, Land Girls were not an entirely new phenomena as prior to the formation of the Women's Land Army, organisations like the Women's National Land Service Corps, (this organisation was not exclusive in its recruitment of women during the war although it was recognised by the government as the central body for organising the training of educated women in agriculture) recruited women and provided short courses of training if required of between 3-6 weeks at a cost of between 15-25 shillings a week. No training was provided for seasonal work.

Cottages were requisitioned where possible but failing that, women were housed in hostels. Despite the reluctance of some farmers and villagers to house Land Girls at the time, offers were forthcoming in some other areas.[5]

Hostels were often large cottages requisitioned to house war workers. They were frequently situated in idyllic villages and some women could boast of living in comparative luxury when compared to the billets of other Land Girls. On a visit to a hostel in Oxfordshire, the editor of The Landswoman described the halcyon scene that greeted her.

> "The [basket] girls are living in a lovely old house, (I rather want to live there myself) in a most picturesque village and they seem to have a very happy time of it. When I am tired and dumpy I am going down to that hostel for a whole weekend."[6]

One Land Girl, (who was taking part in a rally) described her billet, which was in the foreman's cottage. She mentioned that a sitting room was located in a hut outside and that she and the other girls staying there had to take turns at being an orderly.[7]

The Chair of the WNLSC wrote to The Times newspaper in the summer of 1916 in an attempt to appeal to women aged between 18-35 of average strength to work full time. The details that were printed informed girls of where hostels were available. The owners of large, country estates had lent buildings to house any suitable women that came forward having seen the appeal. They were located all over the country in counties such as Berkshire, Essex, Northamptonshire and Surrey.[8]

Land Girls often mention how little comfort there was in hostels. Accounts naturally vary but one evocative account was recollected by a young woman, who worked in Nottinghamshire during the autumn of 1919.

> "Let your thoughts wander to a hostel set in the midst of trees, with a few fine fruit trees in the front, but not exactly an orchard. Then again, as it were, in the gloom turn your eyes from the trees to the windows of the hostel. Through them you see a bright light and by the aid of it you see a cosy kitchen, with a big fire glowing in the grate and round the fire are

seated a dozen or more Land Girls with Miss Leach, (the lady in charge) in the midst of them."[9]

In stark contrast, a high school girl described what her billets were like in the winter of 1917. She had come to work on the land as part of a scheme run by Wiltshire War Agricultural Committee that specifically targeted high school students. The Land Girl was trained at Longford Castle from January 1917 and then went to work on a farm in mid-Wiltshire until April. Although she describes being happy overall, testing conditions greeted her and her fellow workers.

A property may have been pleasing to look at from the outside but after long, hard days working in biting cold winds, snow and hard frost, to return to a cold house, lay a fire, prepare meals and do housework took some sticking.

Camaraderie and sharing hardships enabled girls to get through tough times such as these. However, if groups were split up it meant they had to cope with everything alone. This could finally tip the scales with regard to what they could endure.[10]

The same girl recounts her subsequent farm placement in North Wiltshire, (from April 1917 to November) which was in complete contrast to her previous one. Here she lived in a nice house provided by the village 'Squire' who, (in this instance was female) showed a genuine interest in her workers. Feeling valued really mattered. Land Girls were often placed on tenant farms and as a result, their experiences varied. This particular girl clearly enjoyed her time at this farm as she recounted it fondly, describing how lovely the gardens were and its proximity to a river.[11]

In the early years of the war, efforts to house women land workers were trialled as experiments as nothing quite like it had been attempted previously – not on such a scale at least. Where accommodation was just too difficult to acquire for the number of women workers who required it, mobile gangs were the ideal solution. They could be housed temporarily in village halls or tents if necessary as they moved from farm to farm to work. These gangs frequently cycled long distances in order to get to the farms where they were needed or were driven in trucks or taken on carts!

Established organisations joined forces on an 'ad hoc' understanding and formed links with new trainees, trained women and experienced women. An ambitious experiment was trialled by the National Land Council in the summer of 1916 at Dunnington Heath in Warwickshire. 70 girls, (known locally as 'War Brownies' because of their instantly recognisable brown uniforms) were housed in outbuildings that had been hastily transformed into sleeping quarters, a recreation room and even a hospital! These girls were ill-prepared for what lay in store, having had next to no experience of the hardship of manual work or the rougher side of life!

The 400 acre site had been completely transformed. Brick barns that contained the sleeping quarters resembled Swiss Oberland huts. The whole camp was run with military precision and the girls appeared to genuinely enjoy their disciplined existence. An orderly was allocated to each of the seven sleeping huts and there were platoon leaders in charge of the girls as they worked in the fields. They enjoyed facilities such as a canteen, a field kitchen and two bathrooms.[12]

In contrast, the 'War Brownies' based at Evesham were billeted in lodgings or cottages. This type of accommodation allowed them to furnish their living quarters themselves, if of course they had the money to do so. When asked about the camp at Dunnington, the Evesham Brownies were uncertain about camp life and questioned if it would suit them.[13]

Everybody's day was physical. Organisation was a key factor and the various seasonal camps were careful to have a regimented daily schedule that ensured things ran like clockwork. For the women who were fruit-pickers, their day started especially early, with reveille sounding at the unearthly time of 4am by the night watchman's bell. After an early morning bite to eat and a cup of tea at 4.30am, the women began to head out towards the strawberry fields. 7.30am saw them return for a hearty breakfast having already worked up an appetite. Dinner and tea was served at the same time every day and after tea, an hour was set aside for socialising. Unlike the other Land Girls, fruit-pickers retired to bed an hour or so early due to their exceptionally early starts. Any chatter or reading after 8pm was strictly forbidden in the huts.[14]

In this particular camp, a good balance appears to have been struck between work, food, breaks and socialising.

Where seasonal flax-pullers were concerned, another set of exceptional circumstances had to swing into action. Organising accommodation for 90-

100 girls during the summer of 1919 in North Yorkshire was a case of thinking on your feet! Four camps were established and billets ranged from an empty swimming baths to cottages, a school and a soldier's hut!

Another successful, albeit small-scale trainer of Land Girls was located at Moulton in Northamptonshire, (a site well-known for its training of Land Girls during the Second World War). Moulton County Council Experimental Farm as it was known during the Great War was taking women onto its 200 acres in 1916 and providing them with general training over the period of a month whereby they were then able to take up employment on farms with immediate effect.

At Moulton, the bailiff's house provided accommodation for the Land Girls. Three, neatly furnished bedrooms housed six trainees throughout their month-long course. A large, shared sitting room was also allocated. The Land Girls also had the responsibility of electing a 'Mess President' who would take charge of the catering each week. They were however under the watchful eye of the forewoman who was also billeted there. The course fee was £3 with board and food provided at the rate of 15 shillings a week.

It must have been reassuring to parents and trainees alike if billets were comfortable and managed well. The experimental farm clearly accepted women from further afield as two new students had travelled from Swansea to train there.

It was probably best to have low expectations regarding accommodation, that way any disappointment was dealt with more easily.

On a train journey made in the autumn of 1916, a Vicar's daughter quite by chance chatted to a magazine columnist about a particular issue that had been troubling her about women working on the land. She was obviously a thoughtful, sensitive girl and deliberated about the strange times she was living in, pondering over the dilemma that must have faced many Land Girls – that of how to obtain a bath when there seemed so few of them in the countryside. She told her fellow passenger about her cottage billet, which had commanding views over the Downs in Sussex and how, having worked there for a fortnight, she politely asked if it was possible to have a bath. Her request was met with absolute disbelief from the farmer's wife - so much so that the Land Girl swiftly retracted her request and asked for some hot water in her room instead!

The farmer spoke to the Land Girl the following day and said that his wife had been unable to sleep because of what she had asked and was still very upset about it. As a direct result of this innocent and perfectly reasonable request, the Land Girl had to vacate her billet. The farmer's wife then proceeded to spread malicious gossip about the girl in the nearby village, the result of which meant she had terrible trouble finding a new place to live.[15]

This rather sad tale was probably not uncommon. An unintentional misjudgement on the Land Girl's part had created an intolerable situation. It may have been that the farmer's wife was jealous of the young woman living in her home and merely looked for any incident, however trivial to cause distress to her. Such narrow-minded, jealous and spiteful behaviour was completely unnecessary.

A harrowing story involving an 18 year old Land Girl made the news in February 1919. At the time, the girl was working on a farm in Worcestershire and was unable to secure suitable accommodation in the village with a fellow Land Girl. As a result, they were forced to secure an alternative place to reside in for themselves. The girls worked 9½ hours each day and had no comfort or privacy when they returned in the evening. The report remarks on the untidy surroundings and how the efforts made by the girls to attempt to address even the most basic of problems were met with catastrophe. The billet provided no privacy for the girls as there were no curtains or blinds at the windows. One of the Land Girls, who was dressed in a landworker's smock at the time, attempted to hang her dressing-gown over the bedroom window. As she tried to do this, her smock caught fire in the flame of a candle and she sustained life-changing burns as a consequence.[16]

The case saw the launch of an investigation. The Women's Branch of the Food Production Department would have been responsible in the first instance for the girls' welfare so why had these girls not been better supported whilst trying to locate a suitable billet?

Despite the Land Girl's harrowing injuries, the authorities showed no compassion, common sense or reason. They failed to pay for the expenses incurred when the injured Land Girl, (on the advice of the doctor) was taken to a nursing home having sustained life-altering injuries. Incredibly, the outstanding expenses had to be settled by her parents who were not well-off.

The girl's mother naturally wanted to visit her child, who was gravely ill but officials from the Food Production Department initially refused to provide a railway warrant. They finally agreed to pay 12s 6d a week for a few weeks; a month at best.

The report from the investigation was damning towards the Worcestershire branch of the Food Production Department. Its findings had clearly recognised and acknowledged the enormous insensitivity that had been directed at the Land Girl and her family. It was decided to place the case into the hands of a higher tribunal in order for an appropriate decision and outcome to be reached. Authorities that had pledged to look after this young girl had failed both her and her parents and they needed to be brought to account for these failings.[17]

Food and lodgings were not cheap. In some areas of the country, it could total 15 shillings or even as much as 17 shillings. This figure did of course vary if the arrangement was a private one. If you were billeted with a farmer then the charge was generally fixed at 13s per week.

Land Girls started on a living wage and as each individual gained further knowledge and expertise, (perhaps specialising in a certain aspect of their work) they saw an increase in their wages. In mid-1919 the maximum wage for women land workers had increased from 22s 6d to 25s a week, (after 3 months satisfactory service).

Usually, a fixed price was agreed for the billet before the girl arrived at her post. Items such as milk and vegetables were occasionally included in the price. In May 1918, once deductions had been made, every Land Girl should have had an average of at least 1 shilling left in her pocket each day. An angry parent from Aberdeen wrote a scathing, anonymous letter to a local newspaper about the unfair treatment she felt her daughter was receiving whilst serving in the Women's Land Army. She described how her daughter received 16 shillings a week in wages and how 14 shillings and 6 pence went on food, fuel and light which only left her with 1 shilling and 6 pence after her living expenses had been paid. She urged other parents to really think twice before letting their daughters join the Women's Land Army as she had been required to meet additional expenses for clothing out of her own pocket which she could ill-afford.[18]

In the monthly returns, many villages kept silent with regard to how many women were working on the land in their particular district. Villagers feared that younger girls would be taken from their families to work elsewhere if their names were revealed to the village registrars. In order to try and put a stop to these fears, the Women's Land Army acknowledged that any woman coming forward would see efforts made to keep her, (if she so wished) working within travelling distance from her home.

Whilst they received their precursory training, board and lodging was provided at the training farm or college, (with 4 shillings pocket money given additionally during the last fortnight). Usually, a suitable billet was found in a building on the farm itself or in a village nearby. If the Land Girl passed an efficiency test her wages increased from the usual minimum wage of 18 shillings a week to around £1.

Women that worked on tractors were better off as they were paid at a rate per acre that was fixed for each district. This rate varied but they earnt a good wage aside from any overtime worked.

Due to the remote and inaccessible geographical locations of some farms, the provision of even the most basic of facilities was nigh on impossible. Therefore, living conditions were often far from favourable and wrangles frequently ensued between Welfare Officers, Travelling Inspectors and farmers to try and improve the living conditions for the unfortunate Land Girl(s) placed there.

Rumours flew around Land Girl circles that it was hard to secure billets. This hearsay, although having a provable, underpinning element of credence damaged the sheen that the Women's Land Army publicity machine wanted would-be recruits to see.

The Women's Land Army were quick to counteract these rumours by stating that all accommodation meant for Land Girls was inspected and that anything that was heard to the contrary was incorrect. It also said that Land Girls had, at the very least, one shilling left each day after expenses for board had been deducted. This information was clearly up for debate as it was patently clear that not all billets were inspected, despite being adamantly stated to the contrary and as a direct consequence of these failings, many Land Girls really struggled.[19]

The countywide support network was required to swing into action if there was a problem and attempt to resolve any issues that arose quickly. Welfare Officers needed to be a regular, visible presence in the lives of the Land Girls in order to build trust and sense how relationships were between farmers, villagers and Land Girls. Also, the health of the women was paramount and as such, required careful monitoring.

The feelings of injustice felt, not just by the Land Girls themselves but also by their parents regarding inadequate wages was acknowledged at a meeting of Ramsgate Employment and District Committee during June 1919. The committee fought the corner for the downtrodden Land Girls having received a letter from a demobilised member of the Women's Land Army.

The letter highlighted the disparity between the other female services, such as the WRNS, WRAF and WAACs who received 25 shillings a week. In contrast, if Land Girls found themselves out-of-work for any reason they received a mere 15 shillings. The Ministry of Labour supported the cause at the meeting and unanimously decided to 'make good' the unfair deficit.

Group leaders continued to make visits to Land Girls on farms and also those working in the timber supply departments in order to see for themselves their working and living conditions. They also monitored how efficiently the concern was being run and judged if more labour was needed. By mid-1919, demand for accommodation was declining. Some depots closed and women who still required a billet were referred to nearby YMCAs.

Throughout the lifespan of land organisations, all manner of schemes were trialled to see if more unusual locations could provide suitable accommodation for recruits. A meeting was held in Lincoln in late December 1917 whereby a suggestion was put forward to the Board of Agriculture that would see contingents of Land Girls billeted in private houses. This initiative came to fruition and Land Girls were indeed billeted in many large country houses and worked on country estates the length of the country. Sandringham, Chequers, (the country residence of the Prime Minister) and Burghley, (where Land Girls were trained) were just three estates that temporarily gave land and farms over to the national war effort.

Four trained women were placed to work in the King's gardens at Frogmore, Windsor Castle, (having received special training for two years previously). They worked in the glasshouses replacing the male gardeners who had left to serve their country. They were accommodated in houses located within the royal gardens, in close proximity to their place of work.[20]

The idyllic slope in front of Barwick House, near Yeovil, Somerset was home to 563 women and young girls during the summer months of July 1918.

For the university and college girls, one of 94 little white tents, (which made up a carefully planned camp) was their home. A quizzical folly called 'Jack the Treacle Eater' watched over the camp!

For girls that appreciated a far-fetched tale, they would no doubt have enjoyed the legend of Jack, a messenger who was supposedly fed treacle in a bid to make him run faster, speeding up his deliveries to London! 'Jack' may have even become a whimsical role model for the Land Girls!

Certainly during any free time, women who had travelled to the county for work would have appreciated a chance to explore what it had to offer socially and historically. Some local ladies made sure that there were also additional recreational activities laid on for the girls in the house itself. Some rooms had been made specially available for this purpose.

The 'flaxettes' ate their meals in big canteen-style marquees which provided an opportunity to catch up with any news or gossip! No doubt the shade of the marquee was most welcome having spent hours working under the blazing summer sun. Women could, (aside from their own rations) also buy additional items at their own expense in the canteen.

Large numbers of women travelled from all over the country to partake in seasonal work. During the summer of 1918 over a few short weeks, 2000 women infiltrated Somerset and 3000 went to Dorset. All of them required accommodation, so logistically it was a large scale operation to establish such well-regulated camps.

Prisoner of war labour was also utilised and under guard, the prisoners constructed the camp at Barwick, (which proved hugely successful). Another camp that used captured Germans as a labour-force was at Dorchester, where 300 were deployed to assist with the whole chain of operations required to grow, harvest and process flax.

Processing flax required an additional infrastructure to be in place in order to support the raw material coming in directly from the fields. Additional factories and sites to enable deseeding to be carried out had to be found in the first instance and made fit for purpose. In addition, the workforce actually required to carry out these processes, (if not drawn from the local area) would also require some form of accommodation.

In early April 1917, Veniscombe Hostel in Newchurch on the Isle of Wight boasted an inaugural batch of fully trained Women's Land Army recruits.

Veniscombe was the first hostel to be opened under the National Service and Board of Agriculture's Scheme and as a result, conditions inside were favourable.

As further training centres were established, so too were more 'gang' hostels. This temporary accommodation was dotted all around the country, usually housing between 40-50 women at a time. Some hostels even had land adjoining them where women could become part of an allotment scheme.

For Land Girls living in a hostel under the strict supervision of a Matron, life was regimented. Uncompromising routines were imposed on the girls simply to maintain order and discipline. For the 20 or so Land Girls who lived under military-style conditions in a Wesleyan School during the summer of 1918 their billets were stark. The main area of the school was divided into a communal living space and the other part became a dormitory where mattresses were laid on the floor.[21]

A Land Girl, working in the Fens documented her primitive yet relatable living conditions in a warts and all poem that was printed in The Landswoman in November 1918.

My Little Straw Bed on the Floor by 'Bodge'

When the golden sun sinks in the Fens
And the toil of a long day is o'er,
Though the hour may be late - we retire about eight -
I forget I was cheery before.
Close at hand, where the centipedes crawl,
I shall slumber 'mid beetles galore,
And the spiders will race to alight on my face
On my Little Straw Bed on the Floor.

I've a neighbour who sings in her sleep,
And a mate with a musical snore,
While somniloquists talk and somnambulists walk,
And the cats shriek and howl near the door.
It's a corner of Bedlam itself,
Though it's only a bag stuffed with straw,

> But with comforts so rare, why, no place can compare,
> With my Little Straw Bed on the Floor.
>
> At the call of my Country and King,
> I have left all the comforts of town.
> O! The tears I could shed when I think of my bed.
> Such a snug little nest lined with down!
> Yet I know in the sweet by-and-by,
> When these rural delights are no more,
> I shall long to be back with those beetles so black
> On my Little Straw Bed on the Floor.[22]

By printing this poem, it shows that the editor was not afraid to share stories with readers that showed the harsh reality of serving in the Women's Land Army.

If a Land Girl was happy and harmoniously billeted, there was much fun and enjoyment to be had aside from work with trips into the nearby town to the theatre with the other workers on the farm.

The wider community was frequently called upon to help the Land Girls' cause. Pleas from aristocratic ladies were printed in local newspapers and advertisements appeared that appealed either for monetary donations to be made for furnishings or for items such as books, cushions, comfortable chairs, games, gramophones and even pianos to be donated to hostels. Such items would provide Land Girls with at least a degree of comfort after long, hard days. Many of the girls would have left behind pleasant, affluent lifestyles and it would have come as a genuine shock to have to sit on hard stools or benches at best at the end of an arduous day.[23]

Coming together in the evening to share the experiences of the day would have been something they no doubt looked forward to but for those billeted alone on desolate farms the loneliness would have taken some sticking!

For the 10 Land Girls who were billeted in a hostel at Draughton, Northamptonshire, they paint a picture of a particularly well-run and comfortable establishment. Training centres generally-speaking were the places that struggled to provide even the most basic of comforts so these girls were incredibly lucky. For £1 a week, training, board and lodging was covered. The services of a Matron too were included.[24]

A further favourable account of what appears to be a recently repurposed, whitewashed cottage, (now serving as an airy and pleasant billet for Land Girls) was in the Cornish town of Restormel. Ironically, the young women lived under the supervision of Mrs Cowman, who had been trained at an agricultural college herself!

Another training centre was established for recruits in The Women's Legion at the hunt kennels at Cottesmore in Oakham, Rutland. Cottages that were attached to the premises had been converted into 'pensions' for the women. In addition to the cottages set aside for 11 volunteers, another special cottage was adapted into a depot. If a volunteer found herself unemployed through no fault of her own, she could stay in the depot until another employer took her on. It had space for five such volunteers at any one time.[25]

Official rules and regulations were now formerly set out in the Women's Land Army L.A.A.S Handbook in the 'Copy of the New Terms and Conditions of Service' section. The rules regarding depots stated that free maintenance would be given providing either two weeks, (for those women who had signed up for six months) or four weeks was not exceeded. This of course depended on the reason why a woman had become unemployed. If it wasn't your fault then this rule would apply. For women that had signed up for a year, they would be entitled to maintenance in a depot for four weeks if it was required. If, for any reason women took it upon themselves to return home without seeking permission from the Secretary, then no claim could be made.[26]

The L.A.A.S Training Camp at Glanusk Park, Crickhowell in Breconshire was opened on June 22nd 1918 and was situated on the bank of the picturesque River Usk. Wooden huts were used as a kitchen, store rooms and washhouses ensuring that the women living there enjoyed sanitary, hygienic living conditions. A water supply was readily available and a boiler and camp oven was also built. There were 18 tents in total, 15 sleeping tents, a mess tent, outfit store tent and a recreation tent with a piano too!

This structured set-up had been purposely designed; with meticulous attention being paid to the welfare of the women. It paid dividends because the 68 recruits that passed through were recorded as being happy and cheerful despite having to work in inclement weather.

It appears that the positive attitude displayed by (a) the women towards their situation, (b) to each other (c) their approach to work and (d) how they operated as part of a large unit in the area – went some way to convincing even the most reluctant of farmers in the area of their worth as a workforce. Ironically, many women were kept on by the very same farmers!

In some counties it just wasn't logistically viable to get Land Girls onto farms and even if it had been, there was no available accommodation for them to live on site. Dorset was once such county. The rail network in Dorset was poor and links to more populated areas negligible. Scarcity of fuel made firstly, the transportation of not only Land Girls to and from isolated farms to work nigh on impossible but secondly, any goods that the farm grew or reared too. The incentive for farmers to produce any additional food in this particular county was lacking because there were few, if any markets for them to sell their produce onto.

For those women placed in harsher landscapes such as Exmoor, they spent much of their time alone and items such as a gramophone were indispensable. Singing along to familiar songs helped them to unwind at the end of a tough day. The simplest of comforts were cherished the most, especially when the weather was at its coldest and the nights were at their darkest.

"It is 7 o clock on a drizzly night in October 1917. Do you see three weary Land Girls pushing their bicycles down the muddy lane to that barn-like building which is to be their billet? The doors and windows stand hospitably open but no welcoming light shines forth into the gloom. Let us follow them into the kitchen, a bare, sparsely furnished room in which an exhaustive search reveals neither candle nor matches. A parcel of groceries, straight from the shop, stands in the corner, but horror of horrors, the bread has been forgotten! A walk to the farm, a few hundred yards away, procures a light and half a loaf of bread and the girls make their supper from it and the remains of their sandwiches. Thoughts of tomorrow's early breakfast turn their attention to the grate, but, alas, it's choked with cinders and the remains of half-burnt letters. We slip away with a sigh, but a hearty laugh from within reminds us that it takes a lot to knock the fun out of the lasses."[27]

Some Land Girls who were in a threshing gang had been placed in the village of Newington, (about two miles from Folkestone).

Their accommodation was:

> "Situated almost at the foot of the cliff, hills I like to call them, they remind me so much of home."[28]

Farmers also had reservations about the low wage offered to the Land Girls. As an employer, accommodation had to be found and as a result, the girl or girls instantly became an extra responsibility for him. These women were mainly outsiders and would be unknown in the locality. There was also his own workforce to consider. Village girls who were living at home with their families were viewed as a more convenient choice.

There was however a need to employ village women <u>and</u> Land Girls due to the shortage of labour and yet many village women left the land to work for higher wages in the towns.

It was hard to continue to make land work attractive to young village girls as many did not want to stay in the isolated communities they had grown up in having spied an opportunity to leave it behind. The war offered young women like these, new and exciting chances to escape the difficulties and poverty of village life or at the very least, aspire to work their way out of it.

By having new workers arrive and live in otherwise uninhabited cottages or buildings in a village, a revitalising effect would often have been felt.

For girls that had lived a more sheltered life, (perhaps those from affluent backgrounds) to share a billet with others and work shoulder to shoulder with the same women every day, (all of whom were very different to you) must have been a great leveller and incredibly character-building. Wherever women came from, they would have undoubtedly felt useful for perhaps the first time in their lives and developed personal characteristics they never knew they actually possessed; qualities which one could argue had made them better human beings!

Chapter 8

Wasp stings and weary heads!

> There was a young woman,
> Sick, nervous and blue,
> She had so many troubles,
> I know what I'd do,
> I'd give her a kit
> Without any skirt,
> And I'd soon have her whistling
> And shovelling dirt.[1]

The mysterious fascination that working on the land held for many women all too often turned out to be a fallacy. A Land Girl's 'lot' during the Great War was punishing and with the turn of each season, many new challenges were thrown their way.

Seeing a new day dawn was a new entity for many women; it was now witnessed whilst hard at work in the fields instead of from a comfortable window seat. There were positive and detrimental effects on their general health both physically and mentally. They had, after all, taken up completely new occupations, suffered great upheaval and immediately had jobs imposed upon them that tested their capabilities to the limit.

Improvements or deterioration to health would manifest piecemeal as their service continued with differing levels of severity; from the common seasonal coughs and colds to developing asthma, bronchitis and even pneumonia. It was not unheard of for other medical conditions to develop during the course of service such as allergies and skin conditions due to working with animals in close proximity, lack of adequate sanitation or damp, ramshackle billets.

Lethargy and a lack of enthusiasm crept in too, especially during tough weeks of bitter cold, incessant rain or intense heat. A Land Girl described meeting her friend, (who was a VAD) and during their discourse they both discovered that they were suffering from a case of 'war disease.' In other words, they were sick of their jobs!

It must have felt very easy to feel undervalued at times and that your contribution was not making that much of a difference to a farm or impacting the war effort as a whole. For those women who joined land organisations pre-Women's Land Army, without the camaraderie or umbrella of a regulated organisation to fall back on, support was somewhat scant and it was left to the individual more or less to decide whether to stick at a job or move on.

Threshing is an example of how respiratory problems could be caused or aggravated. Women often wore protective hoods and masks to protect them from the incessant dust created by handling the hay. Threshing tested every girl to the extremes of their patience! It was incredibly dirty work and girls sneezed, coughed and nearly choked as a result of inhaling the dust and soot that emanated from the engine. If the wind was in the same direction as the hay being fed into the drum, these problems were only exacerbated. At the end of the day, girls had red, irritated eyes, (caused by crying dust-induced tears) and their clothes were covered with dirt. When they undressed, the dirt even lay thick on their skin![2]

For town and city women, working on the land was not an obvious draw. There were countless hardships to overcome and difficult working conditions to endure day in day out. Hot summers and bitter winters tested even the toughest! Weather was both friend and foe to the farmer and for the Land Girls too. Extreme weather conditions did of course mean that there could also be enforced, long periods of inactivity on the land. If the land was near to a river or by the coast and excessive spells of rainfall had resulted in flooding, no work could be done. Hard frosts, excessive snowfall and then subsequent periods of thaw saw fields waterlogged and roads become impassable. This was a huge problem for the farmer as he would not be able to find jobs for the women he had employed and they could find themselves out of work, having to return to a depot until they could find employment again. It was also impossible for girls to actually reach farms in such extreme conditions.

Fluctuations in the weather triggered different emotions. Intense cold and intense heat created different problems for Land Girls and the animals that they worked with. Land Girls struggled with the intense cold of winter and recalled how bad their hands and feet suffered. They welcomed the new growth and fresh, sunny days that the coming of spring heralded.[3]

Often, when women reflected on their service, they recalled the trials of working on the land but also the sheer beauty of nature; how the sun rose over a river, throwing hues of red and orange onto the surface of the water or the magical tinges of rainbow colours refracted on the rime frost that encased the trees, hedgerows and everything else that it had touched during the night! The deeply-felt magic of the land was a powerful lure that pulled women back to it even if they had initially chosen to return to their previous occupations after the war had ended.

Cold weather inevitably meant chilblains, sore, cracked and chapped hands, aching joints and backs but ploughing continued despite sleet or snowy conditions. Each season brought with it, its own, specific challenges. Heavy rain and windy days could signal mild weather but biting winds made working conditions miserable.

Mist, thick fog, thunderstorms, hail and blizzards were all part of life on the land. At the other extreme, working for lengthy periods of time in the unrelenting, blazing summer sun also brought with it its own challenges; heat exhaustion, sunstroke, sunburn, bites, stings, allergies and injuries were a constant threat to both Land Girls and animals. Land Girls and horses alike were driven to distraction by swarms of flies that buzzed around their heads as they worked. Measures were taken in an attempt to try and counteract the intense irritation they caused. Land Girls placed elderflower branches in the harness of the horse to try and deter the flies. This had a limited effect and horses were known to speed up in an attempt to escape the flies, leaving the Land Girl to almost run behind them in order to keep pace! After so many plough rows had been completed, both horse and exhausted Land Girl afforded themselves a short break under the welcome shade of a tree.[4]

Tempers were known to fray through sheer exhaustion and even the most placid of Land Girls became frazzled and irritable. One extra flick of the traces may have seen her regret her actions! The horses would continue at a ridiculous pace for up to an hour at a time, leaving the poor Land Girl desperately trying to control the plough, which jolted and thumped along in the stony ground.[5]

Many girls said that they preferred working in the winter to summer because they were less inclined to take frequent breaks or become distracted as they simply had to keep working to keep warm!

Such conditions pushed everyone that worked on the land to the extreme limit of their endurance and patience at times. One Land Girl described how she reached the point where she could take no more of the pace in the heat. Every muscle and joint ached with the exertion. The summer heat was intolerable and she had come within a hair's breadth of giving up. In her desperation, she climbed into the bottom of the hedge and lay in the shade for some considerable time not caring if the farmer caught her there or not, such was her exasperation. Having cooled down both in temperature and mood, the Land Girl recovered herself and continued with the ploughing until night fell.[6]

Humour undoubtedly got Land Girls through the long, challenging days. Land Girls generally took things completely in their stride and laughed their way through the many challenges that came their way! One described how she and two other women were transporting hurdles from one location to another on a farm in awful, wet and windy weather. This involved moving large loads down a rutted lane and through a turnip field; a journey that, at times, almost saw the hurdles slowly wobble off. The horse also struggled to keep itself steady and wobbled along too. For the Land Girl that sat atop the loads in an attempt to keep them steady - the movement nearly threw her off. Despite these trials, they all still saw the funny side of a situation![7]

Several seasons of weather could be experienced in one day. Muddy fields saw boots caked with heavy clods and shoes covered up to the ankle with slimy, wet mud in the morning then sodden with rain in the afternoon. On some days, rain would give way to sleet, then to snow. Visibility could deteriorate so quickly that in a matter of minutes Land Girls could lose sight of each other if they had been working on opposite sides of the field. In truth, having trudged home, they resembled little more than snowmen! Severe weather could severely disrupt work patterns and schedules, delaying jobs for days or in some cases, weeks.[8]

Special measures were taken during the colder months to maximise safety. Horses that had to pull heavy loads up hills in icy, hazardous conditions required 'frost nails' in their shoes so that they could safely maintain a firm grip as they went back and forth from the tillage fields.

No task was easy and drilling wheat into ploughed land proved to be an arduous task. The ground was very difficult to walk over as it was always uneven or sometimes it sloped; factors which all took their toll on feet and legs!

Land Girls adapted their uniform in an attempt to keep warm during the coldest months. Improvisation was often the key to making themselves fit for purpose. Polar exploration was of course a prominent story in the news during the Great War but perhaps not one that was foremost in the minds of Land Girls! They were often forced to requisition bags and sacks and protect themselves from the elements as best they could. A Land Girl working in Scotland described how she and her friend made the best of it in tough circumstances. They each wrapped themselves up in several sacks, tied twine around their wrists to prevent the wind getting in and ventured out looking like members of Shackleton's polar expedition![9]

Land Girls regularly mention the intolerable state of the country lanes they were expected to take horses and loaded carts along. Lanes were frequently impassable either because of mud that was knee-deep in places or because of the ruts which were of a similar depth![10]

Farming machinery often became casualties of mud and frequent stops had to be made to unclog jammed mechanisms or blades; a laborious, repetitive, dangerous and time-consuming task. Land Girls were frequently tasked with mending or patching up the dilapidated roads around the farms or country estates where they had been placed. On one estate, 100 tons of stones were used to patch up the dangerous areas and fill the deep ruts on the surrounding roads.[11]

Poor roads and deeply rutted tracks and lanes meant that cycling was almost impossible hence Land Girls had to revert back to two legs in order to travel anywhere. Walking wasn't without its problems either. Traipsing miles back and forth over rough and uneven earth meant that some women developed problems with their ankles, heels and feet.

The physical nature of the work also saw them develop new muscles and gain considerable strength. One Land Girl, (along with a soldier who also worked on the same farm) planted seven acres of wheat, continuing their work long after the daylight had faded. As a result of doing such continual, repetitive, physical work, she began to compare her legs to those of her brothers; comparisons which would not otherwise have been made had it not been for the Great War, which saw women having to perform such heavy work.[12]

Over time, Land Girls became astute in minimising the impact seasons had on their bodies and their working days. They were also aware of the constant visual changes on the land that occurred over the course of a year and how these changes helped or hindered their work. One Land Girl working in Wiltshire commented on how lovely the hedges looked in autumn. They witnessed the leaves gradually transform into autumnal hues and noticed how the vibrant colours of the many different berries looked like decorations dotted along the hedgerow.

Ultimately, at the end of a long day, any Land Girl worth her salt would have been exhausted from her efforts, (even to the point of feeling too tired to utter a word) but nonetheless contented by her contribution.[13]

Injuries were commonplace as were a gamut of common ailments such as blisters and chafing. Delicate joints and muscles, unused to walking in tough boots on uneven terrain for hours at a time became sore and strained. Being bent almost double for hours at a time when picking potatoes saw Land Girls having to lay flat on their backs for short periods of rest throughout the day in order to literally unfold again!

Farm implements could be dangerous if used incorrectly as Land Girl, Ethel Looby found out. Ethel worked on a farm at Salford, Bedfordshire and sustained a wound to her face whilst examining an old muzzle-loading pistol, (used for scaring crows) when it discharged. Ethel had to be admitted to hospital as a consequence of not being au fait with the pistol.

Another serious accident occurred to a Land Girl who was working at Ousegate, Selby in November 1918. Whilst passing through a railway underpass, the Land Girl, (who at the time was sitting on top of a load of flax) sustained a serious head wound caused by the ironwork coming into contact with her head. She had to be taken to a nearby cottage hospital for treatment.[14]

Men and women even died as a direct result of working with flax. Schoolmistress Christina Chatley of Enfield Lock pricked her finger on a thistle whilst pulling flax which led to her dying of septic pneumonia.

The WNLSC Chair, Mrs Willis attempted to allay any fears women may have had about joining a land organisation by reassuring potential recruits in April 1916 that strength was not always a necessity. Recruits would be introduced to the work gradually so that they could get used to it over time. By doing it this way, the shock to the body was minimised and good health was largely maintained.[15]

The WNLSC were very conscious of the effects that arduous land work could have on the women in its ranks and made efforts to safeguard the health of each Land Girl as did the Women's Land Army Welfare Committee. The committee in each county produced periodical reports that detailed the overall health of members of the Women's Land Army and of the other organisations associated with it. One such report stated that enrichment activities such as dancing and swimming had been organised where it had been possible to do so during the winter months. Likewise, in the summer months, wealthy ladies had invited land workers to their gardens where various forms of entertainment had been organised for them. The women's health had held up well throughout the influenza epidemic although sadly some Land Girls did die having contracted it.[16]

A multitude of health-giving products were aimed at Land Girls, (such as reviving, rich fruit tonics). Advertisements promised a cure for every conceivable minor ailment. Land Girls may also have needed to visit the Women's Land Army assigned panel doctor if their health problem was more complex or serious.

Health problems occasionally arose where there were several Land Girls billeted together. If a cottage was dark, damp or cramped or if they had been billeted in tents or wooden huts, their work clothes could not be dried adequately overnight hence women had little choice but to wear their uniform again the next day.

If a Land Girl had to take milk to a market or factory regularly, inclement weather frequently made the journey difficult and women were soaked or frozen stiff by the time they arrived.

Rest Clubs were established by the Women's Agricultural Committees to enable women to secure dry clothing and a well-earned cup of tea! Simple things like this meant the most to Land Girls who endured these testing situations week in week out.

Poorly maintained cottages on farms had few, if any facilities. Thatched roofs often leaked or allowed drips to fall onto bedclothes. Mildew and mould became an issue if ventilation was poor. This of course saw some Land Girls develop respiratory problems such as coughs, asthma or chest infections. Any contagions could be passed on easily whilst living in such close proximity. Running water was a non-existent luxury. Often the only source of water was from the village pump so it always had to be carried to the billet.

Although the Welfare Committees had stated that in order for good health and restorative sleep to be maintained, Land Girls should not share beds, circumstances made this impossible in many instances. Rooms in cottages were generally small so only one, large bed, (as opposed to the ideal scenario of two smaller ones) would fit in them. Land Girls therefore had no choice but to share.

A report stated how a Land Girl had caught a skin infection from sharing a bed. This was more than likely to have been ringworm or impetigo; easily spread once there was an initial outbreak due to living in such close proximity to one another. Working in dirty environments with animals during the day and then returning to a billet with inadequate washing facilities at night meant that hygiene regimes, through no fault of their own, were not always stringent enough.

When and where possible, Land Girls loved to bathe and swim in rivers and streams. This was certainly the case for some Land Girls billeted in a hostel near the River Tweed! Matron also pumped water so that the girls could have baths after their day at work and nursed the girls if they became ill. A reporter, having witnessed the routine of the hostel remarked on the quirkiness and eccentricity of the establishment.

For less severe ailments, numerous, popular brands of the day were more than happy to assuage Land Girls with their comforting products, (that is of course if they had the money to spend on them).

For the girls that could afford these little luxuries, they would have been most welcome. Girls who were not dependent on the wage they were earning, having joined organisations like the Women's National Land Service Corps arrived quite unused to such demanding toil.

Advertisers therefore saw an opportunity to target such girls with their products. It was imperative that they looked after their hair and delicate skin now they were working outside in all weathers.

On receipt of a completed coupon and four penny stamps to cover postage, free product samples were sent out as part of a National Hair-Health Campaign in October 1918. Land Girls were highlighted as a group of war workers who would benefit from using such products. The condition and health of their hair could deteriorate as a result of the strain that war and war work placed on the body.

A promise of several free gifts would no doubt have appealed to women as many were concerned that their femininity and attractiveness would be compromised by having to wear such a utilitarian uniform and perform such work. It was perhaps inevitable therefore that some went to great lengths to maintain the same high standards regarding their personal appearance despite it being totally impractical. Many women had quirky personalities which, to some may have seemed somewhat perplexing! It was reported that some girls still continued to wear pearl earrings and rings as they worked whilst another regularly used a powder puff to maintain the impression of a flawless complexion. This was of course fruitless as the wind blew the powder off as quickly as it was applied! Mud, rain, wind and onion weeds did not lend themselves well to jewellery and vanity![17]

In 1918, creams promised to soothe and relieve heat-irritated skin, abrasions, sore, chapped, chafed, roughened skin and scratches. Also to maintain a healthy, clear complexion. Ointments and jellies promised to cure chilblains, heal cuts and wounds and alleviate the discomfort of midge and insect bites and stings.

Tonics were sold to revive and fortify. Talcum powder promised to cool skin and minimise irritation and specialised soaps removed stains on the skin and hygienically cleaned filthy hands! Land work was unforgiving and even the best products would not have helped girls with more severe and flaring skin problems such as eczema or dermatitis.

Wholesome, warming, nutritious soups and yeast extract beverages appealed to Land Girls and fortified products that aided stamina such as cocoa were popular.

A Land Girl had invited a friend to supper in her cottage billet and she noticed her friend staring at her. When she enquired as to why, her friend remarked on how full of health and vitality she looked.[18]

Their complexions were commented upon time and time again. Newspaper column inches reported on how radiant the Land Girls faces looked, (a radiance that had been achieved without the need of any make-up). Many were suntanned; the benefits of living an outdoor life were obvious for everyone to see. The girls looked fit, cheerful and relaxed.[19]

Positive observations were a huge boon and strengthened the overall image and objectives of the Women's Land Army. During the summer of 1917, the first women-only agricultural competition was held in rural Hertfordshire. 300 plus women took part. Once again, spectators commented on how confident the Land Girls looked as they worked and noted the variation in their headwear and uniforms.[20]

During rare periods of leave, family and friends were shocked at how working on the land had altered the figures, faces and outlook of their loved ones. One particular Land Girl even had to have her wedding dress taken out to accommodate the changes in her figure!

Land Girls were a hardy bunch and nothing stopped them from eating their well-earnt lunch! They became more in tune with their environment, commenting on how much colder the countryside was when compared to the towns and cities they had left behind. They also became very adept at improvising, especially when the weather was bad. Makeshift shelters were made by draping a tarpaulin over the machinery, (in this case, a drill) in order to form a tent. Carts were also tipped up and used for the same purpose. A fire was then started and although smoky, it provided welcome warmth, cover and a brief respite from the cold, wind and rain.[21]

Land Girls who were in potato picking gangs often suffered from an age-old problem. They were particularly susceptible to developing the painful inflammatory condition traditionally known as 'housemaid's knee' as they crept along on hands and knees in rough, uneven soil. Back pain was also a hazard of the job as women had to stoop and bend in one position for hours at a time. Sore, burning feet and aching calf muscles were the bugbear of all Land Girls whether part or whole-time workers!

Minor and more serious injuries were sustained from working with animals such as bites or kicks from horses and crush injuries from bulls.

Feeding calves meant very early starts and the break of day was the time that saw Land Girls tumble out of bed all over the country groaning, stretching and yawning! Many had to cycle miles to their farms before starting work.

Calves required a special routine and Land Girls treated them as if they were tiny infants. Milk had to be at the correct temperature and there was an order to the feeding process with the smallest calves needing to be fed first, the largest second and all the others afterwards. Gruel was mixed up too. All of the utensils had to be washed thoroughly and left ready for the feed in the evening.[22]

Weather affected Land Girls in some way every day as they worked but never their determination to finish a job. One remembered a day that was particularly muggy and how, as she worked, she had sweated profusely. This, although very unpleasant, did not deter her from keeping focused on her work.[23]

Another Land Girl spoke of the hazards she encountered when working with young horses. Land Girls were very careful not to have their feet trodden on as they turned at the end of a field, especially if it was a double plough pulled by four horses! Immediately they got wise to this and did some nimble side-stepping in order to avoid injury! As with most agricultural jobs, there was a skill in doing this as the horses got extremely close whilst turning.[24]

This farm was fortunate to still have horses remaining on it as most had been requisitioned by the army for service overseas. Young horses posed problems, more so if conditions were difficult. Land Girls spoke of ropes becoming entangled and of one horse going one way and one another way resulting in complete chaos! Being able to see the funny side of any situation despite the risk of injury was thankfully a characteristic that Land Girls possessed in spades![25]

Most problems encountered by Land Girls were overcome by using common sense but for more serious problems that could not be solved by the Land Girl alone, Welfare Officers were put in place to ensure that women had a point of contact in the first instance. They oversaw up to 200 women and their role spanned many facets; from advising women on various matters that related to their personal wellbeing or work to queries about health or accident insurance. Although welfare work was more difficult to administer when girls worked individually or in pairs in remote locations, they did travel to such places and attempted to solve issues connected with accommodation or wages and deal with more serious problems linked to harassment or exploitation.

A Travelling Inspector also attempted to sort out the multitude of problems that materialised in workplaces up and down the country. There was no precedent to refer to, so everything that happened broke new ground. In order to appropriately manage and deal with all the problems that a new organisation such as the Women's Land Army threw up, every option had to be carefully considered before any final decision was made. Any resulting penalties or punishment(s) dealt out would set the benchmark for similar cases in the future.

It was the responsibility of each woman to get an Insurance Card once she was enrolled in the Women's Land Army. The rules as laid out in the L.A.A.S Handbook clearly state that should they be without insurance, an approved society must be contacted whereby they must ask for insurance but only to be taken out under the National Health Insurance Act. Once the card has been received, they are entitled to free medical attendance.

Their names must also be registered on the Panel in the area that they are working in. If their circumstances should change, the card should be presented to the Panel Doctor immediately. Women will be entitled to sickness benefit, 7 shillings 6 pence a week, (at the end of six months) should they fall sick.[26]

If women fell ill, depending on the severity of the illness, relatives were notified or sent for. If in a billet, inspections were made to make sure they were being appropriately looked after.

If a woman was in a depot at the time, maintenance minus sick benefit was paid from depot funds. For any Land Girls that required a longer period of convalescence, arrangements were made for them to be received into a YWCA home on the coast. In November 1918, Mrs Edith Lyttelton, Deputy Director, Women's Branch, Board of Agriculture and Fisheries made a groundbreaking announcement. She stated that provision had been made for the first time for land workers in a women's hospital; a bed had been made available for those women that required hospitalisation.[27]

If a woman had an accident, they were required to claim compensation under the Workman's Compensation Act. They were also urged to report an accident and make a claim within a week. Some made the mistake of trying to claim weeks after the accident took place which of course compounded the risk of their employer refusing to pay any compensation.

The Landswoman magazine regularly ran advertisements for insurance for all women workers.

Despite the risk that having no insurance posed, some farmers still didn't opt for it when they took female workers on. One Land Girl suggested that the reason behind it was that the premium was too high. A further, efficient system needed to be put in place that protected women from other matters that could potentially arise.

The Welfare Fund was one such example, established to assist Land Girls who, during the course of their service experienced all manner of problems, ranging from private personal issues to periods of poor health, to difficulties with billets and general financial hardship through unexpected or unavoidable expenses arising.

The fund also endeavoured to provide comforts such as the provision of furniture in communal areas when and where it was required. It also organised social events that encouraged interaction and friendship between women. A proactive and visible Welfare Officer was worth their weight in gold!

It appears that even in mid-1919 the public still needed to be made further aware of the vital contribution that tens upon tens of thousands of women had already made and were still making in order to ease crippling food shortages. With the Armistice many months past, the public consensus appeared to be that these emergency war workers were no longer required. This was of course, far from the truth. They had much work to do and were still in demand.

Women never intended to cause unemployment for those men returning from service. They simply had no alternative but to continue filling the gaps that had been left in agriculture. Shortages of skilled labour were as severe as they had ever been, if not more so by mid-1919. Responsibility therefore fell at the feet of these same women as they still remained best suited to solve the most urgent of shortfalls. Appeals made by the Welfare Fund continued to raise awareness of the women's work; highlighting to the public that any contributions and donations made would demonstrate the high regard and debt of gratitude that the country felt for the service given by the Women's Land Army.[28]

Testimony shows that Land Girls continued to serve their country right up until the organisation was officially demobilised on the 30th November 1919.

Many women continued to work on the land having joined the newly-formed National Association of Landswomen. They were offered several opportunities which enabled them to continue their path in agriculture.

And yet, in spite of all their hard work, their contribution never really gained the respect and recognition that it truly deserved.

Chapter 9

Quirks, oddities and curiosities!

"It was awful fun!"[1]

Great War Land Girls encountered numerous quirky and unorthodox situations. For the women who had volunteered during the early years of the war, jobs were not always tied to the land, forage depots or woods. More than the odd eyebrow or two was raised by local men and women on catching their first glimpse of the new female workforce! Life on the land however, was, more times than not taken on with a keen, irrepressible sense of humour and a sprinkle of irony thrown in for good measure!

Land Girls often recounted funny stories of how they genuinely thought they would start to take on the characteristics of a turnip should they see one more of them. They spoke of absolutely loathing fields and machinery some days, feeling that if they didn't have a break from the monotonous job of pulling turnips, they themselves would sprout green, mouldy hair, grow rotund and resemble every other turnip in the world![2]

A Land Girl who worked in Kent as part of a threshing gang highlighted a recurrent problem; one which seriously impacted their working day.

The elderly driver that took the women to work clearly had a fondness for drink. He had been reprimanded about his drinking and unreliability before as he had often been in an unfit state to drive the women safely to and from their place(s) of work. Having temporarily heeded the warning he soon lapsed back into his old habits.

"We moved from Eccles to Detling yesterday. He stopped at each public house on the way and when we arrived at Detling it was nearly dinner time. He made for the village pub and stayed there until after 2 o'clock and was no good for any work, so we just had to walk back home again!"[3]

Land Girls had to be quick, practical thinkers with a natural aptitude to solve problems and improvise. One Land Girl recalled in her diary how she swiftly solved a problem. Rather than wasting considerable time trying to scour a huge area to search for a pin that had come out of one of the levers on the cultivator she was working on at the time, she used her hair pin as a temporary solution to the problem and simply carried on!

Something as simple as giving a friendly smile in an attempt to win over the more uncertain folk or the cynics was high on their agenda too with Land Girls both sides of the Atlantic stating how important it was to exude the affable side of the Women's Land Army. Take for instance, the very aptly named "Laugh-a-Lot Club" of North Charlotte, North Carolina. Their club ethos was to:

> "Suggest a form of relaxation that would benefit everybody in these over-strenuous days. When economy in every form of heat and light is being urged as a patriotic duty, it is well to remember that one may still indulge in the warmth and illumination of the friendly smile without a thought for the Food Controller."[4]

In Britain too, determined efforts were also being made by individual girls to warm the hardest of hearts. In spite of often feeling homesick and lonely themselves, they still went the extra mile to brighten other people's days. It sadly wasn't always reciprocated.

A Land Girl wrote about her determination to wear down any hard-heartedness or resistance that she met on a daily basis from some local people. Despite her efforts, it seems that the only bond she formed was with the pony that assisted her with her daily milk round.

It could be the simplest of things that lifted the darkest of days. A Land Girl who had been placed in a village in Nottinghamshire had received a letter the previous day which had left her downhearted. As she went about her duties, she described seeing a very old dustman on her ride.

> "He had a very grandfatherly old face, round and rosy, such as you only find in the country and as soon as he saw me he just stood still and stared, his jolly old face crinkling up into the most engaging and friendly smile that I have ever seen."[5]

She was overjoyed at this simple gesture and the ensuing interaction; how he complimented her on the colour of her hair and her pluck.

> "I felt so bucked up with the smile and compliment that I drove all the way there and back again, (from the farm to the large institution it supplied with milk) blissfully unconscious of anything else but that dustman's smile."[6]

Those broad smiles from thereon in continued to be exchanged every morning! She continued with her smile experiment and logged the 'stages' of smiles that people gave her.

Firstly - the uncertain smile.
Secondly - the surprised smile.
Thirdly - the silly smile and even the insolent smile.
Lastly - the friendly and jolly smile.

> "Yes, it is a small thing and costs nothing but it is worth its weight in gold."[7]

Mail and parcels from loved ones were just as welcome as those sent to soldiers in the trenches. A Land Girl working in Wiltshire recounted the moment she took delivery of a new hat, made for her by her mother. As soon as she knew it was from her mother, she left her breakfast and ran upstairs to see how it looked. Land Girls still liked their creature comforts and fashion after all, even if their life on the land did not afford them much glamour! Home-made things were special and were always appreciated just that little bit more as they lifted the many dreary and repetitive days of winter.[8]

Land Girls were usually more than happy to accept any challenge that was put their way. During Doncaster's Tank Week in June 1918, eight willing girls from Plumtree Training Centre became the human 'fillings' in sandwich boards which had been hastily made the night before from any available cardboard and posters!

Tank Weeks took place all over the country and the 'Tank Bank' was a fundraising campaign created by the British Government to encourage investment in War Bonds and War Savings Certificates.

The green and yellow colours of the Women's Land Army adorned the front of posters along with patriotic, emotive slogans such as "For your children we are growing food." Each girl had one letter fastened onto her back, which collectively made up two key words. As the Land Girls marched alongside Egbert the tank in their smart uniforms, the public craned their necks to see what words these letters formed. As they passed by, the delighted crowd shouted out "F.O.O.D P.R.O.D.U.C.T.I.O.N!"

This was a publicity stunt that had the desired effect. Not only did it thrill the gathered crowds, it also raised the public profile of the Women's Land Army. The Land Girl sandwiches gimmick proved to be a terrific success as the recruitment booth was filled with eager potential candidates afterwards!

Land Girls absolutely loved jokes! One informed the editor of The Landswoman that she had named all of the cows in her charge after the staff at Headquarters. Thankfully this tongue-in-cheek humour aimed at your superiors was taken in the spirit it was made in. the response was:

"I was sold the other day so I understand and fetched a very poor price!"[9]

Land Girls cropped up everywhere in the popular culture of the day. A play called "Summertime" by Mr Louis Parker provided an ideal opportunity for the escapist-starved public to transgress from the stress and worry of their daily lives. The plot saw a bachelor stir up trouble for himself by pledging love to three Land Girls, having penned the same letter to each girl - only to find himself residing in the same place as them along with three further bachelors![10]

Genuine affection was shown towards the Land Girls but despite this, stubborn sentimentality stuck like glue and negative representations of Land Girls still appeared in the media.

There were distinct differences in how men and women approached animal husbandry on farms. The Land Girls clearly brought instinctive, maternal, nurturing skills to their employment and farmers noted that they were more patient with the animals in their care. They invested the time to encourage weak animals to fight for their life that would otherwise have died. Farmers stated that most male workers would not have done this.[11]

A Land Girl placed on a farm in Wiltshire witnessed a young colt resisting being put in traces. A boy was trying to gain control of the obstinate animal but had lost his temper with it. She witnessed the unsuccessful use of ash switches on the colt and how shouting had made its behaviour worse, in-turn also exhausting the angry boy. She asked the boy if she could have the animal and attempt to calm it down. By behaving in a calm manner, she was able to take the colt by its halter and as she spoke quietly to the animal, it immediately responded favourably to her. Land Girls often chatted away to their horses as they rode along country lanes![12]

The manner in which Land Girls approached tasks gave rise to better farming practice universally - especially if the benefits were witnessed and proven to enhance the running of any given farm. Herding, ploughing, shepherding could all be done much more calmly and efficiently if different approaches were adopted by the 'old hands.'

During the summer of 1917, three Land Girls briefly made a visit to their former boss at the Mansion House as they delivered straw in London. The story made the news as prior to joining the Women's Land Army they had all worked as servants in the Lord Mayor's household! The Lord Mayor came out to welcome his 'old' servants, who were sat atop a load of straw bound for Whitechapel and invited them to have luncheon with him. They had to decline as there were many jobs still to be done. The call of war work never ceased![13]

Occasionally, Land Girls made the news for reasons that were injurious to their war service. Miss Victoria Coleman of Shire Hall, Hawley, Dartford fell foul to the slanderous tongue of widow, Mrs Fanny Jenkins of Wilmington and made the news as a victim of slander. Answering to her crime, Jenkins gave an apology and indemnity. It soon became apparent what Mrs Jenkins had got into trouble for. In her world, two and two had made five! A young child was being raised by the grandparents of Miss Coleman who was 20 years old. The young woman was working on a dairy farm that was owned by a young man called Mr Moss. Mrs Jenkins had been spreading gossip that was unfounded and this is what had landed her in trouble.[14]

Land Girls were unquestionably newsworthy. There was the ever-present requirement to be seen as a virtuous and honourable representative of the Women's Land Army and anything less would not be accepted. Luckily for Miss Coleman her name was cleared, justice was seen to be done and her reputation remained untarnished.

A curious story involving a Land Girl appeared in May 1919. Two men had argued and come to blows over a rude remark made about two Land Girl's wearing puttees! It just goes to show that the Women's Land Army uniform caused controversy and not everyone liked what they saw.

On hearing this remark, Amos Baggley assaulted Walter Dimmock on April 26th and was fined £2 at Rotherham!

Due to the ever-present need to find more available acreage and turn it into productive land, ever-more bizarre places were being given over to cultivation. Potatoes were being grown on the fairways of some golf courses just outside of London. Members themselves were set to work planting the precious crop.[15]

In Stoke Poges, Buckinghamshire, a cottage was occupied for a few weeks by Land Girls who had been engaged in mowing the lawns at the local golf club! It seems that the Land Girls temporarily stepped in to do the jobs of the former caddie-master and greenkeeper, (who had recently been evicted from the cottage).

A Land Girl called Margaret Robinson wrote to The Landswoman to tell fellow Land Girls about this rather humorous story about the bullocks in her care.

> "They went to market last week and were some of the fattest at Norwich and Walsham. A profit of £15 was made on each bullock. One was so fat that on the way to North Walsham he lay down and in the end, he absolutely refused to walk any farther. They had to get a cart for him."[16]

Many Land Girls seemed to possess a previously unknown flair and natural aptitude for rearing calves and prizewinning bulls. Prior to joining up, one young woman had been an assistant in a ribbon department in a large store in the Midlands! It merely proved what was already known by so many, that women were more than capable of adapting to almost any situation.

High commendation came from Major Behren, (his estate had employed Land Girl, Miss Doris Raper since 1917). Doris worked almost single-handedly with Shorthorn bulls and seemed to have a natural affiliation with the breed, confidently taking them into the sale ring. Working with such animals was difficult and required courage and a fervent nature.

> "Very few women would have had the courage to undertake such work and still fewer have been able to carry it out so well."[17]

During the summer of 1916, Land Girls were engaged in overseeing the work of conscientious objectors who were being taught how to carry out land and farm work.[18]

Women that were involved in team sports possessed qualities that easily transferred to land work. They were good team players, strong, fit, adaptable and usually had an active temperament and organised disposition. Members of many hockey clubs turned their hand to all kinds of work, opting to study gardening, do fruit-picking or partake in general farm work.

In their pre-war lives, Land Girls were often talented, versatile sportswomen, excelling in multiple disciplines. None more so than the Land Girls who took part in the sports during the peace festivities, held in the village of Itchingfield, West Sussex in the summer of 1919. Land Girls got involved in all manner of competitive events such as the '100 yards race: Demobilised women and Land Girls.' Most organisations had, by this time been demobilised but not the Women's Land Army, which had four further months of official existence.

Every minute of any time off was savoured. One Land Girl who had toiled ceaselessly for nine months without a holiday spent her leave enjoying picnics and swimming. By knowing that she had served her country to the very best of her ability up to that point, she was able to enjoy every single minute of her hard-earned break with a completely clear conscience.[19]

Chapter 10

Unshakeable camaraderie

The rules laid out in the L.A.A.S Handbook clearly stated that free time should be spent wisely as a woman's health depended on it.[1] Free time was a real luxury and it always seemed as if a Land Girl's work was never done! Discrepancies in the number of hours that should be worked frequently became blurred, culminating in resentment and a thorny working environment for the placed worker. For others, a hard day in the fields or woods did not appear to tire some and they had plenty of energy left to enjoy social activities.

What was the social life of a Land Girl actually like? Social activities had to appeal to women of all ages so who actually formulated the social calendar that was so enjoyed by Land Girls? Where were these events held? Who attended and how were the events organised? What else did they enjoy doing during their spare time?

The answers to these questions encompass a real cornucopia of ideas; often hatched quickly on an ad hoc basis or for some events, more stringent planning and inventiveness was required. The Land Girls were not averse to being spontaneous and often burst into song, played a tune on a musical instrument or danced to a hornpipe without needing much encouragement!

Free time was mindfully spent as although the women were off duty, they were still serving members of the Women's Land Army and other land organisations. They needed to be aware of their behaviour at all times and how any deviation would reflect badly on their chosen branch of service! Good Service Ribbons were hard earnt after all.

Contrary to popular belief, a Land Girl was more likely to suffer from boredom than exhaustion! They brought an effervescent energy and a refreshing, new dynamic to any village where they were placed. The fact that they were undertaking work of national importance gave many an extra spring in their step and an added determination to really savour this unique time in their lives.

They were typically imaginative and started handicraft meetings in villages which encouraged interaction, which in-turn enabled better working relationships to be established between local women and themselves. It was viewed as imperative that the women were provided with suitable outlets for any surplus energy they might have! With limited or no budget for entertainment available to them, Land Girls simply had to be inventive and capable of carrying momentum on right through to the actual fruition of any event.

For those 'blinkered' villagers, trapped in the cyclical grind of land work, life as it always had been and in their eyes always would and should be, was turned on its head by the injection of zestful enthusiasm. Uncertainty and suspicion about the new women meant swift and unfair judgements were frequently made and despite their best efforts to become acquainted with the locals, Land Girls were often snubbed and made to feel unwelcome.

Where their input was embraced by villagers, the new yet temporary inhabitants not only whetted the social appetites of the villagers but quite clearly made some keen to encounter further diverse social experiences. Friendships were forged and perhaps once flimsy, fraught working relationships were strengthened outside of the farming day.

The danger was that having thoughts such as these may have been seen as getting ideas above one's station. The blame of course, would have lain solely at the feet of the incomers! Villagers that dared to fill their heads with any pie in the sky ideas or new-fangled thoughts would have been swiftly admonished.

One village which appears to have struck a correct balance was Wivelsfield in East Sussex. The ultimate aim of arranging a social event was usually to raise funds for valued institutions such as the village club; a place where local people and newcomers could mix. It was however the 'respected' ladies in such villages whose opinion and thoughts carried the most weight at the time. They decided on a plan to seek out a suitable venue that was located in Wivelsfield itself whereby young, unmarried men and women who were living away from their homes could all meet up and socialise together during the winter months.[2]

In this particular case, a huge effort was made to seek out a venue suitable for hosting both regular and one-off events. It had been hoped that a YMCA hut could be secured for the purpose but it proved to be too costly an option to have to relocate the hut to the village so other alternatives had to be found.

The village Reading Room therefore became a further option. Despite plans to extend the building, the cost once again put pay to the plans. The Reading Rooms were still chosen as the venue and were redecorated and furnished as well as it was possible to do so in wartime. The spirit of 'making the best of it' epitomised the villagers of Wivelsfield.[3]

This combined effort demonstrates the lengths that some local people went to in order to make Land Girls feel part of the village where they were temporarily living and working and of the wider community too. It also exposes the many difficulties faced in actually implementing these well-meant ideas both practically and financially. Certain individuals within the village clearly recognised the importance of minimising the amount of time Land Girls spent alone during bleak winter nights missing their family and friends back home.

Women of all ages and backgrounds were now working and socialising together in a way that was totally unprecedented. It was not just Land Girls that were responsible or to blame, (depending on your viewpoint) for invigorating village life.

Organisations such as The Arts League of Service also formed to trial a short experiment in Sussex that took plays, songs, theatre and variety performances 'into the sticks' during 1919. The primary aim of the organisation was to revitalise and enhance village life via arts and culture. Land Girls had taken an energy into the villages where they had been placed that influenced and reinvigorated those it touched. Subsequently, this was one of the main factors behind a new hunger that had developed to experience new ideas, interests and entertainment.[4]

A similar point was made in November 1919 stating that women from as far away as John O'Groats down to Lands End were influencing the way that villagers socialised. These women were part of mobile gangs that worked on farms for a short period of time before moving on. They brought many different facets of life with them that hitherto, rural areas would not have been exposed to; facets which ultimately broadened the outlook of those who chose to listen.[5]

Land Girls were indeed a pivotal force in their own right and created new social opportunities for the communities in which they were placed, (whether that was by themselves or with the collaboration or input of their Welfare

Officers). Organisations such as TALOS aimed to make different kinds of entertainment, (some of which were viewed as out of reach to many) accessible to all. This could apply to pursuits such as music, crafts or art.[6]

What was a given to a woman of means was not part of life for women who had had little choice but to remain, through sheer necessity in often remote villages all of their life. By taking a variety of good quality entertainment out to rural audiences who perhaps had never seen anything like it before, it provided a chance for everyone to enjoy themselves. Not only was it exciting to anticipate and subsequently attend, it lifted the spirits of the war-weary population.

For the generation that was already familiar with some of the types of entertainment now on offer, harking back to the good old days, (in part) was a nostalgic journey many were willing to retake. The music hall era faded away after 1918 and was rebranded as variety, so this experiment was indeed audacious in that it saw rural audiences being introduced to new forms of entertainment and stimuli. Moreover they were also exposed to art, crafts, sculpture, textile and furniture design. TALOS presented culture that villagers could learn from and about and then organise or interpret their own responses to what they had seen in their own individual ways in their own, familiar setting.

Land Girls were never averse to singing and performing themselves and they formed groups such as the "Flaxen Follies." This group performed popular songs and choruses to audiences in locations such as village schoolrooms to raise money for causes such as parish funds.

Things were slightly different if the Land Girls were seasonal workers, (summer saw an additional influx of college or university-educated girls who harvested crops such as flax). They were frequently housed in temporary hutted or tented accommodation in large camps or in village or school halls. In these circumstances it often fell on the shoulders of the Welfare Officer assigned to the flax camps to organise suitable entertainments for the women in their off duty hours.

For young women billeted in camps, during their free time they swapped their uniforms for more fashionable, feminine clothes. They naturally wanted to disassociate themselves from the long days of work carried out in their utilitarian uniforms. Their suntanned faces and rosy cheeks however gave them away![7]

Perhaps some of the feistier girls saw this brief getaway from the camp as a genuine opportunity to kick-back! Woe betide anyone that disregarded the strict curfew! Nowhere seemed to be off limits for Land Girls and even if their uniforms were a little muddy, they regularly met up in groups in stylish, expensive tea shops on their days off or were spotted laughing and chatting as they enjoyed a meal in a restaurant.[8]

Land Girls that were part of mobile gangs would often have been placed in locations far away from their own homes for short periods of time before moving on. They would likely have had an air of mystery about them and been a source of fascination to the local people, perhaps even more so when they were off duty.

A social event that was a rip-roaring success took place at Santon Bridge, (then in Cumberland, now Cumbria) where a Land Army club dance was held on August 15th 1919. The Land Girls decorated Drigg's Schoolroom and attended the dance in uniform because the Welfare Officer for the district presented three girls with Good Service Ribbons. The dance drew quite an attendance as the night wore on and was a triumph in Land Girl public relations!

> "A most attractive musical programme made everyone ready to dance, and as the evening advanced the room became very crowded."[9]

No doubt, word had got round the village that the Land Girls were dancing to the music ensuring many dropped by to nose!

A group of Land Girls, billeted in a rural hostel in Nottinghamshire wrote of their excitement on hearing that a social evening was to be organised to take place in their rest room where as many Land Girls from the surrounding area who could attend, would! They were:

> "As excited as school children would be at a Sunday School Treat."[10]

When planning such events, Land Girls needed to assign tasks fairly and work well together. It was no wonder they looked forward to such evenings and felt a friendly, competitive spirit towards any visiting Land Girls. There must have been many impromptu rehearsals to each other in the fields, forests and forage depots - perhaps even a cow was a captive audience as the girls ran through their items for performance!

Anticipation of the night itself would have made long working hours go past much more quickly too. Who would do well? Not so well? Who would give the best performance? This pre-event buzz was great for lifting the morale of the girls especially if they were struggling, were homesick, didn't feel well, had heard sad news regarding their families or were just plain fed up! On the eagerly awaited night itself the girls:

"Flew breathless here and there, so that none should be late."[11]

Often at these social gatherings the county Welfare Officer or Secretary would attend. 'Socials' provided the ideal chance for them to interact with Land Girls in an informal setting where the atmosphere was relaxed and where the women felt more able to chat freely and openly about their life on the land. It also provided ample chance to speak to the girls individually and get to know them by name and to find out more about their home lives without being intrusive and how they were settling into their new working environment(s). They were of course also away from the watchful eyes of any farmer or farm bailiff so were perhaps more inclined to open up about any concerns they may have had.

Authority figures attended social events to announce items of interest or details of forthcoming events. There needed to be something to look forward to all the time, whatever the season as this was crucial for maintaining collective optimism, especially if women were billeted alone on isolated farms.

Dancing, in whatever form it took appeared to be a favourite pastime of the Land Girls. They were certainly versatile and could dance a hornpipe as well as a waltz! In all corners of the country, dancing lessons were set up for them to attend throughout the darker months. The chief aim was to teach them a skill that, if new, would enable them to interact better socially within their new communities.

These dancing skills certainly never went to waste. Land Girls improvised lighting for an event, (in the form of candles stuck into empty bottles). This system not only illuminated the makeshift ballroom but also the fancy dress costumes of all who attended.

The rule in this instance was that costumes must not incur any cost; emphasizing the 'make do' ethos that wartime placed upon everyone. The

"Flaxen Follies" sang choruses in colourful outfits to raise money for the parish hall - which was also the location of their billets!

The party, held on Christmas night in 1918 in an unnamed hospital realised a kaleidoscope of colour as the partygoers danced in inventive and colourful fancy dress costumes. What appeared to be on trend at this particular party were traditional, old-fashioned styles of fancy dress.[12]

Dances such as Veleta waltzes, quadrille-lancers, galops, schottisches, (a slow polka) saw Matron dance with a military man of high-rank, that is until the signal came for all of the other impatient dancers to grab a partner and head onto the dancefloor.[13]

What followed was the most glorious, incongruous merging together of fancy dress get-ups worn by serving men and women of various professions and ranks. There were many unique dancing combinations too! A woman dressed in a kilt danced with an Ace of Spades and the Padre had dressed up as a chef![14]

The Land Girls who were present had done themselves proud and were dressed up in male attire - real soldiers in green smocks!

Rather poignantly, many convalescing soldiers attended the party; perhaps patients at the hospital. Although invited, they were dressed in the customary hospital blues and due to their injuries were unable to dance. They stood forlornly along the wall watching the joyous scene in full swing before them with longing in their eyes.[15]

The swathe of happy men and women in fancy dress dancing together in such colourful costumes, letting their hair down after long, drawn out years of war must truly have been a wonderful sight. The Land Girls who were at this dance however had not yet been demobilised. They still had a further 11 months left to serve.

The dancers lost track of time and could have danced all night but on the stroke of midnight, all the 'lights' went out and the partygoers were stopped in their tracks. Matron was not going to let fun get in the way of discipline![16]

As people said their goodbyes and drifted away in separate directions their laughter echoed down the draughty, cold, long hospital corridors. Weary revellers headed back to their various billets and camps in need of a cup of tea if one could be found![17]

During the Great War, wealthy ladies often invited Land Girls to their opulent homes and sprawling, manicured gardens in order to provide entertainment for them. The Women's Land Fete held at Bredon's Norton in Gloucestershire during the summer of 1917 enabled Land Girls to discuss farming practices with veteran farmers. This interaction attempted to allay any preconceived ideas that people may have harboured about the Women's Land Army.

Informal occasions such as these gave the curious and misinformed the opportunity to either watch from afar or directly speak to the girls about their war work in a relaxed environment. Demonstrations in food preservation such as bottling fruit were also given and younger girls were invited to take part in such activities. At its core, the purpose of such fetes was a serious one; promoting the crucial war work being carried out by women during wartime.

Whenever Land Girls attended social events they were required to wear their uniform therefore rules regarding behaviour and conduct always had to be at the forefront of their minds! Local people took part in competitions and various sporting activities, individual and team races and the ever-popular tug-of-war, often against teams of Land Girls! Many attended just to browse the many stalls that sold artwork, kitchenware, chintz, lavender and flowers and of course those of the various organisations that took part.

There was also the chance to enjoy a quintessentially English tea. As the public savoured their tea, they would often listen to a band or watch a concert party who had perhaps come from a nearby barracks to entertain. And, if that wasn't enough, a multitude of other amusements came in the form of roundabouts, swing-boats and conjuring tricks. Injured or wounded Allied servicemen were also invited along and mingled with the crowds.

An event held in Cockermouth in Cumbria during the summer of 1919 saw The Cockermouth Club, (formed by the Land Girls of that area) set up a stall that sold items, (made or contributed by Land Girls all over the country) to raise valuable funds, (in this case for the vital 'Comforts Fund') for its members.

Emphasis was placed on the need to have faith in the youth of the day in order to keep Britain's soul alive. Every effort possible was being made to ensure that the comfort of female war workers outside of their working hours remained a priority.

The Vice President of the National YWCA, the Hon. Mrs Stanhope stressed the need to raise money to provide a new club room; which would be available for use by members of the WAAC, WRNS, Land Army women and also for those women who worked on the docks. All of them were invited to socialise together as comrades.[18]

Welfare organisations such as the Young Women's Christian Association were immensely proactive where the Women's Land Army was concerned. Popular fundraising events such as fetes and sales of work were organised under its auspices. These were always popular with those serving their country and the wider public as well. Monies raised went to funding and providing clubs housed in YWCA hostels that Land Girls could attend. This meant that Land Girls had access, free of charge to attend such clubs for three days a week in some cases.

Accommodation was also provided in hostels, typically for 15 women. A residential club at 51 Upper Baker Street, London charged the following for its services in early 1918. Rooms were charged at the daily rate of 3s 6d or at the weekly rate of £1 1s. Alternatively, a cubicle could be hired from 2s per night, (this price included other expenses such as lighting and a bath). A simple breakfast could be obtained for 9d, a meal started at 10d and if tea was required, it was an additional 6d.[19]

During their free time or holidays, Land Girls often attended large events in the nearest town or city. The two day War Fete and Sports event held at Franklin's Gardens, Northampton in August 1918 was attended by between 8000 and 9000 people and raised money for the Northamptonshire Prisoners of War Fund. £300 was raised on the first day alone. It was reported that lots of Land Girls visited Northampton on August 5th 1918 as part of their holiday. Their presence in the town caused many people to comment on their appearance; remarking on how healthy and tanned they looked.[20]

Whilst events predominantly raised money for a variety of good causes and charities, they also raised money for social trips for the members of clubs that Land Girls had formed themselves. For girls that had been placed near to areas that were holiday destinations where there were tourist attractions, any money left over was spent on treats such as a boat-trip. Some Land Girls in Cumberland enjoyed a trip on the 'Lady Betty' to Keswick.

Some communities proved difficult to interact with. Miss Calmady Hamlyn, the Travelling Inspector for Devon War Agricultural Committee spoke about the loneliness that many girls felt and the awful solitude they experienced when placed on remote farms. One particularly distressing case was reported which involved a Land Girl who was working in a village in North Devon. She had not had a word uttered to her by the villagers for three weeks.[21]

This only intensified the need to have readily available, open lines of communication. Where possible, visits were made regularly to women on isolated farms. During these visits, attempts would have been made to improve dialogue with farmers and the wider community. Regular post from other Land Girls who could offer support and from friends and family also went some way to lift flagging spirits or alleviate homesickness.

Feeling disconnected to others was a major problem and yet this 'disconnection' was experienced by many Land Girls. Measures were put in place to try and reduce the impact that, over time, emotions like this could have both mentally and physically on an individual who was trying to work efficiently in an unfamiliar part of the country. Just as it was important to provide social outlets for wounded, convalescing soldiers, it was deemed equally so to provide adequate support and welfare to women workers.[22]

On the Club Page in the February 1918 edition of The Landswoman, mention is made of several Land Girls who were feeling extra lonely and would be glad to receive letters. A rather pathetic little list follows of the names and addresses of four Land Girls. Becoming a pen-pal and writing letters was always actively encouraged by the editor of The Landswoman. Receipt of letters alone did not solve the immediate and pressing problem of loneliness that many girls felt so other solutions were sought such as knitting and sewing clubs, poetry and writing competitions.

Alternatively, organising a location where social events or classes could be held specifically for Land Girls who were working on remote or neighbouring farms was also an option, (that is if it was logistically possible for them to travel to the venue in the first place <u>and</u> arrive back at a reasonable hour). Land Girls generally speaking were good at cycling but didn't necessarily want to cycle long distances after work on bad roads in the dark!

A way had to be found which enabled regular get togethers to be arranged so that women could enjoy themselves with other Land Girls and gain access to the visiting Welfare Officer. In many counties, ladies of social standing and the local vicar and his wife invited a Land Girl(s) into their homes on Sundays, providing a change of scene and an opportunity for social interaction.

Land Girls appreciated anyone, (personnel or otherwise) that invested the time and effort into getting to know them personally. Miss Cook was one such woman who knew only too well the importance of this in her role as Secretary of the Women's War and Agricultural Committee in Winchester, Hampshire. A meeting was held at Embley Park and hosted by the owners, Major Chichester and his wife. A vote of thanks was proposed to Miss Cook personally in front of some of the women she had represented so well.

Lunch breaks for the women in the Forestry and Timber sections often meant sitting or leaning against piles of logs and having a well-earned rest. They took food and drink out with them and during their breaks, chatted and read letters. Some girls may have received bad news about their brothers or fathers who were overseas serving so breaks may have been respectfully quiet. During the busy weeks of harvest, food was taken out to the fields for the hungry workers.

For the relay of students from St Hilda's Hall in Oxford, who spent the summer of 1916 working on the land in a tiny village in Northamptonshire, their lunch breaks looked idyllic. Wherever women were placed, they would have read local newspapers and parish magazines to find out what was happening as well as keeping abreast of the national picture of how the war was unfolding. Gaining local knowledge would ultimately have helped them to integrate more effectively.

Land Girls did not appreciate anyone that grumbled or moaned about their lot. There was a sense that they had all joined up for a common cause and like soldiers, if the attitude of one person was negative, it generally affected everyone. Any tension felt within a group would undoubtedly have had a ripple effect on working relationships.

"Girls who continually say they are 'fed up' we have no time for but I do not think we have any of these girls to contend with."[23]

One Land Girl who made no attempt to 'cloak' the real grind of land work was Olive Hockin who is remembered today as a militant suffragette, arsonist, author and artist and Land Girl for a year on a Dartmoor Farm. Olive disliked the monotony of farm work and wrote famously on the subject.

Her book "Two Girls on the Land: Wartime on a Dartmoor Farm" was first published in 1918 and provides an account of what working on the land was really like; from the prejudices experienced by middle or upper-class women such as her, right through to trying to cultivate challenging rocky soil for food production.

When Land Girls struggled, they only needed to think of one of the Land Army mottos, 'Stick it if it kills' to spur them on! A Land Girl nicknamed 'Tubby' Keyes stuck at potato picking even though it was a nightmare for her back.

"I'm alive after 5 weeks of it and don't feel like dying yet."[24]

'Tubby' comments on the strangeness of the war years and of how some people struggled to understand what she was 'meant to be.' A convalescing Tommy had once asked her if he could accompany her for a walk. Tubby eventually saw him home as he had to be back at the hospital for 7pm.

"Rather a funny arrangement isn't it? But still, it's wartime and very funny things happen nowadays."[25]

Accounts vary with regard to how swiftly problems were dealt with or how accessible Travelling Inspectors and Welfare Officers actually were. Some Land Girls endured terrible hardship and often long-standing issues were never satisfactorily resolved. There were of course exemplary reports, one of which came from a Land Girl in Enfield Wash.

"No-one could have done more or worked harder for us. We are all doing our utmost to repay them for their many kindnesses and thoughtfulness and to uphold the dignity and honour of the Women's Land Army."[26]

If local people genuinely didn't want Land Girls in their village then it was a tough ask to sway those entrenched attitudes whatever efforts were made. Official intervention could actually exacerbate the problem rather than appease it. Ever resourceful, the Land Girls themselves found their own way around many problems by forming local committees that comprised of usually 12 girls. These committees met weekly to discuss any matters that had arisen during the week so that any issues could be resolved effectively and speedily if it was possible. Suggestions were also made as to what activities might be beneficial for the girls to attend throughout the year.

During the warm, light, summer nights, Land Girls enjoyed a variety of activities, ranging from punting, swimming or enjoying a trip out in a motor car. However, as petrol became scarce, these trips were curtailed and social events such as sing-a-longs and concerts were organised on farms and at venues in villages during the dark, winter months. Land Girls simply loved to showcase their musical skills! One Land Girl regularly played the piano accompaniment as the classically trained farmer's wife sang alongside her.[27]

If you were able to forge a solid, amicable working relationship with your employer then you clearly reaped the rewards. The very fact that you wanted to mix socially with your boss after long hours working for them says a lot about the kind of people this particular girl was working for; also that the girls were invited into their employer's home for sing-songs too is telling of the cordial yet respectful relationships that were formed.

Individual club funds were established whereby each Land Girl voluntarily contributed a small amount of money each week. If a situation ever arose where a Land Girl experienced unforeseen problems and was unable to afford the travel expenses to return home, the fund would step in and assist her with financial help. The well-meaning and inclusive sentiment behind the fund was based on genuine experiences and was no doubt a reassuring, albeit last resort for any self-respecting yet struggling Land Girl.

Grassroots fundraising for the 'Land Army Comforts Fund' was a perennial favourite cause. Attempts to rectify any shortcomings were made by organising white elephant stalls and giving concerts and recitals. St Bees Land Army Club in Cumberland was a case in point as all of the women mucked in and raised £15 9s and 6d. All positions, such as doorkeepers, those who got the room ready or produced programmes right through to the women that managed the stage curtain were filled by Land Girls.

The causes that the women raised money for were numerous. It could have been to fill the coffers for the parish hall, local church or large organisations such as The British Red Cross Society. Flag days were immensely popular in Great War society.

Whatever the total sum raised was and whatever the cause, it had the fringe benefit of enriching the girls' social life along with being able to do good and perhaps more importantly be seen to do good.

One large-scale fundraising event saw a Land Girl ride a pony, (decorated with red, white and blue ribbons along with two collecting boxes either side of the saddle) around Ledbury. For those that donated, a buttonhole was given out made of corn and tied with a dash of the Land Army colours of red and green.

Land Girls may have occasionally gone to the cinema if the distance was near enough for them to attend but it is doubtful that it would have been a regular social treat for those girls billeted in more isolated communities. After a long day, many were just too tired to travel any great distance to see a film, even if they were close enough to do so. They would have been aware however of the many plays, love stories, other entertainments and film screenings being advertised in the press that either featured Land Girls or had them as a central part of the plot.

A popular weekly event open to Land Girls within travelling distance from London was "The Landswoman Sunday Guild." The editor invited Land Girls to share tea between the hours of 3pm and 7pm. In addition, The Landswoman Office, (which was also the editor's home) had a club room that was open to all members.

Women were invited to write letters, talk and sing. Don't be shy was the predominant message and this was yet another example of the hand of friendship that was outstretched to all Land Army recruits. Concerts and talks were planned for future gatherings if the venture proved successful. Attendees were asked to wear their uniform as proof they were members of the organisation and their friends were also welcomed, (no doubt the hope was to draw in more recruits this way). Directions from the main railway stations were supplied and local girls were encouraged to use their bicycles to travel to the address.

A group of Land Girls based in Middlesex were fortunate enough to have a large club room that catered for their many different interests. One evening a week was set aside for gymnastics and another for dance classes. There was even a Land Army football team!

"We have a gorgeous ball and a real live man to coach us."[28]

In June 1919, another team of Land Girls who worked in the Bury St Edmunds area of Suffolk raised money for clubs associated with the Women's Land Army against a team of discharged soldiers, (who played dressed as clowns). Crowds gathered to cheer them on. It was noted by one Land Girl that the soldiers certainly did not play in a clown-like manner! Both sides performed well and approximately £17 was raised. The final score was a draw at 5-5.

A number of Land Girls sold programmes to attendees at a fundraising gymkhana event at Tonbridge Racecourse in Kent in aid of The Red Cross and The Red Triangle. A team of Land Girls also successfully competed there against a team of soldiers in the tug-of-war contest! It was held on a bank holiday and an estimated crowd of 4000-5000 people attended! The Land Girls eventually went on to triumph overall!

The variety and provision of both indoor and outdoor activities aided the wellbeing of those recruited into its ranks as it provided choice. The need to have readily available private and personal spaces, (such as rest rooms and communal spaces) allowed the women to relax and partake in less strenuous activities such as board games, writing letters home or simply immerse themselves in a book and mentally escape for an hour or two!

The Women's Land Army was never an organisation to pass up an opportunity to be patriotic. Land Army girls from London and Middlesex combined a presentation of Good Service Ribbons with a celebration to mark Queen Mary's birthday. They enjoyed a plentiful supper, after which dancing and games were enjoyed.

Establishing new working relationships however proved tricky at times for many reasons, some glaringly obvious, others a little more subtle. Appeals were made in every county newspaper using every available means to attract educated recruits and provide a reason as to why it was so crucial. Educated women aged between 18 and 35 were being called upon to join the WNLSC to undertake a course of training for six weeks on a farm. Once trained, such women would become leaders of groups of village women. This venture was not well received by local women as they resented being under the leadership of these educated women who had, until relatively recently, had no experience of working on the land and yet immediately earnt more than they did.[29]

More work manifested itself with the turn of each season, meaning that the shorter and longer daylight hours required not only the farming day to be adapted but also the workforce too. These factors were exactly the same for those women who worked to meet the demand for timber in the woods and spinneys all over the country in the Timber and Forestry sections.

The women needed to adapt quickly to their surroundings and be amicable with those around them. It would have been a miserable, lonely existence otherwise working in such close proximity if you did not all get on or at the very least remain on good terms with each other.

For a huge number of young women, it was a definitive shift from their stifled, restricted background. Working outdoors most of the time, carrying out laborious manual tasks was in sharp contrast to the comfortable and cosseted lives they had left behind. For those at the other end of the social spectrum, (the young women embroiled in and somewhat resigned to a life of drudgery in domestic service) it literally was an escape route to a hitherto, out of reach world of opportunity!

Emphasis was placed on attracting young women to the Women's Land Army and as a result, older women felt that they were being ignored and overlooked. In June 1918, highly contentious viewpoints appeared in newspapers stating that, what was deemed to be the best 12 years of a woman's life, (from 18 to 30) was the age range that employers ideally wanted working on their farms.[30]

If however the individual was fit and well, there should be no reason whatsoever why she would not be able to carry out the work regardless of her age. Many people defended the position of the older worker saying that the experience and steady nature that older workers provided was in fact of more use to farmers than the eagerness and good intentions demonstrated by the younger, newly-trained women.[31]

Despite this argument, older women, (especially married ones with children who could offer part-time hours) frequently struggled to secure positions. They were not offered the chance to even try in some circumstances in spite of the labour shortages - despite childcare being offered.

Older women who came forward to work on the land, whether it was through the Women's Land Army or any of the other land organisations passed on invaluable wisdom and skills to the less experienced. Miss Cissie Wood of Rickarton, Kincardineshire was 83 years old when she set a new record in early 1914 by taking part in a ploughing match with the best of the other all-male competitors.

It was claimed that Mary Alcock from Norfolk was in fact the oldest member of the Women's Land Army. Although her exact age wasn't stated she was probably well into her eighties!

Times changed rapidly in farming during the Great War years and women often had little choice but to take over the farm that had previously been owned and run by their husband if he died. Women were strictly prohibited from taking a farm lease on in some parts of the country (an example of this was in some parts of Cheshire).

For young girls, born into farming families, it was often assumed they would continue to assist with the routine of agricultural work as they grew up which meant that many girls only received a basic education. Their lives were simply given over to being yet another devotee to the land; generational grist for the agricultural mill. For many, there was no opportunity to break free. War however changed those expectations.

For the young girls that remained, they helped out on the family farm as they were too young to join the Women's Land Army proper. Younger girls were ideal candidates for what became known as "The Flappers Land Army." This 'junior' Land Army was first mentioned in the summer of 1918. Girls under the age of 18 were allowed to undertake light duties such as market gardening and working in parks under supervision and just like their older counterparts, they too had to enrol for a set period of time, wear a uniform and were housed in hostels.[32]

Many young girls however were well under the stipulated age and had already been working for years in an agricultural capacity quite successfully before this idea was even conceived. They often wore an armband which denoted that they were doing their National Service. Photographs frequently appeared in newspapers, proudly informing the readership that despite their youth, they had already won many illustrious prizes. They had competed fairly

Nine Women's Land Army recruits, having arrived with suitcases at Tregavethan Farm, Truro, Cornwall, (a Women's Land Army training centre) April-May 1917. The names of the women are as follows from left to right: possibly Ms. Vera Dunfrane, Ms. Northey, Ms. Trejeweth, Ms. Nora Lock, Ms. I. Crowther, Ms. Dorothy Phyllis Martin, Ms. Brown, unknown, Mrs Ford. Photographer: Arthur William Jordan. © From the collection of the RIC. Image archive of the Royal Cornwall Museum. Image licensed from Media Storehouse.

Nine members of the Great War Women's Land Army in working dress, Tregavethan Farm, Truro, Cornwall, April-May 1917. These women were possibly the first recruits that were trained at Tregavethan Farm, a Women's Land Army Training Centre. The names of the women are as follows from left to right: possibly Ms. Vera Dunfrane, Ms. Northey, Ms. Trejeweth, Ms. Nora Lock, Ms. I. Crowther, Ms. Dorothy Phyllis Martin, Ms. Brown, unknown, Mrs Ford. Photographer: Arthur William Jordan. © From the collection of the RIC. Image archive of the Royal Cornwall Museum. Image licensed from Media Storehouse.

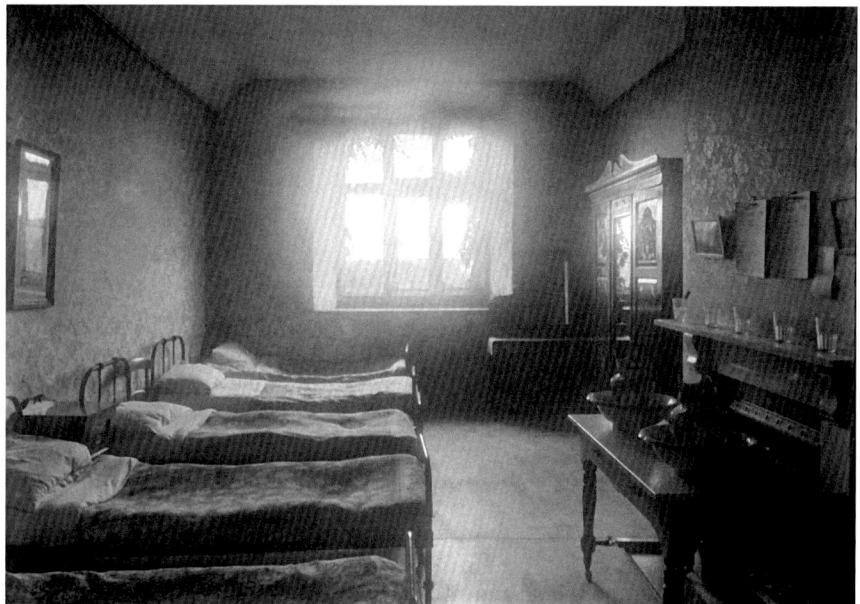

The sleeping quarters for the Women's Land Army at Tregavethan Farm training centre in 1917. Rules and a timetable are pinned to the wall above the wash-stand. 5 glasses stand on the mantelpiece, 2 jugs and bowls sit on the table and the 5 beds have been pushed closely together. Photographer: Arthur William Jordan. © From the collection of the RIC. Image archive of the Royal Cornwall Museum. Image licensed from Media Storehouse.

Fourteen members of the Women's Land Army standing in a line eating Cornish pasties at Tregavethan Farm, a Women's Land Army training centre, April 1918. The pasties were more than likely a traditional reward for passing their efficiency test! Photographer: Arthur William Jordan. © From the collection of the RIC. Image archive of the Royal Cornwall Museum. Image licensed from Media Storehouse.

The 1916 year group photograph of students studying at St Hilda's Hall, Oxford. The girls that worked on the land during their summer vacation at Brockhall in Northamptonshire in 1916 appear on this photograph. Photograph by kind permission of the Principal and Fellows' of St Hilda's College, Oxford.

Setting out from The Dairy House at Brockhall. Four students from St Hilda's Hall, Oxford set out for a hard day, dressed in their work clothes, carrying farm implements, a jug and a bag of food for their lunch break later in the day. Photograph by kind permission of the Principal and Fellows' of St Hilda's College, Oxford.

Two students from St Hilda's Hall, Oxford holding thistle-pulling tools. They spent their summer vacation in 1916 working on the land in the leafy manorial village of Brockhall for the Squire of Brockhall Hall and a local farmer. Photograph by kind permission of the Principal and Fellows' of St Hilda's College, Oxford.

Pulling thistles in corn. Four students from St Hilda's Hall, Oxford moving thistles with thistle-pulling tools under the watchful gaze of the farmer. Photograph by kind permission of the Principal and Fellows' of St Hilda's College, Oxford.

Three St Hilda's Hall students wearing rather impractical work clothes as they hoe. One is wearing a covering over her face to protect her from bite and stings. In Verse IV of the poem called "Farming Song" penned by one of the working party, a reference is made to one girl being stung on the hand and nose! Photograph by kind permission of the Principal and Fellows' of St Hilda's College, Oxford.

Four St Hilda's Hall students in work clothes, working with scythes under the supervision of a farmer at Brockhall, Northamptonshire during their summer vacation in 1916. Photograph by kind permission of the Principal and Fellows' of St Hilda's College, Oxford.

Two St Hilda's Hall students pitching hay at Brockhall. Written on the back of the original photograph is "Grace pitching." The high wall of the hall's kitchen garden is visible in the background. Photograph by kind permission of the Principal and Fellows' of St Hilda's College, Oxford.

"Grace pitching" holding a long pitchfork whilst working with two other farm workers. Photograph by kind permission of the Principal and Fellows' of St Hilda's College, Oxford.

Two St Hilda's Hall students and a farm labourer carrying stooks in a harvest field. In the background, the chimneys of Brockhall Hall can clearly be seen. Photograph by kind permission of the Principal and Fellows' of St Hilda's College, Oxford.

The original photograph had the words "Co-workers" written on the back. This group of nine soldiers assisted with the harvest and were probably drafted from the nearby barracks located in the village of Weedon, just a few miles away. Photograph by kind permission of the Principal and Fellows' of St Hilda's College, Oxford.

Horse and cart with the name of the Squire, T. W. Thornton Esq, Brockhall, Northamptonshire painted onto the front board. A farm labourer is pitching hay onto the cart. Other farm machinery can be seen in the background. Photograph by kind permission of the Principal and Fellows' of St Hilda's College, Oxford.

The words "Gladys on the stack" were written on the reverse of the original photograph. Gladys is photographed atop the huge hay stack, working alongside five other farm labourers and boys. Photograph by kind permission of the Principal and Fellows' of St Hilda's College, Oxford.

Four St Hilda's Hall students enjoying their lunch break on the Brockhall Estate. One girl is pictured eating a banana. A farm implement leans against the estate fence in the background. Photograph by kind permission of the Principal and Fellows' of St Hilda's College, Oxford.

Four St Hilda's Hall students relax during a break from their labours on a bank. A piece of paper in the foreground shows the word 'Weedon' clearly written on it, (a nearby village). Photograph by kind permission of the Principal and Fellows' of St Hilda's College, Oxford.

The first verse of the "Farming Song." This six verse poem was written by one of the relay of students from St Hilda's Hall, Oxford and describes in rhyme the ups and downs of their time spent on the land during their summer vacation in 1916. Five verses appeared in the local Weedon Deanery Parish Magazine. Photograph by kind permission of the Principal and Fellows' of St Hilda's College, Oxford.

"We all go the same way home." A group of Land Girls walking back to billets in single file, climbing over a stile. The Landswoman, September 1918, p13. © Successor rightsholder unknown.

"Sunday hair-washing" is written on the back of the original photograph. One girl pumps water as another washes her hair and three other girls look on in the cobbled courtyard at the back of The Dairy House. Photograph by kind permission of the Principal and Fellows' of St Hilda's College, Oxford.

A procession of women who were serving in the Timber Section of the Women's Land Army. One of their officers holds the cross at the head of the group of women as they march towards the new Church Hut erected at the Timber Camp at Chilgrove, near Chichester. The money raised to construct the wooden church and the furniture inside it was raised in small sums and donated by the Girls' Friendly Society. The Landswoman, September 1919, p21. © Successor rightsholder unknown.

The initials, "GM" are written on the back of the original photograph. One of the St Hilda's Hall students is photographed here sitting in her work clothes with her arm tenderly around a small child. It shows how good relationships were established with some of the villagers over short spans of time, (a month in this case). Photograph by kind permission of the Principal and Fellows' of St Hilda's College, Oxford.

Two of the St Hilda's Hall students enjoy bathing and swimming during some free time. Photograph by kind permission of the Principal and Fellows' of St Hilda's College, Oxford.

Fourteen Land Girls showed great initiative when they were inspired by hunger and a railway station refreshment room! As part of Tank Week they wore hastily created sandwich boards adorned with advertisements for the Women's Land Army and took part in a recruitment drive in Doncaster during the summer of 1918. The Land Girls walked alongside Egbert the tank and fastened onto their backs a huge letter which spelt out F.O.O.D. P.R.O.D.U.C.T.I.O.N much to the delight of the gathered crowds. The recruiting booth was filled with potential recruits as a result! The Landswoman, June 1918, p11. © Successor rightsholder unknown.

"The Long and The Short Of It." The physical differences of the women that joined the Great War Women's Land Army. The Landswoman, 1 July 1919, p156. © Successor rightsholder unknown.

The lighter side of working on the land! Some Land Girls playing leapfrog after their efficiency test at Tregavethan Farm, Truro, Cornwall, 13 September 1918. Photographer: Arthur William Jordan. © From the collection of the RIC. Image archive of the Royal Cornwall Museum. Image licensed from Media Storehouse.

Four characters in play called "Hannah Comes Round" written by Mr J. G. Griffith. Land Girls were a hot topic and this play demonstrated how people that were opposed to the new women on the land were eventually won round by the sheer determination of Land Girls to succeed. The Landswoman, 1 April 1918, p16 © Successor rightsholder unknown.

A seasonal, mobile gang of Land Girls. These women often moved from farm to farm to assist with the harvest. This particular gang picked 100 acres of potatoes in less than six weeks. The Landswoman, 1 December 1918, p48 © Successor rightsholder unknown.

The Women's Land Army of America. The first contingent of the Women's Land Army of America to leave Los Angeles for farm duty. The Landswoman, 1 February 1919, p4. © Successor rightsholder unknown.

This "Peace wedding" took place at Holy Trinity, Hotwells, Bristol on Peace Day, 28 June 1919. It was the first Women's Land Army wedding in Bristol. Miss Violet A' Court married Private Harry Collins of the Australian Imperial Force. The Armistice brought the couple together. It was their intention to run a farm in New South Wales. The Landswoman, 1 August 1919, p12. © Successor rightsholder unknown.

The wedding certificate of Violet A' Court and Harry Collins. They married on Peace Day, 28 June 1919. Theirs was the first Women's Land Army wedding in Bristol. Violet recorded her profession as a "Land Girl" in box 5 on the certificate. This is a rare example as many serving Land Girls left the profession box blank. It shows that Violet wanted her wartime service in the Women's Land Army to be recorded forever in the official register. Image by kind permission of Bristol Archives: P.HTC/R/2/c and successfully against other experienced men and women and won prizes for their skills and ability at demonstrations, (events designed to showcase specialised skills in specific categories which were subsequently judged and marked).

Miss Truscott, of St Veep, Cornwall was photographed ploughing with two horses. She was one of the youngest members of the Women's Land Army at 14 years of age and had already won a raft of prizes for her skills in harnessing and harrowing. During 1916, Miss Truscott, (without any assistance) raked an astonishing 80 acres of corn.[33]

72 women took part in the demonstration at Cartuther Barton, Liskeard in October 1916. Some of the results were so close that two prizes had to be awarded or split when necessary.

Younger still, little Elsie Gray was just 10 years old when she took part in a demonstration in Lincolnshire in March 1916. Little Elsie wore a red tam-o-shanter whilst working which made her stand out from the rest of the competitors. Little Elsie was clearly quite at ease walking behind the two big horses called Big Dolly and Nell as she harrowed alone.[34]

Although far too young to be in any organisation, Elsie clearly was confident when working with such large, powerful animals and machinery having witnessed her parents and other men perform the same tasks right from her earliest years.

The public had a genuine interest in and fascination with the Women's Land Army. For those women who were curious to learn more about its work, public places such as the cinema or theatre also became useful tools for targeting the undecided, dithering women. Short films, (that had an underlying serious message) or official films, (that promoted the important work of the Women's Land Army) were shown to captive audiences before the main feature.

Two popular actresses of the day, Violet Hopson and Ivy Close starred in a film where they played the part of two apathetic, privileged young women who discover the benefits of working in the Women's Land Army. Any woman that saw the film, who wasn't doing war service of any kind would surely have felt a pang of guilt as they saw the advantages of joining unfold before them on the big screen![35]

Films were often shown twice a night over several days. The Women's Land Army was a hot topic!

Sunday was usually a Land Girl's day off and many attended church or chapel. Every individual had the right to follow whatever religion they wished to. In its handbook however, the Women's Land Army did encourage L.A.A.S girls to attend public worship if it was possible to do so although it was undenominational itself as an organisation.[36]

Many Land Girls attempted to seek out a place of worship near to where they were billeted. This was not always possible as it may have been just too far away to travel there and back in a set time. Potato gang member, 'Tubby' Keyes wished to attend chapel but she felt too tired to walk or cycle the 2½ miles there and back on her day of rest, opting to take a book and sit by the river and read instead!

The students from St Hilda's Hall, Oxford, (who spent their summer vacation in 1916 working on the land in Northamptonshire) attended the village church. They rang the bell for Sunday service, sang in the choir and pumped the organ bellows. These women clearly made a concerted effort to participate in village life during the short time they were there.

Efforts made by Land Girls were clearly appreciated in certain villages. Two resident Land Girls based in Hampshire were asked to ring the peace bells and a rector in Dorset asked a Land Girl to plant an oak tree to commemorate peace in the village churchyard.

Land Girls would have been very aware of other people's strength of faith, (as well as having their own or in some cases, not) and also of the strong bonds that the church had to the land and agriculture. These deep-rooted, ancient associations would have seen people regularly attend services, especially those that were linked to the agricultural year, namely Plough Sunday, (Plough Monday in some areas) Rogation Sunday, Lammastide and Harvest Festival.

Participation in such services was unavoidable as rallies and church parades were frequently conjoined. At a Rogation Sunday service at St James' Cathedral, Bury St Edmunds in May 1918, the presiding canon welcomed everyone but brought to the fore the vital work being carried out by landswomen. He informed the congregation of what high regard all decent people held them in. They had risen above all of the prejudice, mocking and scoffing and shown how invaluable their service was to the nation. This had been the best way of proving to those who had foolishly demonstrated such behaviour that they had been utterly misguided in their assumptions.[37]

Traditional harvest hymns such as "We Plough the Fields and Scatter" and "Come Ye Thankful People Come" would have been sung with grateful thanks in village churches and other places of worship up and down the country.

A large congregation, (comprising of a number of Land Girls) participated in a Harvest Festival service in November 1918 at St Peter's, Mancroft, Norwich. Thanks was given for the collective efforts of all the people that had worked on the land to gather the precious harvest. A further fitting acknowledgement of the high esteem and respect that the Land Girls were held in was given during the address made by the Bishop of Thetford who stated that the service:

> "Was really the harvest festival of the members of the Women's Land Army."[38]

The plough became a symbol of contention during the war when the concept of Sunday ploughing was first suggested and later introduced. It was reported that ploughing on the sacred day, (after much wrangling with and reluctance) had finally been given the blessing of both the secular and ecclesiastical; due to sheer national necessity resting upon the outcome of the harvest.[39]

The Sabbath was indeed sacred to so many people and the very idea of having to work on it, even in times of such need posed a real dilemma. Despite protests, work did indeed progress on the sacred day. Allotment holders also worked on their plots on Sundays to maximise productivity.

For the girls and women based at Barwick Park flax camp in Somerset, special provision was made for those that wished to attend a service. The local reverend arranged services for the women on Thursdays and Sundays.

Having access to clergy and regular services would have given comfort and solace to so many of the women; allowing them to pray, sing, take Holy Communion or merely collect their thoughts. It is important to remember that women would have received all kinds of happy and sad news from home and overseas whilst they were away. All manner of things would have been read and discussed under the canvass of 94 little tents and lots kept private too!

Sunday was also the day when polite invitations were taken up by Land Girls to visit ladies in their homes. This break from toil was seen as necessary in order to maintain a healthy workforce who underneath must have been experiencing all manner of emotions.

Just in case any Land Girls got carried away with their social life they were starkly reminded in the L.A.A.S Handbook of the standards that were expected. It was clear that any behaviour that was noisy or unruly would not be tolerated as it tarnished the reputation of the Women's Land Army as a whole and brought disgrace upon the individual wearing the uniform.[40]

To many Land Girls, singing seemed a favourable way to get through the endless hours of work. Some mention reciting patriotic songs as they worked. This helped them to establish a rhythm which in turn alleviated the monotony of the work. Familiar songs that reminded them of home or their brothers and fathers, (who would no doubt sing similar songs many miles away) were always favourites!

Miss Beatrice Smith was an office girl in London in her previous life and had been a member of the Women's Land Army of one or two years standing by 1919. Beatrice had been placed on various farms in the surrounding area throughout that time. She clearly loved singing and performed in a competition organised by the "Nonsense Concert Party" who presented the programme at The Bohemia Theatre in Broadstairs, Kent. She captivated the audience with her performance and received rapturous applause, going on to win first prize in the competition!

Launched in January 1918, priced at 2d and edited by Meriel Talbot, (the lady in charge of recruitment, regulation and coordination in the Women's Land Army) The Landswoman was the official monthly magazine of the Women's Land Army and the Women's Institute. It was a new and significant tool aimed at firstly establishing and secondly maintaining a united, cohesive spirit for women who may have felt isolated whilst working or being billeted alone in a far flung corner of an alien county. Its aim was to extend a hand of friendship to all recruits by way of involvement in various club and societies.

A competition featured every month and Land Girls were encouraged to contribute. Land Girls were also invited to suggest further ideas. If their ideas were chosen, they were awarded a prize. Some of the prizewinning ideas submitted were:

1. My most exciting adventure since joining the Land Army.
2. A farm alphabet.
3. Notes on an ideal Land Army club.
4. The best set of three photographs illustrating the Land Army's work.
5. The best cure for toothache and bee stings.
6. Some strange tricks and habits I have seen with animals.
7. What I would do if I had the power?[41]

During the busiest times of the year, such as the harvest months, when the daylight hours were significantly longer and more pressurised, most Land Girls were too weary to think about doing anything else at the end of the day apart from cleaning themselves up, preparing and eating a meal and making sure that they got plenty of sleep.

> "No time again this week, (to submit drawings, photographs or letters etc) but we must get the corn in."[42]

During the dark months of winter, Land Girls passed the long, cold evenings playing games, singing, dancing, drawing, writing and submitting a wide variety of material to the magazine. Recipes, remedies, poems and sketches portrayed the lighter side of working in the Women's Land Army and were constantly being sought!

Other items frequently requested by the editor, (with an eye to publishing) were essays on aspects of agriculture and animal husbandry and articles that marked and reflected important events in the calendar. Women were invited to become part of a countrywide network by way of actively seeking out more knowledge and gaining more expertise in their chosen field(s). They could send for instruction leaflets which aided and assisted their training; leaflets that imparted invaluable tips and advice from experts.

The Shopping Club was always a popular feature and it was through this regular column that Land Girls could request items that they needed. The requests were always eclectic, such as a handbook for a special type of tractor through to a patent boot polish! Other items were:

"Books on rabbits and bees, to hats and coats; from watches to patterns of all kinds of underclothes, smocks and frock coats."[43]

Some Land Girls wanted items of uniform and were willing to exchange them for another item that was in good condition thereby avoiding the much higher cost of replacement. They were thrifty and recycled where it was possible.

A scheme called "Landworker Libraries" appeared to be another successful venture. Approximately forty centres, (also called Guilds) were established in England and Wales. These centres held between 50-100 books. Stock was changed as new books were required. This circulation enabled each county to receive new stock before it was eventually given back to Headquarters.

An additional aim was to send five books at a time to Land Girls who were perhaps feeling isolated or alone in the location where they had been placed.

One such Guild was set up in Yorkshire. It met once a week on a Sunday. A qualified librarian was put in charge to advise women when selecting books for their agricultural studies.[44]

There were also books to read for pleasure. Any interested girls had to contact the Secretary in writing at one of the centres and provide the name of their District Registrar. The Land Girl also had to cover the cost for postage one way.

Land Girls were a rich source of inspiration for established authors of the day such as Berta Ruck who wrote "A Land Girl's Love Story" in 1919. The novel was advertised for sale at 6 shillings or alternatively, people could purchase a particular newspaper and read it as a serial. People could also pay one shilling for Ian Farquhar's "The Land Army Girl" which was one of fourteen amusing stories or maybe purchase Olive Hockin's "Two Girls on the Land" for 2/6 paper or 3/6 cloth!

Many Land Girls kept diaries which chronicle this unique window of time in their lives. It must have felt very important for the women to record what the war had allowed them to do for their country. Many describe the prevailing public mood of the day and recall the strangeness or unsettled restlessness that war effected in people.

These recollections stand now just as they stood at the time they wrote them down; a proud record of their service. A genuine realisation and desire to put down in writing the fact that "I was there."

The conviction of and confidence in the performance of women employed on any particular farm had to be assured if more land was to be planted with crops such as corn. If the farmer knew that he could rely on his allotted female workforce to put in the time and effort to produce more food then it was a risk worth taking.

Over time, bonds were formed with people and with the land itself. A Land Girl's bond was first and foremost to duty but many women were surprised at just how deep and profound their love of the countryside became. Many found it hard to break away after the organisation had been demobilised.

Organisations were set up in an attempt to provide women with guidance and direction with regard to the employment options still open to them after they were no longer required for war work. The Overseas Settlement for British Women encouraged women to consider emigration, (to countries such as Canada). These were countries where female labour was still in demand.

In January 1919, the Women's National Land Service Corps appealed for £10,000 to set up a small holding cooperative whereby women could continue to work in agriculture and farming when the war came to an end.

Many enterprising Land Girls considered resettlement almost as a natural progression. After all, their wartime 'career' was now over and this next step was something that had merely evolved from it. It all depended on the individual circumstances of each girl and how tied or restless they still felt.

One young woman who chose this path was Elizabeth 'Bessie' Edwards. Bessie was born on the 22nd February, 1896 in Denbighshire, Wales. Bessie completed her training and worked in the Sutton Coldfield area. In 1921, she travelled to Wellington, New Zealand aboard the ship "Robert Fenn." Bessie had received assistance with her resettlement from the Girls Friendly Society, (a Church of England organisation). Their members met Bessie in Wellington and later in Lyttelton. A minister found her employment in Hinds, (a small town on New Zealand's South Island).

Her first few weeks were lonely ones, with a less than favourable first impression being made of Hinds. Bessie however clearly stuck at it as she married a man called John Henry 'Jack' Ellis on the 16th July 1924 in Allenton, Ashburton.

After their marriage, Bessie and Jack farmed a 75 acre dairy farm and supplied a local cheese factory with their milk. Her previous training and experience in the Women's Land Army proved to be invaluable.

After Jack's death, Bessie lived alone for a while on their farm before eventually going to reside at a residential home. Rather touchingly, the local community showed just how much they loved Bessie. They certainly had not forgotten her. Over 30 people provided wool, including some children who donated part of the fleece from their pet lambs - from which 10 local spinners created a colourful, crocheted knee rug which was presented to a delighted Bessie. The young Welsh Land Girl who had shown such courage to resettle in a new country had clearly left an indelible mark on the population of the town she had called home for so many years. Bessie died on the 16th September 1984 aged 88 years.

After demobilisation, efforts were made to utilise the swell of comradeship generated by service in the Women's Land Army. Ex-Land Girls were heartily encouraged to keep in touch and events such as reunions were organised in order for women to reconnect and reminisce by way of large-scale dinner events. Who else after all would best understand the wartime trials and tribulations of a Land Girl *but* a Land Girl?

There would have been few individuals unaffected by loss during the Great War so the need to preserve the emotional link with your Land Army 'kin' would have been a priority, especially in the months immediately following demobilisation. Memories that encompassed every emotion would have been recalled.

Maybe there was one special memory that each time it was thought of, would always bring a smile back to the faces of those who were part of its creation, no matter how many years had passed by.

> "We had a sing-song and seldom has that lane heard such shrieks of enjoyment and delight as were heard that night over the excitement of the penny game. Then good night and to bed and next morning happy, laughing girls, singing their hearts out, wandered across the meadow to their milking, all the keener on their work this morning for the fun of the evening before."[45]

Theirs truly was an unshakeable camaraderie!

Chapter 11

Farmerettes and friends

It wasn't just the women of Britain that joined up to serve their country in the Great War. America had a Land Army and also other countries too such as Canada, France and Belgium.

America's Land Army was organised along similar lines to those of the Women's National Land Service Corps. 'Units' of 'Farmerettes' were swiftly recruited, organised, trained and posted. American women came forward and volunteered to do similar jobs to their British counterparts although the difference in climate determined the types of crops that were ultimately cultivated and harvested.

Women in both countries participated in food preservation initiatives at pulping plants in order to save and preserve any surplus or substandard seasonal fruits from being spoiled.

Wealthy, young American women forwent their summer holidays which were usually spent in their country homes at Newport choosing instead to assist the war effort in the less than salubrious surroundings of the New York docks. There they spent time rescuing food that would otherwise have been considered not fit for human consumption and subsequently destroyed. This food was then made available for those in need. 2000 women were at work in the state of New York alone.[1]

Schemes were established all over America. Wellesley, Massachusetts set up a land training scheme and Home Economics departments at colleges and universities also ran courses. Any avenue which saw food conserved and preserved was explored, right down to individuals cutting down their consumption of white flour, meat, bacon and fats.

The Women's Farm and Garden Association had initially piqued and stimulated any potential new recruits to come forward. The recruitment ethos was much the same with regard to the types of patriotic females the organisation needed to attract: college students, (who were readily available for seasonal work) women who perhaps were at home and wanted the opportunity to live away, married women with a family who could perhaps offer part-time hours and women who wanted to switch an indoor career for one outdoors.

After being trained, the units of American women could be as small as 6 or as large as 73. They also worked individually on farms. Farmerettes were billeted in a centre and were deployed to work wherever they were required. There was inevitably a swell of patriotism when America entered the war in 1917.

Canada also attempted to promote the ever-present need for women to consider working on the land as a viable option for national war service. Prejudice against women working on the land was not as keenly felt in Canada as it was in Britain. As a nation, it didn't appear to consider land work a derogatory occupation for females.

As time wore on, a regular Women's Land Army of America came into being; based on a reflection of the sister organisation that was working hard across the Atlantic.

The National Political League's Land Council also had a sturdy relationship with their American equivalents. The two organisations enjoyed exchanges of constructive information and advice which only hastened the development of the American Women's Land Army in 20 states countrywide by the summer of 1918.

A farmer in New Jersey stated just how hard the women worked:

> "Pitching corn stalks: Two girls working together lifted from 8-10 tons of stalks per day.
> Hay: Two of his girls could load as well as a man.
> Oats: One girl pitched 310 sheaves in 19 minutes, each sheaf averaging 8lb and she could pitch 19 tons in a day."[2]

The New York National Farm and Garden Association expressed a genuine desire to collaborate with and link the two Women's Land Armies together which would have further cemented their respective bonds and encouraged shared ideas. It was suggested by the chairman that an exchange programme might be established that permitted Land Girls from America to study at an agricultural college, (by way of a scholarship) in England and for English Land Girls to travel to America to do likewise.[3]

At the time, American Land Girls expressed a wish that they wanted people to see how important women's work was with regard to the future of their country. The women wanted the wider public to gain a better understanding and appreciation of what they were doing for the war effort by working on the land and in food reclamation and not feel threatened by their existence as an organisation. They had gained strength by being unified in their cause and it was this strength that continued to propel them ever forward.[4]

This idea had been considered for some months as it had already been mentioned in the February edition of The Landswoman. The editor however stated:

"I doubt whether it can be done."[5]

It did not stop American Land Girls lapping up the stories and information contained within this magazine specifically produced for and by the Land Girls. Weekly subscriptions sent to America numbered into the dozens!

British Land Girls also learnt a great deal about the type of crops being harvested in America; far removed from the ones grown in the British climate. They saw photographs of almonds being gathered, apricots being dried and beans being harvested. Many of these fruits were dried or canned and supplied to the troops.

Wartime also saw the creation of approximately 5 million additional 'Victory' war gardeners in the United States in 1918 alone, (the intention was to double the figure in 1919). In late 1916, Britain also had a similar scheme called 'Out for Victory' which saw approximately 1.4 million additional areas of land put over to cultivation in just over a year. These plots were tended not only by adults but by millions of schoolchildren too.

The women of France had also answered the call of their country to work on the land; they had worked exceptionally hard in the early years of the war. The harvest of 1915 was so abundant and of such high quality, it had led some to claim that there hadn't been a better one for nigh on 40 years.[6]

Had it not been for the women, this would not have been so as there were no younger men to assist with the land work. Only old men were available.[7]

The government of France had appealed to its women in August 1914 stating how vital it was that agriculture should be kept going, not only to feed the army but its citizens too.

A farmer's wife residing in a small, French village expressed concern at the deep bite that had been felt from requisitioning and how it was leaving farms with no carts, motor cars, horses or even oxen to pull the ploughs. Women, (often elderly) out of sheer necessity pulled ploughs themselves chained into pairs or threes.

The formation of the Women's Land Army in Britain aroused great interest amongst French women who were living in Britain or in their native France. Rather interestingly, a little heard-of French 'unit' was formed that coexisted within the structure of the British Women's Land Army proper. A lady called Madame Veron was appointed to the Women's Branch of the Food Production Department to oversee its efficient running.

French women were patriotic just like their British counterparts and keen fundraisers. In July 1918, London held 'France's Day' and its buildings and streets were resplendent with the bright colours of France's Tricolour flag. Flags appeared everywhere, even in buttonholes! A huge sum of approximately £250,000 was collected in tins for the French Red Cross. In the same year, a French Legion and a Belgian section of the Women's Land Army had also been formed.

French Land Girl, Gabriel Fleury was working in England in December 1919. Acting on her own initiative, she showcased her new tractor to the press. Gabriel had set up her own business venture at Wantage, Berkshire. As a result of this, she was being employed by many farmers in the area. Gabriel had continued to work in agriculture despite sustaining severe burns to her face after helping another man whose machine was on fire.

Female labour on the land was not viewed as such a new or groundbreaking concept in countries like France, Belgium and Germany. It was reported that in late 1916, there were 8 million German women working on the land, 6½ million of which were working on holdings of less than 50 acres.

Young children and young adults aged between 8-18 years old from various countries formed their own labour forces which enabled more men to be released from agricultural work to serve. Staggering numbers of French schoolchildren were mobilised during their summer holidays in 1918. 5,000,000 voluntarily worked in fields or in gardens. In the previous year, 215,000, (90,000 of which were girls) volunteered to work on farms. They worked in many different areas, including 12,000 villages and as a result of their combined efforts, a total of 2400 acres of land was cultivated. The food produced on these 2400 acres was estimated to have had a value of £222,000. Even greater totals were being hoped for should every one of France's 5,000,000 schoolchildren be able to cultivate 100 square yards of soil. Instead of 2400 acres – it was hoped that 100,000 acres could be cultivated in 1918.[8]

Collective effort spread over the allied nations undoubtedly provided the impetus that kept each individual motivated through what must have seemed like a never-ending war.

Chapter 12

Royal approval

The efforts of the Women's Land Army were supported by the Queen and her daughter, Princess Mary. They attended events that endorsed and advocated the inclusion of women in agriculture. The Queen regularly invited women war workers to garden parties held at Buckingham Palace and presented Good Service Ribbons and Distinguished Service Bars to deserving candidates at special ceremonies. Other members of the royal family attended prize-giving events, such as Princess Helena Victoria, (a granddaughter of Queen Victoria). In late September 1917, the Princess presented members of The Women's Legion, (who had partaken in agricultural competitions) with their well-earned awards at Oakham.

The National Anthem was usually sung at the end of any meeting as a mark of respect and at church services throughout the land. King George V and Queen Mary were never very far from the minds of the patriotic members of the Women's Land Army.

The Queen personally sent for the Director-General of the Women's Land Army, Miss Talbot to enquire about and discuss matters concerning the conditions that landswomen were working in and about the uniform they wore. In February 1918, the Queen even enquired how waterproof the government issued boots were!

The genuine and constant interest shown by the royal family won both respect and admiration from landswomen. The Queen and her daughter visited "The Women's War Exhibition" at Whitechapel Art Gallery in 1918. It opened to the public on the 7th October and was free to enter. Over the course of 6 weeks, 82,000 people visited it. The exhibition represented all of the wartime industries that women were employed in. More poignantly, there was a women's war shrine dedicated to those women who had died whilst serving their country.

The Queen's close association with, what were then, fledgling organisations saw her actively involved with projects set up to benefit landworkers by furthering their knowledge about specific aspects of their work. The Queen sent a request through her Lady in Waiting who in-turn wrote to the Secretary of the Landworkers' Libraries.

"Her Majesty is sending forty volumes to the libraries for the use of the workers and gives permission for Her Majesty's gift to be mentioned in the papers."[1]

Queen Mary also issued frequent messages at various times of the year. They often marked significant points in the calendar. These messages appeared in newspapers all over the country and must have lifted morale and spurred women on. The Queen travelled all over the country to observe the new female recruits at work and was clearly impressed with what she saw on her travels. Her Majesty commented on how the Empire required its womenfolk to rally to the cause, now, more than ever.[2]

Such rousing words galvanized and enkindled the already recruited and aimed to rouse the dithering and uncertain.

The King and Queen welcomed 3000 female war workers into the quadrangle of Buckingham Palace on the 29th June 1918. The women had marched in procession from Hyde Park to Buckingham Palace. This incredible spectacle or "review" as it was called drew together Land Girls, munition girls, anti-gas girls, (mask making) Naval Wrens, Endell Street nurses, VADs, members of the Women's Legion, Post Office mail van drivers, tramway conductors and policewomen.

The event was of course an opportunity for the royal family to express their appreciation and see with their own eyes the varied roles now taken up by the sex. The review also coincided with the celebration of their Majesties' Silver Wedding!

It must have been heartening to see the many groups of trained, skilled women adorned in their respective uniforms proudly standing to attention.

A royal welcome also awaited the Land Girls that took part in a rally that passed by many famous landmarks of London, eventually culminating at Buckingham Palace. After lunch at The Savoy, a recruiting meeting took place in Trafalgar Square prior to the Queen's inspection of the three sections of the Women's Land Army - even the cart horses were subject to a brief inspection by Her Majesty!

The visiting registrar clearly made the most of her visit to London because she attended the Opera House in the evening!

The Queen must have been struck by the gravity of the task that still lay ahead. What would the future hold for those gathered before her when the war came to an end? All of the skills that the new workforce had acquired needed to be nurtured if possible, not wasted. 6000 women intended to continue working on the land in some capacity after demobilisation.

The route forward for those 6000 women would have been employment, either sought independently or through the National Association of Landswomen that was formed in January 1920 under the patronage of Princess Mary. Certainly for the women that had enjoyed being part of the Women's Land Army, (or any of the other wartime landworker organisations) the chance to continue their agricultural career under the umbrella of yet another ground-breaking organisation would have been too good-a-chance to miss and as such would have been seen as a somewhat natural progression.

It is worth taking into consideration that many hundreds of thousands of women came forward in some capacity to work, (for the first time) either part or full time on the land and yet their contribution has received scant acknowledgement since. Their success can also be measured by way of individual achievements and of the countless milestones passed by their sex at a time when convention said it was not possible or appropriate for women to do such things. Recollections and stories passed down through the generations have dissipated through the intervening decades to the point of being all but lost to the wider public. The existence of the Women's Land Army during the Great War was overshadowed by its successor in the Second World War.

Good Service Ribbons, Distinguished Service Bars and other badges and medals for long service were awarded to women for their devotion to duty. Each woman received a certificate of appreciation for services rendered after demobilisation, (this however was not signed by the Queen) but no other individual, formal acknowledgement of service was awarded in the succeeding years.

At the time, there was a need to proudly acknowledge and publicly be seen to demonstrate an appreciation of the Land Girl's National Service by presenting candidates with the highest honour that could be awarded to them – a Distinguished Service Bar. It had been proposed that Her Majesty the Queen would present these prestigious, deserved awards at a special rally.

A letter from The Food Production Department, Women's Branch dated the 8th May 1919 shows that the Board of Agriculture and Fisheries had decided that a very large rally should take place in the town of Northampton, (chosen for its centrality) towards the end of June or in September whereby participating Land Girls could travel relatively easily from most counties to attend. At this spectacular event, the nation could officially say thank you and acknowledge the war service of all land workers who had come forward to serve.

Further correspondence showed that this idea was postponed for predominantly two reasons:

1. The Treasury needed to exercise further economy at the time.

2. That an alternative date needed to be decided upon, one which took into consideration the unavailability of participants during the vital harvest months.

The same letter contained evidence that showed that the demand from farmers for Land Girls outstripped the possible supply. Despite a rise in wages, this had not brought forward enough women and this caused a major headache as labour requirements fell way short of what could actually be provided.[3]

The impracticality of allowing hundreds of Land Girls to leave farms and other employment from all over the country to travel to Northampton for two days was, in the end, neither feasible or economically viable.

The Treasury viewed this proposal as one that simply could not justify the expense it would incur. It was not a national necessity. Northampton therefore did not host what would have been a fantastic spectacle befitting of its purpose. As a consequence, Land Girls did not have the spotlight shone on them in the way that they deserved to, neither did they receive their deserved medals for bravery and devotion to service from the Queen.

Princess Mary instead attended the Farewell Rally of the Women's Land Army some months later at Draper's Hall, Throgmorton Street in the City of London on the 27th November 1919, 3 days prior to the official demobilisation of the organisation. It was at this significant event that 56 Distinguished Service Bars, (or "Land Girl VCs" as they were more commonly known as) were presented to deserving recipients.

A supper ensued afterwards in the old dining hall, where the Princess was guest of honour. The evening concluded with a concert made up of 'turns' from talented Land Girls!

And then, it was up to each, individual ex-member of the now demobilised Women's Land Army to make their mind up as to which direction their future was to go in. Was each woman going to continue to stamp their own mark firmly in the furrows they had ploughed so patriotically throughout their war service?

The window of opportunity was still open but the clock was ticking.

Chapter 13

An epidemic of marriages!

Wartime did not stop romances from blossoming and many Land Girls got married during the Great War. Photographs show fellow Land Girls making a guard of honour with their customary pitchforks or a triumphal wedding arch of hoes as happy couples emerged from town and country churches all over the land. Land Girl weddings were even featured on the front pages of national newspapers!

Farm wagons were traditionally decorated with corn, ivy and ribbons and were the preferred mode of transport for the betrothed Land Girl as she was paraded along familiar village streets and country lanes to the church, ensuring that the villagers all got a glimpse of the bride-to-be.

For those men who had sustained life-changing injuries during their service, adapting to civilian life again after demobilisation was incredibly tough. The physical and psychological effects of war caused relationships to fracture over time and become increasingly strained. The husband that returned was often unrecognisable to the one that had left and children frequently recoiled from their fathers as if they were strangers. During the long absences, things often changed immeasurably at home too.

For soldiers that were fortunate enough to return to their native villages, towns and cities, (whether permanently disabled or otherwise) they often wanted to continue their working life where they had left off. For many men, farming was the only kind of work they had ever known. Many of course wanted to settle down and start a family or at the very least try and attempt to adjust back into the rhythm of life with their families having endured such long years of separation. Many Land Girls also wanted the same.

The autumn of 1919 saw a cluster of marriages take place in one locality. Three Land Girls who had been placed in the same area married local men.[1]

Despite all the positive work done by various land organisations, women were still often viewed as commodities or an asset to be acquired by returning servicemen, especially now that they possessed the necessary skills to become a useful farmer's wife! Derogatory statements appeared in the newspapers stating that men from overseas might also want to take a souvenir back home with them once their service had come to an end. The 'souvenir' being referred to was a woman that would be useful to him; a Land Girl was viewed as an ideal choice.[2]

Reading such disrespectful statements like this of course would have left a bitter taste in the mouths of the women that had done so much to reverse deep-rooted prejudice. When these words were written, (in late August 1918) the organisation <u>still</u> had a further 15 months of work to do!

By the time soldiers returned home, Land Girls who had remained on a particular farm for any length of time had generally established good working and personal relationships, not only with the soldiers' families but also formed friendships in a wider social network with the villagers, so it was inevitable that they were going to be vied as potential wives!

A 'fairytale' wedding took place in Ashow, a village in Warwickshire in the spring of 1919. Annie Edwards was a Land Girl living in Kenilworth at the time. Although she was not a local girl, she married a local man, Private Albert Seccull on the 29th March 1919 in Ashow Parish Church. Annie was working on a farm in the Ashow area and must have met her husband-to-be, (who was a farm labourer) whilst working on the same farm as each other or by coming into contact with him in the village socially.

Rather strangely, no mention is made of Albert's regal connection! A traditional, large farm hay-cart, (the property of the late farmer for whom Annie had worked for) was bedecked in Union Jack flags. The bride-to-be sat with her six Land Girl bridesmaids who sat holding rakes aloft which had been decorated with ribbons.

As the smiling newlyweds came out of the church, they walked through the traditional guard of honour formed by Annie's Land Girl friends. They then led a happy procession of Land Girls to their reception in the village.

Annie had found her very own Prince because on the marriage certificate to Albert, his full name is written as Prince Albert Seccull! Maybe Albert was a little embarrassed about his first name and chose to use his second name instead. It does however show the strength of popularity that members of the royal family enjoyed in the Victorian era and how their names influenced the choices made by parents.

Prince Albert fell in love on his home patch near to Kenilworth and its historic castle. On her wedding certificate, Annie did not record her profession or occupation as that of a serving member of the Women's Land Army. It was left blank. For her own reasons, (now lost to history) she chose not to record her wartime profession. Similarly, and for reasons known only to them, many Land Girls chose not to record their wartime service on their marriage certificates.

Miss Laura May Fisher, (known as Peggy) of Hastings, East Sussex received the highest honour awarded by the Women's Land Army - the Distinguished Service Bar for her act of heroism - that of rushing to the aid of a man who was in grave danger of being gored to death by an enraged bull. Mr Marshall was a young ex-soldier who had served with the Royal Sussex Regiment during the war but was now a cowman/stockman. He fell over in a cow-stall and was being gored when Miss Fisher, who saw the danger he was in, kicked the bull on the nose with her hobnailed boots until this action had the desired effect of making the bull retreat.

Peggy was one of 56 deserving candidates to receive this prestigious award which was presented by Princess Mary at Drapers Hall in London on the 27th November 1919. By the time she was presented with her decoration she had been married to Mr Marshall for almost a fortnight!

This remarkable 'bull' wedding as it came to be known was witnessed by throngs of well-wishers from her village. The wedding day itself was a rather typical, misty, dull November day but the story that had led to the couple marrying transcended the leaden skies overhead.

Peggy's employer had pulled out all the stops by decorating a farm wagon with corn, wheat and bracken. Six horses pulled the wedding wagon which was flanked either side by farmworkers wearing white smocks. Peggy travelled from her billets to the church in the beautifully decorated wagon; its wheels and shafts were also adorned with ivy and a white lovers knot had been placed in the centre of each side. On arrival, a large group of Land Girls and 12 uniformed L.A.A.S girls, (all of whom had travelled to be at the happy event from all over East Sussex) ushered Peggy excitedly into the church where her husband-to-be, Mr Arthur, Samuel Marshall was waiting![3]

Another local character who met her at the church with a bark was a faithful but almost blind old collie dog; a seasoned attendee of all church ceremonies! Peggy was observed polishing her already shiny boots moments before the ceremony began and she got married whilst wearing the uniform of the Women's Land Army.

The couple took their wedding vows in front of a full church and the service itself was choral. Having signed the register and with the formalities now over, the couple walked out of the church to see two lines of Land Girls forming a guard of honour with crossed pitchforks! The newlyweds ducked through the archway and headed to the waiting wagon which then took them to their reception at the nearby Griffin Hotel.[4]

Heart-warming love stories would have been widely embraced – not just in rural communities that welcomed women like Peggy into the fold but the country as a whole, who shared in their joy too.

A speech was given by the Lady Mayoress in Leeds after a successful Women's Land Army rally. She announced to the gathered crowd that she had been raised in the countryside, recalling an old farmer's wife saying to her that she would in effect be throwing her life away by marrying a man from the town! The farmer's wife had hoped that she would marry a farmer instead![5]

Difficult decisions were made by many women after demobilisation; ones which must have given rise to heated discussions and arguments with family and friends who steadfastly disagreed with the eventual choice(s) made. Nevertheless, many women continued to follow their hearts or acted on their gut instinct.

Land Girls realised that all of these chances needed to be seized and seized quickly because after the 30th November 1919 it really would become a case of 'now or never'. Regret was not an emotion Land Girls dwelt on for very long. They had learnt to live much more for the here and now and were often forced to make impulsive decisions as a result of living through years of what a country at war had imposed on them.

Do not dither. Only DO!

Chapter 14

Misbehaving Misses!

Land Girls often made the news but not always for the right reasons. Crimes were committed by both serving members and ex-members of the Women's Land Army. Some crimes were petty, others much more serious hence the punishment meted out to the offenders ranged in severity. Land Girls were victims of crime too and high-profile cases were covered by national newspapers.

Disobedience or any bad association linked to the Women's Land Army was swiftly dealt with. In less serious cases, Land Girls, (whether official or unofficial members) whose behaviour caused concern should have been reported to the Welfare Officer in the first instance. A report would then be passed onto the Women's Branch whereby the facts were established and dealt with accordingly. This however was not always the case as the lines of who should exercise authority and any subsequent punishment occasionally became blurred across counties and rules were enforced and penalties dispensed by different means.

Low level disciplinary matters could be dealt with by the trained and educated women who had joined the Women's National Land Service Corps. Once these women had received their special war training they became leaders, who, unabated, formed up 'squads' of female part-time village workers to maintain supply and demand. These leaders were under the supervision of a local registrar but also had to be accountable to the farmer. In addition, they had the task of ensuring that the farmer's orders were rigidly adhered to.

Travelling Inspectors had to investigate any claims made against members of the Women's Land Army as rumours, true or otherwise circulated from time to time.

Given that it was the tiniest minority of women that appeared to prove problematic to the farm or establishment that they were placed on, any discredit that ensued or that attracted widespread attention was disproportionate.

Further investigation was however always required in order to conclude if any allegations were true.

It was glaringly obvious that not every woman would adapt well to the work she was being asked to do; likewise she might also struggle physically to undertake the workload of a man.

Sweeping generalisations, perhaps made by loose-tongued, misinformed farmers or villagers about how women 'replacing' men was useless were unjustified and hugely damaging not only to the organisation as a whole but also to the wider food production campaign and its intended targets.

This is true in the case of some female hay balers who were investigated. The conclusion was subsequently drawn that the two women employed in the particular district in question were indeed unsuited to the work. However the Travelling Inspector was concerned that as a result of the investigation, the two women involved would unfairly bring widespread condemnation to all of the other women at work in the Women's Land Army.[1]

This demonstrates the plight of the vast majority of Land Girls who worked diligently throughout their National Service. It must have saddened them to hear or read about cases such as this that cast a shadow over their genuine and united efforts.

A case where the forewoman wasn't effectively enforcing rules strictly enough was that of Colonel and the Hon. Mrs Abel Smith who had provided a furnished house for use as a training centre, (Stapleford Training Home for Girls in Hertfordshire) for younger girls, (under supervision) in farm work.

The bad behaviour of some of the girls housed at the training centre had led the committee to believe that supervising girls under the age of 18 was indeed fully justified.[2]

The girls' bad behaviour at Stapleford saw a claim being made by Colonel and the Hon. Mrs Abel Smith in January 1920 for the damage caused to their furniture and other items that were in the house.[3]

Their claim was successful and they were granted £31 8 0d.

Clearly for the younger girls, living away from home without parental guidance meant that the responsibilities that automatically came with being a member of any given land organisation proved just too difficult to cope with. Living all together merely exacerbated the problem and exposed their immaturity.

It is important to remember that for the young girls, it was their first experience of living away from home. It is little wonder that a few went a bit wild as it would have been unlikely that the other girls they lived and trained with would have known each other prior to joining up.

Land Girls were usually 'let go of' because they could not be relied upon, were too noisy, immature and irresponsible and loathed working in the really tough seasonal weather. For some women, it merely came down to the fact that they simply were unable to stick the daily grind.

Some Land Girls were at the centre of bitter relationships with farmers' wives, who felt jealous or threatened by the sudden presence of (often) younger and rather mysterious newcomers who now spent a lot of time with their husbands. Any resulting tension could make day-to-day life really unpleasant.

There were naturally fracas and disagreements all over the land, however, some relationships were cohesive and cooperative right from the start. Which way it went was entirely dependent on the attitude of the Land Girl herself, the farmer, the local workforce and villagers.

One farmer clearly thought a great deal of the girls in his employ. Every day, the girls travelled six miles from their hostel to his farm in a charabanc to work all day pulling thistles, (an unpleasant and hazardous job). When the seasons permitted, he brought them peaches and strawberries from Lord Tankerville's garden, (his seat was Chillingham Castle, Northumberland).

Another heart-warming story saw farmers form a committee. They regarded the Land Girls in their employ almost as if they were their own daughters and did everything they could to make the girls' time at the hostel and on their farms as pleasant and straightforward as it was possible to do so.[4]

The ages of Land Girls who worked or lived together varied, so, potentially there could have been women who had children to support whilst their husbands were overseas working alongside more frivolous, scatty girls. This could create problems, especially if the girl(s) did not pull their weight.

Women joined the Women's Land Army for a multitude of reasons. Becoming a member was not merely borne out of a desire to serve their country. Married women saw it as an escape per se or an escape from a difficult or violent relationship. It could have been as simple as wanting a change of scene, taking control of their own life and finding a new and different direction, putting a toe into an area of work they had never considered or tried before or to gain new, life-affirming skills and make new friends from different walks of life.

Joining up might even have provided the ideal opportunity for some women to turn their back on a life that was difficult or on the fringes of criminality; a lifeline in effect, where they could stay on the straight and narrow without any familiar distractions and attempt to make a fresh start in an organisation that gave them structure and a clear purpose. They would be told what they needed to do, how to do it <u>and</u> were paid a wage.

The burden of survival which plagued many women would have been lifted temporarily if they were able to join the Women's Land Army. For many it broadened their horizons. It brought shy women out of themselves, especially in situations where good decision-making, newly acquired skills and cool judgement were crucial.

For those that persistently showed more challenging behaviour, a willing and suitable compromise might have initially been made with regard to what it was felt they could cope with. If this approach failed, they were swiftly discharged to avoid affecting others or to stop problems manifesting further down the line.

The immature, impressionable nature of some girls was highlighted in a case that was held at the Newport Pagnell Sessions on the 2nd October 1918. The crime took place on the 24th September 1918. The perpetrator was, at the time a member of the Women's Land Army, (Forage Corps) having previously worked in a factory.

Private Ruth Gertrude Bissell, aged 17 of 23 St Giles' Street, Stantonbury stole a purse containing £2, 14 shillings and 9½d which was the property of a neighbour, Mr Ambrose William Bull aged 25. Ruth, (the prisoner) entered the prosecutor's house when nobody was at home and stole the purse. Ruth is referred to as a Private because she was serving in the Forage Corps at the time.

Ruth at some point had been on probation and under the supervision of a female officer from the Royal Army Service Corps. The offence appears to have been committed on her return home, having been discharged. The Forage Corps was attached to the Royal Army Service Corps and was a British military organisation unlike the other branches of the Women's Land Army.

Misbehaving Misses! 143

This case proves that by having the weight of an initial good character reference from the Assistant Superintendent, (Miss Nash) from the Forage Department, (regarding Ruth's prior good conduct and also a possible explanation as to why she had gone astray) it had added an additional dimension to her case.

Miss Nash had told the court that when at Oxford, Ruth had been led astray by a female thief.[5]

Having returned home, Ruth appears to have got into trouble more or less immediately after her discharge from the Forage Corps. She had however previously been in trouble with the law, having stolen two bicycles and been sentenced to two terms of 14 days imprisonment for that crime.

She had been due to be admitted to a home in Middlesex but absconded from there with two other girls. It was not until she was arrested again by the Metropolitan Police for soliciting that her other crimes came to the fore.

A plea of leniency came from Mr and Mrs Bull, (a respectable couple who knew Ruth's parents). Details of Ruth's fate are conflicting as one report saw Ruth being committed to a borstal institution for two years. Another stated that the case was bound over but only on the assurance that Ruth would be taken back to the gainful employment from whence she came.

Life for some women serving in land organisations became unbearable very quickly and they clearly felt that they had no other option but to go absent without leave. Desertion is not a word that immediately jumps to mind when thinking about the Women's Land Army but in the case of two 18 year old Land Girls, Priscilla Lilian Sage and Ada Grace Hedge, this is exactly what they did in the summer of 1918.

A landmark case that reported on the Land Girl absentees was brought to Bristol Police Court during the summer of 1918 - a crucial time in the farming calendar. It was the first case of its kind in Bristol.

Under the Army Act, these two girls came before the magistrates. They both worked in the Forage Corps. The rules that the women worked under were therefore much stricter so any bad behaviour was punished along military lines.

The magistrate, having taken into account the evidence and also that it was the first case of its kind, announced the decision made by the bench and fined the defendants £2. This case set a precedent but it was made clear that if any more girls appeared in court under the same charges, they would not be dealt with so leniently. At the time, magistrates had the power to sentence any 'absent' Land Girl to six months in prison.

Reading the reported evidence, it seems fair to assume that Priscilla was homesick as she had deserted after only 3 days. The work itself was not the reason behind her drastic action. She had informed the court that she was more than willing to carry out any war work so long as it could be carried out back home.[6]

This supports the theory that some girls were not mentally ready to live and work away from home for any length of time despite being initially attracted to joining the Women's Land Army having seen the idealistic recruitment posters. Any initial rushes of patriotism, bravado and ebullience perhaps were swiftly regretted when reality struck and with little life experience to draw on, it was a recipe for disaster.

Ada admitted to lying about a letter she claimed had been written by her father, (which the aforementioned, when initially asked, said she knew nothing about). A military representative described how both girls had travelled from farm to farm in a baling squad. The Forage Corps required a longer commitment of a year for service to be made by women who joined it unlike the other two branches of the Women's Land Army. With the familiarity of home once again around them, both girls continued with their work on the land.

The seriousness of the offence was made abundantly clear to both girls. They could not be seen to be allowed to bring both the Women's Forage Corps and Women's Land Army in its entirety into disrepute. Without question, this landmark case had shone an unwelcome spotlight on the Women's Land Army. The outcome and summing up of the case showed that a considered punishment had indeed been given to those in question in order to deter similar cases from happening in the future.[7]

Miss Bannister was a Land Girl who was summoned to Wycombe, Buckinghamshire along with her employer, farmer, James Robertson of Stokenchurch. The case concerned the working of a horse in an unfit state. Miss Bannister cared for ten horses at the farm.

The skin of the horse was so tender that whenever it was touched on the nose or the tail, it became irritated. Robertson claimed that he had taken measures to alleviate the suffering of the animal by either bathing its skin with salt and water and by also using a silk pad to protect the shoulders of the animal. Mr Robertson defended Miss Bannister in court saying how caring she had been to the horses on his farm. He felt that it was unfair and somewhat ironic that she had been summoned as she had often worked very late whilst caring for them and they in-turn were very attached to her.[8]

The outcome was that the summons against Miss Bannister was dismissed but Mr Robertson was fined £2.

An interesting point that arises from this case is how women, once they had signed up, had to be prepared to travel long distances away from their homes to where they were needed. Miss Bannister hailed from Herefordshire and at the time of the case worked on a farm in Stokenchurch some 100 or so miles away.

Two aspiring Land Girls ended up on probation during the summer of 1918 having been charged with theft at Thames Police Court. Ada Crooks and Leah Kaufman stole a diamond ring that belonged to Leah's mother. Their intention was to pawn it in order to get enough money to go and work on the land; hoping to eventually earn enough money to buy the ring back. Their plan failed and they were publicly shamed.

A rather sad turn of events saw 18 year old Clara Beers charged with stealing at Nottingham Guildhall in September 1919. Clara had stolen a frock coat and dress worth £19 18s 6d from Long Row, (a row of retail buildings). As with a lot of women, Clara had initially started her war service in the shell filling factory at Chilwell. As a result, her health had begun to fail, so much so that she made the switch to the Women's Land Army like many other women had done.

Whilst working on several farms in the Derbyshire area, she had made acquaintance with people from much wealthier backgrounds than that of her own. Clara was not able to afford the luxury items of clothing and jewellery that the other women wore so she turned to stealing and committed several thefts to satisfy her taste for fine dress. Her punishment saw her sent to prison by Derby magistrates. Her defence asked for leniency as she had suffered significantly with her health.

Clara appears to have made a promise to turn her life around, start afresh and as a result was placed on probation for six months.

19 year old Lily Weeks of 11 Hawden Road, Tonbridge was charged with obtaining two pairs of boots, (worth £3 1s 6d) under false pretences with intent to cheat and defraud. The manager of the shop Freeman, Hardy and Willis stated that Lily was wearing a Land Girl uniform and at the time had said that Miss Neve, (the Superintendent of the hostel where she was staying) had sent her to get some boots for another girl also staying at the hostel because she was unable to wear regulation boots. This was not true and no authorisation had in fact been given.

Lily had been discharged from the Land Army on the 11th October 1918 and had left the hostel on the same day. She had stated that she wanted money to become a 'hawker.' She had already pawned one of the pairs of boots for 7s.

Miss Neve said that Lily required supervision to keep her under control but that she had some good characteristics.[9]

Lily was remanded for a week whilst arrangements were made for her in a home.

Misleading information appeared in newspapers during the summer of 1918 and the Food Production Department was required to step in and clarify that Land Girls should not in fact be working on the same farm as German prisoners. If any information appeared to the contrary, it was made clear that it was not an instruction given by the department.[10]

Other formal notices began to appear a few months later. The rules were clearly laid out: Land Army women must not be employed on farms where German prisoners are billeted. It was possible for mobile threshing gangs to work on the same farms where German prisoners were billeted but the prisoners themselves are not allowed to carry out the threshing work. If German prisoners travel to a farm each day from a camp, Land Girls must not work in close proximity to them; instead they must work on a different part of the farm. Land Army women were strictly forbidden to drive or accompany

any prisoners between their places of work. If these rules were found to have been contravened, then the Land Girls and/or German prisoners would be swiftly removed.[11]

Inevitably, there were breaches. A case that came before the Borough Bench at Taunton in August 1919 is that of Hilda Mapstone, otherwise known as Hilda Cosh, an 18 year old Land Girl (who was working at the time on Comeytrowe Farm near Taunton).

Hilda pleaded guilty to her crime and was fined 40 shillings, (£2) for sending love letters other than by post, (instead delivered by William Hall, a demobilised soldier) to a German prisoner of war, Carl Muller, (or Charlie as Hilda addressed him).

Hall admitted the first charge against him; that of delivering the letters written by Hilda to Muller without any authority and received a fine. He pleaded not guilty to the second charge of conveying letters on behalf of Muller to Hilda. This charge was eventually dismissed.

Hilda, under caution had been interviewed on the farm by a police sergeant on June 14th 1919. She provided a voluntary statement which detailed how she had met Muller, (who was assisting with forage work) at Claremont Stables some five months prior. It had been Muller that had asked her to write to him, which she subsequently did. Several letters then passed between them. In one of Muller's letters, he had said to send any correspondence via Hall who at the time was working at another stables at Castle Green. This is what appears to have happened from thereon in. Hilda had asked Hall about the ethics of writing to a German prisoner of war and he had reassured her that it was perfectly alright to do so.[12]

The account by Hall, (who was interviewed on the same day) is conflicting. He says that he showed the initial letter to Muller from Hilda to his corporal. Having shown his corporal the letter, Hall then handed it to the prisoner himself. Muller pointed Hilda out to Hall as she drove past the Castle Green horse depot on a milk cart. It was at this point that Hall says he spoke to Hilda and said to her that he couldn't deliver any further letters as he would end up in trouble. He told Hilda that if she continued to send them, he would report her to the police. Thereafter, no further letters were received.[13]

Hilda defended herself by stating that the statement made by Hall was not correct. Hall did not stop her outside the depot when she wrote the first letter to him. She received Muller's letters either through the post or from Hall's own hands.

Hilda did not realise the implications of what communicating with a prisoner of war was to have upon her character. And yet, despite the strict rules, when asked by the bench, both Corporal Garland and Hall had also felt that, having read Hilda's letters, they were totally harmless.[14]

Hilda burnt all of the letters, destroying any potential incriminating evidence. In the event that she had been privy to any sensitive information or had divulged anything, (accidentally or otherwise) to Muller, it could have had far-reaching consequences. It did seem as if Hilda's interest in Muller was purely innocent.

A famous painting produced in 1918 by war artist Randolph Schwabe appears to contradict the information stated in notices to farmers that appeared in early November. It depicts two members of the Women's Land Army working alongside a German prisoner of war who is wearing the distinctive prisoner of war uniform, (with a highly visible, large, red diamond shape on his upper left leg).

The painting depicts the process of threshing and once again contravenes several of the rules that were stipulated at the time. German prisoners worked under guard to assist with tilling and ploughing and the crucial gathering-in of the harvest as they were viewed as a viable, often skilled source of labour. Like men in Britain, many thousands of German soldiers would have come from agricultural backgrounds and it made perfect sense to put their skills to good use, especially during the busiest months of the year.

To some women, German prisoners of war would have been curiously alluring. Tales abound of sloppy sentries, who, there to guard the working parties clearly had lapses with regard to their duties. Complaints were made about the excessive freedom permitted to prisoners on occasion.

During the summer of 1918, the consequences of lack of overseeing had caused somewhat inevitable problems. It had come to light that women and girls had somehow come into contact with German prisoners and written them love letters or given them gifts which of course, was wholly unacceptable behaviour.[15]

It was deemed such a serious problem that new powers were secured under the Defence Of the Realm Act ensuring that if rules continued to be breached then women would be punished severely for their illegal liaisons with enemy prisoners.[16]

In direct contrast, some Land Girls in Warwickshire in late 1918 flatly refused to work anywhere near the German prisoners of war. They downed tools and enjoyed a half-day mini holiday whilst the farmer dispensed with the German prisoners! The girls were lauded for standing their ground on this issue.[17]

In early February 1918, it was estimated that 6000 German men were working on the land and had been for some time. They normally worked in groups of between 30 and 40, usually with four or five groups in each county. Prisoners were billeted in a War Office approved depot or were part of an agricultural prisoner of war camp. They travelled to work by lorry or train almost always within a five mile radius. They were guarded whilst in the depots and supervised whilst out in the field by soldiers or 'policed' by ploughmen. It was inevitable that they attracted attention.

In July 1919, a rather bleak story detailed the pitiful life of 21 year old Fanny Roberts, who had just recently been discharged from the Women's Land Army. She had left the organisation to get married. Fanny had gone home to Gloucester where she had spent 10 days, returning to Dover only to learn that the man had changed his mind. Even though she claimed to be working she had turned to prostitution in order to earn money.

A policeman had spotted Fanny loitering near the Seaplane Base at 10pm on Sunday the 29th June and had stopped to ask her what she was doing. Fanny provided an address and told him that she had just been discharged from the Women's Land Army. Her case contains several damning witness reports and complaints. Fanny was seen speaking to several soldiers and sailors and was asked to move on by a witness but at 4.30am the very same morning the same witness had come across Fanny sitting in a sorry state in a shelter wearing no hat and just one boot.[18]

The witness took her to the police station where it was discovered that Fanny had been sleeping rough for a week. The police had noticed Fanny walking around the town wearing a Women's Land Army uniform some three weeks prior and she had, in the interim period regularly been seen with many different soldiers and sailors.[19]

Accommodation was recommended at a local hostel and she stayed there, that is until she returned at 2am one morning! After that, the owner disowned her.

She clearly did not change her ways and stayed at another shelter, run by a Miss Quance, who did the decent thing, (or so she thought) and contacted Fanny's parents in Gloucester. When told to be in at 9pm, Fanny did not adhere to the rules and never returned to the shelter. Soon after she was spotted hanging about the streets once again.

The Women's Land Army were duly contacted at their Canterbury headquarters and confirmed that Fanny Roberts had indeed been discharged. To have persisted in wearing the Land Army uniform after being discharged would have been a serious breach of the rules as the uniform should already have been returned. Moreover, the reputation of the organisation that Fanny was seen to still represent was at stake; the Women's Land Army had not at this point been demobilised.

Fanny obviously had little intention of changing her ways. A plain clothes constable had also spotted her in Northfall Meadow on Sunday the 29th June. This was prior to the sighting later that night near to the Seaplane Base.

He decided that the only way to try and stop this pattern of behaviour was to charge her. Fanny's home was apparently a good one but her parents did not want her back. Fanny had also refused the chance to return to Miss Quance's shelter. Her parents had assumed that on her return to Dover she was to be married in Canterbury. They had paid her fare and even gave her some pocket money. Her only saving grace was the fact that she had been a hard worker and she herself admitted that she had hit rock bottom and was desperate to try and make a fresh start elsewhere.[20]

At court, Fanny was prepared to consider any type of way forward that was offered to her.[21] The outcome at Dover Police Court was that the defendant was bound over for six months and sent to a home at Maidstone. Cutting words concluded the case from the chairman. He stressed that Fanny would be best served to show how grateful she was for the lifeline given to her by the court by paying the poor box back the money that had been paid out so that she could get to Maidstone. It was suggested that this recompense could perhaps be made once she had improved herself.[22]

Fanny may have found authority just too difficult to deal with despite being more than capable of doing the work or was she just too rebellious to succeed within the confines of the organisation itself?

At Kent Assizes during the summer of 1919, a miner, John Charles Machon, aged 24 was sentenced to 12 months imprisonment, (without hard labour) for bigamously marrying servant Mildred Victoria Stannard, aged 21 on the 27th December 1918 at Minster. After marrying Mildred he returned to his lawful wife in Yorkshire. Machon had at one time been on service at Ramsgate Naval Base.

Mildred, who at the time had been working as a Land Girl at Manston was charged with aiding and abetting although it was Machon who had deceived her and in effect seduced her. She received two days imprisonment which permitted immediate discharge.

Trouble broke out on a farm at Baldwinholme in what is now Cumbria during the summer of 1918. Private Frederick Coates who was in a Labour Battalion at the time, worked on the same farm as Land Girl, Catherine Annie Neil. Coates was charged with assault at The Courts, Carlisle on August 2nd.

The assault came about rather bizarrely because of a disagreement about a bicycle pump. Coates accused Neil of stealing it and it became clear that she could not show him the pump and he threatened her. The pump in question was not owned by Neil but instead by another girl. His temper quickly grew because he sparred up to her and hit her twice on her face with his fist. Her eyes were bruised by the violent blows and she collapsed. The day after, Neil complained to Coates' sergeant-major and superintendent.

Another private gave evidence stating that Coates had told him about the bicycle pump and how he believed Neil had stolen it and that he had intended to slap her across the face on returning to the farm. Private Ritson had heard someone squealing. It was after this that Coates admitted to Ritson that he had hit Neil but that he was sorry for doing so.

Coates stood firm to his belief that he suspected Neil had stolen it and despite hitting her, he was given an excellent character reference by an officer who was present. The outcome of this rather peculiar case was that the assault was a cowardly one. Coates was fined 40s.

During the winter of 1918, reports appeared in the local press about a woman who had endured persistent mental and physical abuse from her husband. The case had been taken to court and Charles Proctor, aged 42 from Bedlington had been summoned. He stood accused of numerous counts of drink-fuelled abuse. The complainant had married Proctor in 1905 and by 1918 had three children, the eldest son was aged 13 and the youngest child was 16 months. Long-term, excessive and problematic drinking appears to have been at the centre of the violence shown repeatedly against her and throughout their marriage. On numerous occasions, Proctor had been known to argue in public with other men only to return home and take his anger out on his wife.

Legal action had been taken previously but not seen through as the accused had promised to give up drinking. Proctor's long-suffering wife clearly saw the Women's Land Army as a way out of her awful life. Mention is made of two references that she had secured that would have supported her application.

How she managed to join up is a feat in itself because right up to the point of her leaving to work in the organisation her husband was accusing her of being unfaithful.

Proctor had plotted a horrific attack over the course of three weeks, until he finally carried it out. His wife sustained terrible injuries as a consequence of his violence. Proctor knocked some of her teeth out and she was covered in bruises on her arms. The attack left her confined to bed.[23]

The woman managed to leave him and went to her Aunt's house but he continued to seek her out. Proctor had brainwashed his son to hate his mother as he, (Proctor) himself did. His warped plot involved sending his son to the relative's house in order to continue the terrible tirade of mental and physical abuse.[24]

It can only be hoped that the woman found some kind of refuge in the Women's Land Army and that it afforded her at least, a temporary escape out of this ghastly situation.

The chilling murder of 18 year old Land Girl, Beatrice Annie Dawes at Edenbridge on October 26th 1919 sparked nationwide interest during the months of October and November 1919. Beatrice's young life came to an abrupt and tragic end at the hands of Ernest Ebenezer Cosham, (variations in the spelling of his surname appeared) who, aged just 17 was well-built and sturdy in stature and looked much older than he was.

Cosham was not a local man. His Aunt and Uncle resided in Edenbridge and he had lived with them as a very young child. He had recently returned to the village and at the time he was employed at Whitmore's Tannery, Edenbridge where his Uncle also worked.

Beatrice had been working as District Postwoman for 3 years as part of her war service. She then became a Land Girl on a farm at Cobhambury Farm in Kent, (where Cosham had been lodging for the past nine weeks). His sweetheart's parents, Mr and Mrs Berry lived at the farm.

Details differ but it appears that her body was found in undergrowth, 3 feet off a country lane. She had been strangled whilst making her way home where she lived with her mother, Mrs Pocock and her stepfather Mr Pocock. She appeared to have left home on the Sunday morning in question sometime around 10am and walked the mile or so to fetch a can of milk along a lane that led from the farm at Shernden to Cobhambury Farm. A can containing milk was found nearby.

At the time she had been wearing a smart, fawn blanket coat and a black picture hat. As soon as she was missed a search was made to find her. On the discovery of her body, the police sent for a doctor who determined that Beatrice had been dead 3-4 hours. There were fingermarks on each side of her neck and also a cut.

The inquest was held at Church House, Edenbridge. Cosham was charged and cautioned at Tonbridge Police Station. At court however it was noted that Cosham showed little interest in the proceedings or any remorse.

At the time of his arrest, the officer asked him about Beatrice's death. Cosham told the officer that he had quite liked Beatrice and had never felt any malice towards her.[25]

He coldly recollected how he had leapt at her and how they had both fallen over at the same time. Cosham clearly thought that he had killed Beatrice by strangling her but she screamed several times after his first attempt. He then proceeded to strangle her again.[26]

Cosham remembered how Beatrice had said good morning to him as she walked past him on her way to collect some milk from Cobhambury Farm. He was out blackberrying and on seeing her he made the decision to wait for her to walk back and spring on her.

He then tried to cut her throat but failed due to a blunt knife and therefore strangled her. He returned home and hid a handkerchief in one of Mrs Berry's fields down a rabbit hole and threw his knife down by a hedge.

'Beatie' as she was known locally was a popular member of the local community and well-known and well-liked by its inhabitants. She had also been a Sunday School teacher for some years in the Presbyterian Church, taking part in organising concerts to raise money for a piano for the day school. She was a proactive, intelligent, energetic young woman.

Rather bizarrely, on the Sunday evening, (the same day that Cosham had committed the murder) he had penned a letter to Miss Marjorie Berry, (who he had been keeping company with) to an address in London where she was staying. The letter contained a muddled mixture of details about attending church, specific locations of where he had been, who he had seen and spoken to, who had read the sermon and of the shock he had felt on hearing the news about Beatrice.

After a sleepless night, Cosham admitted that he was Beatrice's killer.

The prison medical officer had observed Cosham for 3 weeks and referred to his unstable state of mind. When the prosecuting counsel asked if Cosham was fit to plead the answer was no. The jury agreed with this and Cosham was detained at the King's pleasure.

Six minutes was all it took for the jury to find Cosham unanimously guilty of Beatrice's death.

A 21 year old land worker called Gladys Kate Roberts became the main suspect in another harrowing case in 1918. Gladys was described as one of the best of characters and was employed at Brick Kiln Farm, Shipley.

The body of a new-born male child was found some 15 feet away from a closet by the ferret hutch on the farm. The child had sustained injuries which were not consistent with a fall. The coroner was required to ascertain four points in order to consider a verdict. Those being:

1. Whose child it was.
2. Whether the child had been born alive.

3. How it came by its death if it had been born alive.
4. Whether anybody had deliberately brought about the death of the child.

Gladys had apparently made a vague admission to Mrs Turner, the wife of the carter on the farm. She had had the baby and spoke of how the infant had landed on the bricks.[27]

The doctor gave evidence that concluded that the child had been born alive. He stated that the injuries were consistent with the head of the baby probably being hit more than once on the ground. They were simply too extensive to have been caused by one fall alone.[28]

After 50 minutes, the jury had made up its mind as to how the child had met with its death and who, if anybody was responsible. The child had been born alive on the 25th April 1918 and had also tragically died the same day. The jury handed in the verdict of: Death by violence caused by its mother.

One can only imagine the psychological state of Gladys if she felt that there was no other option but to carry out such an abhorrent crime. To have to conceal her pregnancy and the identity of the father and seemingly give birth alone must have been harrowing.

An intriguing story appeared in 1918 involving 24 year old Kensington resident turned Land Girl, Hilda Marjory Holland. Hilda was found not guilty at the Old Bailey on the 27th February for not paying her bill, (£1 14s 7d) at the Castle Hotel in Richmond. The circumstances surrounding the unpaid bill saw her visit the hotel to be near to her young man who was a soldier. He had said that he would settle the bill but was not able to owing to the fact he was suddenly sent to France. She attended court wearing a rather strange uniform, comprising of an American soldier's hat, officer's trench coat and the green armlet of the Women's Land Army!

Despite the formal court setting, her attire caused much amusement. The recorder enquired about the uniform Hilda was wearing to the detective. The detective continued to openly ridicule the Land Girl's unconventional uniform and the recorder was only too willing to pick up where the detective had left off. He too facetiously expressed disbelief at the outfits women were wearing during wartime.[29]

It is strange that the focus appeared to be on what she was wearing and not on the alleged crime that had occurred. Hilda clearly felt that she had to defend both herself and her uniform. Her retort was succinct. She was a proud, serving member of the Women's Land Army and yes, wearing breeches was part of the uniform. It was not a facade.[30]

It wasn't just crime that put Land Girls in the spotlight; controversial stories also appeared.

Firewood was a precious commodity and the price of it reflected its scarcity. In the early years of the war, woods and forested areas needed thinning and the women that could carry out this type of work required relatively little training.

Wherever Land Girls initiated this vital war work they were often met with fierce opposition from local people - especially where ancient rights were seemingly being infringed on Crown land. None more so than for the women who worked in the Forestry Section in the New Forest, Hampshire.

With fuel being scarce or non-existent for many, it was no wonder that any signs of wastage were met with frustration and anger. A lady, (who represented some of the people from the New Forest) wrote candidly about what she had witnessed for herself; the burning of so-called 'dead wood' in the forest. Although she realised that the Land Girls were only following orders set down by the government, she felt compelled to make her views known. She felt enraged that so many villagers were desperately short of fuel and had to pay such high prices for it and yet Land Girls were being paid £2 to gather and burn wood that was often suitable for firewood.[31]

Seeing the heaps of boughs, branches and dead wood left by the timber and motor-cutters being burnt must have indeed jarred those who had no alternative but to pay the extortionate prices for firewood or simply go without. The machinery used in forestry was also destructive to the natural environment as it made its way through forest lands. Winter loomed along with the ever-present threat of starvation. Despite this, when confronted with these concerns, the forewoman, although apologetic, made sure that every last bit of wood had been burnt.[32]

Attempts were made by the local farmers to try and buy wagon loads of the doomed wood but red tape made this impossible.

The existence of the Women's Land Army brought together women from all corners of the United Kingdom, from every walk of life to work together towards a united aim. However, women brought the complexities of life into its ranks too, which would at times impact on its smooth operation. The organisation unquestionably empowered women to see that there was much more out there to achieve. Enrolling may have been an initial gamble but most came away from their service changed individuals with new ideas in their heads about where they wanted their lives to go.

The Women's Land Army attracted much negativity and some women let the organisation down but despite this, it dealt with these problems in the best way it could at the time; after all, there was no precedent to refer to. It always attempted to rise above controversy and aimed to hold its head up high.

The National Association of Landswomen prevailed into the early years of the 1920s. It aimed to keep landswomen connected and provided opportunities and support to those that wanted to continue to work on the land.

Unity was indeed strength for those that had chosen to abide by a Land Army motto:

'Stick it if it kills!'

Chapter 15

Respect and recognition

During its short lifespan, the Women's Land Army took part in countless meetings, rallies, events and demonstrations that promoted both the work of the organisation and encouraged potential new recruits to step forward. It aimed to eradicate the myths that surrounded the new army of women; instead, opting to showcase their skills.

Landworker organisations worked tirelessly from the start of the war, (long before the Women's Land Army was recognised as a bonafide, stand-alone organisation) relentlessly appealing to women to come and work on the land in some way. It must have been with immense satisfaction that in just a few years such success was achieved despite so many challenges and struggles along the way.

As the Great War continued unabated, the underlying principles that had initially underpinned the creation of many countrywide associations and organisations in the first instance became strengthened by the official formation of the Women's Land Army. Individual organisations continued to think ahead in the months immediately after demobilisation as to how demobilised Land Girls' interests would be best served in post-war Britain.

The rallies that took place in towns and cities all over the country clearly had an effect on the general public who went to peer at these rather strange looking women, the likes of whom had never been seen before. Land Girls, when it was logistically possible and when they had been released to attend, travelled from their places of work and converged on towns and cities to meet their fellow Land Girls - all of whom were united in one common cause. Service.

A rally held in February 1918 saw some women unable to participate as the farmers would not release them from their work owing to the weather being too good. So, of the 150 or so women that marched patriotically on that day, although most were still Land Girls, it was part-time village women, (who had worked enough hours to receive the Women's Land Army armband) that also made up the numbers.

Rallies usually included a procession of Land Girls, marching briskly along and singing purposefully. Several large banners were held aloft, endorsed with bold slogans. A band usually accompanied the women and played patriotic, popular songs. One such tune that the women were known to have marched along to was the very apt, "The Great Little Army" which was composed in 1916 by Kenneth J Alford.

Agricultural machinery also rumbled along in the procession and frequently slowed everyone down but it gave the public the opportunity to see Land Girls operating such machinery having completed their training. Rallies were spectacles and a feast for all of the senses! There were hay-laden carts, Land Girls holding agricultural implements and animals being held and led along. All of these features embodied the important work and the purpose of the three branches that made up the Women's Land Army.

Once a specific location such as a town hall was reached, it was the turn of the speakers. Invited dignitaries who were supporters of the cause declared a profound appreciation of the collective efforts of the women, young and old, married and unmarried who had answered the call of their country without a second thought. An opportunity was never missed to laud their efforts. One example even saw the Land Girls compared to the brave, warrior women of many centuries past who saw off enemy invaders! Land Girls vehemently lapped up the comparison and showed their approval through fervid applause!

Both during and after rallies, Land Army women were instructed to be proactive and flitted amongst the gathered onlookers, circulating recruitment literature and invitations to women.

"They explained, exhorted, entreated and every now and again led off a recruit in triumph to the Church Army hut at the corner."[1]

It must not be underestimated how effective rallies were in reaching out to huge numbers of women. It was not unheard of for as many as 500 women to either enquire or leave details with the intention of joining the organisation at such an event. This was the figure mentioned at a rally that took place in London in March 1918. Later feedback and figures showed that in fact 1000 women had actually gone on to enrol as a result of the rally. In addition, an astonishing 5000 copies of The Landswoman magazine were also sold!

A prominent building was selected on the route of any given march as a location for recruits to register or where a display of photographs, (showing the already recruited at work) could be set up. Women would be invited to gather and look at the images; the intention of which was of course to persuade them to take the next step, albeit impulsively to enrol.

The more the merrier was the ideal with regard to drumming up new 'soldiers' and each enrolled Land Girl was encouraged to try and draw at least two further recruits into the organisation through the year, in a bid to continuously swell the ranks. These recruitment drives were also actively encouraged in The Landswoman magazine.

Land Girls were incredibly resourceful and set up their own "Recruiting Clubs." If a girl managed to recruit five new girls into the Women's Land Army, she would receive a token that was a visible acknowledgment of her efforts; that is once it had been authorised as a true and honest effort by the organising secretary of the county it had taken place in! In-turn, the organising secretary forwarded the name of the recruiter to the Editor, (Meriel Talbot) of The Landswoman in order for the award to be considered, processed and all being well - awarded! That reward was a cockade of red and green ribbons, (the Land Army colours) which was worn in her hat and the title of Recruiting Sergeant.

The immense pride felt during public events like this must have been palpable to onlookers. Rallies were often the tipping point for many women who were still dithering about joining. However, perhaps once a 'real life' Land Girl had taken the time to describe first-hand what it was really like to be one then there was simply no other option but to enrol!

Town rallies were large-scale events but city rallies could realise huge crowds. A rally took place in London on the 20th April 1918. It saw Land Girls being deployed from various surrounding counties to take part. The procession started from the Food Production Department in Victoria Street, marched up Whitehall, turned down Piccadilly, went along Bond Street, down Oxford Street to the YMCA on Tottenham Court Road where lunch was taken. Afterwards, uniformed girls marched along in time to the Land Army band escorted by the gathered crowd. The route concluded with them entering

Hyde Park through Marble Arch corner where a recruitment meeting took place at 1.30pm.

For girls who were perhaps unused to the bustle and noise of London life, participating in an event such as this must have been quite overwhelming. Many women spoke of their dislike of being put on show at events like this. Many did not like being the centre of public attention or having to mingle with the crowds to promote the organisation.

During this rally, reference is made to the procession walking up Whitehall which in just over a year would see a temporary, wood and plaster Cenotaph being constructed; a potent symbol of remembrance and a catalyst for the nation's grief and personal loss.

Rallies were frequently incorporated into other large or significant national events such as Tank Week or Women's Day. The county Women's War Agricultural Committees utilised such events to maximise publicity. Also, 'one-off' events were regularly incorporated into the schedule where deserving Land Girls were presented with their service badges and stripes.

The Women's Land Army offices, (The Land Army Enquiry Bureau) was opened at 135 Victoria Street in London in 1918 and outside, the Land Army Band played country airs and marches every day at 11am. After which, the women took the recruiting car out to meetings which were held at various locations during work dinner hours. Maximum coverage of workplaces ensured maximum exposure to the unrecruited or unconvinced!

Members of the Women's Land Army were not permitted to take part in the Peace Day procession that took place on July 19th 1919 in London. The procession in the capital was for military and naval service personnel only and not civilians. However, the Land Girls were allowed to march in processions in other areas across the country and join in with the peace celebrations.

One Surrey farmer however went to great lengths to drive the Land Girls he had working on his farm to London himself in a lorry in the middle of the night so that they could see the decorations in the capital without getting stuck in the crowds the following day!

It must have felt especially moving and strange to see the newly constructed, temporary Cenotaph painted white if you were a Land Girl as your National Service had not yet ceased. They must have felt emotionally spurred on to put their heart and soul into continuing to serve their nation for as long as it was still required.

Doris Gallimore was one such Land Girl whose dedication to the Women's Land Army went far beyond what was expected from an individual. In order to try and swell the ranks, Doris spent some of her own precious leave attempting to get women to enlist into the same organisation she clearly felt so passionate about. During December 1917, she stood in a public square in Stoke patiently targeting any potential Land Girls, telling them about her own, individual experiences and informing them about the type of life the Women's Land Army could offer them. Doris' efforts appear to have been very successful as women were still apparently coming forward to enrol for some time after her very own, personal public recruitment drive had finished.

Girls who were too young to join were certainly not deterred from trying and one girl tried three times to enrol but was rejected on each occasion because of her age, (18 was the minimum age). There were however many instances where girls managed to join who were under 18. It may have been that like many soldiers, they simply lied about their age in order to enrol. Many were just desperate to escape their humdrum lives and spied the ideal opportunity to do it.

At another rally, the Land Girls arranged an impromptu ceremony to present a duck egg, (laid by one of the poultry 'stars' whilst in transit on the train travelling to the rally itself) to one of the munition girls who worked at the Woolwich Arsenal!

Especial satisfaction came when one of the Land Girls said on her journey home, that her fellow female war workers could no longer say:

"Why didn't you tell me why I was needed? I never knew."[2]

The English novelist, Max Pemberton was also clearly won over by these women too as he wrote about their collective efforts in April 1918. He clearly felt that the vast majority of women had answered the national call admirably. Should a balance need to be struck, he felt that the scales were tipped in favour of the efforts made throughout the land by womankind during wartime.[3]

This sentiment is echoed by a reporter who describes how he felt on seeing a detachment of the Land Army, who were participating in a march en route to attending a service at St Paul's Cathedral in London. The sight of the Land Girls, proudly wearing their uniforms he felt sure would make every man, woman and child feel an enormous swell of pride. War was dreadful but it would surely make people see just how far women had come and how far they could now go, should they so wish![4]

Demonstrations and efficiency tests were also part and parcel of a Land Girl's life. Not all women enjoyed the pressure and scrutiny that such events put them under as the gathered onlookers would usually be a mix of seasoned farmers, (only too ready to chip in with a comment or quip, useful or otherwise about how things should be done) and village women who had years of hard, intense agricultural experience behind them. Regardless of the gathered crowds, Land Girls demonstrated their skills against others from different counties. Prizes were awarded and certificates distributed with marks given out of 100% for each discipline.

Wherever these demonstrations took place, those that gathered to watch the Land Girls at work were generally interested in what they were doing and were sympathetic if they showed ineptitude. Better still, they encouraged those that required more training and even applauded or cheered those that had performed the tasks ably. Sometimes, farmers overstepped the mark by giving commands to their horse teams or advice to a Land Girl as she walked within earshot. Any disapproving looks from the women were futile as the farmers saw it as merely offering gentle, instinctive assistance in words or gestures that were familiar to their animals.[5]

The clear reluctance to readily accept assistance speaks volumes for the women despite it being well-meant. There was of course the risk of dented pride to take into account and Land Girls would not have liked to perform poorly in public. Employers would also have been fearful of a poor performance. If such reports spread to neighbouring farms, it may have reflected badly on their farm and farming practice(s).

There were however, some farmers that would have liked nothing more than to see the women fail in public so that their prejudice against employing them was borne out. By actually being able to observe the women closely as they worked in the many disciplines, it tended to put the maelstrom of preconceived ideas to bed. This was not so for a small remainder of the unconvinced, staunch farming fraternity, who looked on with indignation and bitterness as the Land Girls ploughed impeccable furrows right before their eyes. They found fault where there was none to find.[6]

The response from the reporter, rather fittingly was heralded in a quiet yet triumphant tone. From what he had witnessed that day, it was clear that, if petty and resentful mutterings were the harshest words that had been uttered about the Land Girls, then they were not going too far wrong![7]

Speeches were sometimes given in village halls after demonstrations where, (rather begrudgingly) some of the assembled farmers appeared to have, in-part come round to the idea that women were in fact useful! Not everyone could be won over, but winning over the vast majority by operating and conducting yourself in an exemplary manner was not surely too much of a hard task - or was it? Land Girls had to shrug off any detrimental comments quickly even though it must have been difficult to do so.

A demonstration was a special occasion and one that took place in Lincolnshire in March 1916 saw the village Squire, (who was also the vicar) up early, putting up notices everywhere in the rain that showed the way to the demonstration. These guided the many curious local farmers to the spectacle. They had travelled from all over the district so that they could witness for themselves the new, female war workers.[8]

It would not have been possible for Land Girls to have perfected every type of skill that farmwork asked of them in the short space of time they had been in the Women's Land Army. The skills of countrymen and women were acquired, mastered and honed over a lifetime of watching and listening to previous generations. It would therefore have been an unfair expectation to assume as much.

Some women were however naturals at precision jobs like ploughing and surprised their employers and fellow workers.

Women that travelled from other counties to participate would not have been familiar with the plough types being used, the soil, topography of the land or the animals. It would have been with a mix of genuine trepidation that any given task was undertaken and completed and yet, despite this, they set to tasks seemingly unfazed, without requiring any assistance. Some girls were still in their teens but showed great maturity and steadiness as they began to work with the plough and horses.[9]

Now was not the time to compare the work carried out by men and women. It was time for each woman to do her level best - for herself, her sex, as a trained individual and for her country.[10]

Farmers attitudes towards the new war wonders tended to fall into three categories:

1. Those that were willing, (if a little cautious) to embrace the women placed at their disposal from the Women's Land Army.

2. Those that wanted to take the women on but were anxious about housing and how their existing workers and the wider village environs would engage and interact with them.

3. Those that viewed a female workforce, (certainly from outside the sphere that was familiar to them) as an unknown entity and were therefore instantly and staunchly opposed from the off. They totally rejected the idea of any government intervention.

In direct contrast to the latter view, as a mark of respect, appreciation and recognition for the work a 71 year old lady had done over the summer months for the war effort, some villagers had all contributed to getting her a silver brooch. The lady was clearly used to a life spent working on the land. She was assured and nimble, ably carrying heavy bundles of long straw up a tall ladder. Once at the top of the high rick, she started to thatch as if she was still in her youth! She wore a homemade bonnet which shielded her from the sun.[11]

The lady wore a red and green armlet which bore the silver brooch. She had been presented with the brooch due to her age and the fact that she was receiving her old age-pension but had chosen to remain working on the land in order to assist the war effort.[12]

The arms of friendship were readily held out in some rural areas as the arrival of Land Girls was seen as a godsend. For some women, sadly less so. Respect and recognition were hard earnt. Land Girls discovered that underneath the toughened, rough-around-the-edges, tell-it-like-it-is nature of country folk lay infinite rural wisdom. Over time, a mutual respect was, (generally-speaking) quietly gained and Land Girls soaked up any useful information that was imparted from the wisest of the 'old 'uns' as they were often respectfully referred to. They also had to become familiar with the local farming phraseology in order to fully understand the tasks that had been assigned to them.

Land Girls had to become knowledgeable about how weather affected crops and how to contend with any damage caused by heavy rain, frosts, excessive heat, weeds, thistles or pests. They needed to know about crop rotation, soil types, timings of harvests, topography and what to do if a crop was 'light.' Every eventuality had to be considered and executed appropriately. Crops were precious.

They also had to think on their feet and be responsive to the requests of the farm bailiff, (which often meant a great deal more work for themselves) and undertake their instructions without complaint.

Their awareness of nature also became heightened. They recognised colour changes to tree leaves that had occurred in a matter of hours. Shades of green on brown leaves noticed at the start of the day had given way to green by the end!

Land Girls noticed that lots of birds nested in the corn and that the fields were also home to tiny leverets which lay perfectly still and camouflaged as women hoed just feet away. A tillage field was a precarious location for a bird to make a nest, so as they worked, the Land Girls carefully removed plover eggs from the nests that they spotted and replaced them once the horses and machinery had passed by.[13]

Land Girls fondly remembered the call of the skylarks and the sound that their wings made as they swooped above them as they worked. They felt that the call of the skylark was the perfect accompaniment to land work.[14]

Quiet kindnesses were always appreciated by Land Girls and any constructive comments that lightened the workload were welcomed! If mistakes were made by the women, the men that took the time to discreetly and gently steer the women back in the right direction instead of mocking or ridiculing them made life much more bearable for them.

Consider too, the ever present feeling of needing to prove yourself against the established village hierarchies. Fronting it out was usually the best policy. Being made of stern stuff was imperative!

Occasionally, being a Land Girl had its advantages and as part of London's "Land Day" in March 1918, some Land Girls were invited to a luncheon by the President of the Women's Land Army, Lady Gertrude Denman and the directors of The Savoy hotel! Tea followed at Ciro's, (an exclusive restaurant, cabaret club and nightclub) in London.

By 1919, there was a growing tide of feeling that women should be encouraged to remain in farming now that the industry had been revitalised by the swathe of 'new blood.' Land Girls still had much to offer. They were trained, skilled and possessed specialist skills. They had demonstrated capabilities far beyond the nation's expectations and their wealth of experience could not be seen to just go to waste. Food was still short and rationing of some foods continued until 1920.

Land Girls were still going above and beyond the call of duty to serve and their work often meant having to travel to unusual and remote places. Perhaps in Miss Woodgate's case, the word remote was an understatement.

When Miss Della May Woodgate, aged 21 of Dawlish and Miss Dorothy Maud Yeo, aged 18 of Torquay signed up for the Women's Land Army, it seems fair to assume that they could never have guessed the extreme location their war service was going to take them once their six weeks of training had been completed.

They were the only Land Girls to work on Lundy Island, approximately 12 miles off the coast of Devon, (later reports state that Della was in fact the only Land Girl to work on Lundy). Her contribution and exceptional good work saw her deservedly receive one of 60 Good Service Ribbons awarded at a presentation at Victoria Hall, Exeter on Friday, January 31st 1919.

Mrs Calmady-Hamlyn, (the first and only Travelling Inspector appointed by the Board of Agriculture) praised the spirited recruit and her surreal journey to work each day. She told of how Miss Woodgate was transported to and from the island on a special packet boat. Hers was indeed one of the finest examples of pluck and resolve to be shown by a serving member of the Women's Land Army bar none.[15]

Another Land Girl received a Good Service Ribbon as she had worked for the same employer for five and a half years, (others for 3-4 years).

Letters received from employers confirmed just how loyal and committed the women were.

Special mention was often made at these ceremonies of women who had been the first to join the Women's Land Army in any given county or of women workers who had an excellent service record but sadly weren't able to receive any award as they were not officially enrolled in the Land Army. In April 1919, Mrs Quirk, the Chairwoman of the Lindsey Branch of the Women's Land Army addressed 30-40 Land Girls. She proudly remarked how the Land Girls had always worked hard, often with very little reward and whilst they did this without complaint, it lifted them no end when their efforts were recognised and appreciated.[16]

Meetings often took place at the grand homes of some of the wealthy Women's Land Army representatives; where both Land Girls and village women were welcomed. Following such meetings, it was frequently the case that armlets, badges, stripes and Good Service Ribbons were awarded. This was exactly how proceedings unfolded at Embley Park in Hampshire during the summer of 1918. The owners, Major Chichester and his wife, (who was the District Representative) held a meeting which saw 50 Land Girls and village women in attendance.

The Chichester's home had been the main home of the Nightingale family, who had resided there from 1825, when Florence would have been five years old. The connection to such an influential and inspiring female figure was no doubt a huge bonus when addressing members of the Women's Land Army, (an organisation that, at the time was barely into its second year of existence).

The meeting was held in the imposing entrance hall. 27 village women and two Land Girls received armlets and stripes. Several of the village women already had three stripes, (each stripe represented 6 months of work). This indicates that they may have worked in a land organisation before the Women's Land Army had been established. One village woman was presented with four stripes! After the formalities at Embley Park the women were allowed to take a walk in the beautiful grounds of the house shortly before enjoying a concert played by a small orchestra under the baton of a corporal from a local remount depot.

The two main awards of merit awarded by the Women's Land Army recognised length of service and good conduct. Firstly, the Good Service Ribbon, (inaugurated by the Women's Land Army on October 5th 1918) was issued to 8000 recruits. This was awarded to all workers for six months of completely satisfactory service both inside and just as importantly, outside of working hours.

Secondly, the Land Army's 'VC' known as the Distinguished Service Bar was issued to just 56 members, (55 was also a figure regularly reported). This honour was awarded to women who had demonstrated exceptional loyalty, bravery and devotion or had proved to be especially proficient in a particular discipline.

During a presentation at the Nottingham Exchange Hall in March 1919, forewomen and instructresses were awarded their Good Service Ribbons by the Duchess of Newcastle alongside Land Girls.

Not all armlets, stripes or other awards were presented in such salubrious surroundings. Many girls had their armlets presented to them in a farmyard from a farm cart which acted as a makeshift stage!

The Women's Service Club at 252 High Street, Grimsby, (although nowhere near as grand as Embley Park) was nonetheless still an appropriate setting for yet one more county presentation of 30-40 awards. All of the deserving candidates belonged to the Lindsey Branch of Lincolnshire's Women's Land Army. A stirring address was heard and a lavish lunch followed at a restaurant. There was a cinema show at the Corn Exchange and to round off proceedings there was a tea at the Club Rooms!

Two further special awards were presented to eight Land Girls. The Royal Society for the Prevention of Cruelty to Animals presented a bronze medal to three girls along with certificates of merit to a further five girls.[17]

Other awards were given out, such as the Long Service Award.

"The Long Service Prize of £1 offered by Mrs Payne, Chief Inspector of the Women's Branch, F. P. Depot has been awarded to the: Misses Emma and Fanny Webb of Hatton Farm, Faringdon. They were trained as war workers under the government scheme begun in March 1915.

On April 1st 1918, they had worked for the same employer for three years and one month and had been members of the Land Army for eleven months. There were 112 entries and Mrs Baynes hopes to give a similar prize later on."[18]

The Minister for Agriculture had called for women to come forward early on in the war to work on the land in some way. The Forage Corps was established in 1915 to, (among other things) assist with the production of hay and fodder for horses in the army. The Forage Corps was a military organisation under the control of the Army Service Corps, (unlike the other branches of the Women's Land Army). It did however contribute to the formation of the Women's Land Army proper in 1917, surviving until 1920. It was therefore possible for women to serve for a considerable amount of time gaining stripes and for some, promotion along the way.

A further two Land Girls were recognised for their long service. Hilda Walesby was the first girl to enrol in the Women's Land Army in Berkshire and continued to work in the organisation until it demobilised on the 30th November 1919. May Higgs' lengthy duration of service was also acknowledged as being the longest period of satisfactory service in the country.

Two letters survive that detail the intended plan to hold a very large Victory Rally that, had it gone ahead, would have seen hundreds of Land Girls descend on Northampton in late June or September of 1919. The first letter, dated 8th May 1919 made it clear that on no account could it go ahead during the critical harvest months of July and August.

It was expected that the Queen would be in attendance too, not only to witness the national pride felt and shown by the Land Girls themselves and a grateful public but also to present Distinguished Service Bars.

The second letter dated the 27th May 1919 sees the Victory Rally deferred until September. The content is very telling of what was happening in the country at the time. It describes that the postponement was due to the fact that Land Girls were still in huge demand. The department simply could not meet the huge amount of requests now being received from farmers. It was therefore deemed virtually impossible to remove women from their work in order to take part in the two day rally.[19]

Their importance as a workforce cannot be disputed here as this letter was typed six months after the Armistice and still the thirst for a Land Girl labour force was insatiable and proving problematic to quench. Despite wages being increased, this was clearly not enough of an incentive when trying to continue to attract enough women to swell the ranks into 1919.

Consequently the Victory Rally did not take place in Northampton during the September of 1919. It was instead held at Draper's Hall in London on November 27th 1919, just 3 days before the Women's Land Army was officially demobilised.

Rather poignantly, in late 1919, a newspaper reported on the demobilisation as if a much-loved individual had passed away. The metaphoric 'death' of the much-admired and respected organisation was keenly felt by the public.

The final ceremony and presentation to members of the Women's Land Army saw Her Royal Highness Princess Mary present deserving Land Girls with various awards. The presentation of a further medal and diploma, awarded to just 10 members of the Women's Land Army by the RSPCA, recognised the humanity and courage shown by such Land Girls in protecting and saving the lives of animals during the course of their service.

The National Association of Landswomen was formed in January 1920 with the sole intention of retaining as many of the skilled female workforce as it was possible to do so. It eyed a membership of at least 8000; encouraging farmers to join it as well as Land Girls, thus maintaining and ever-strengthening the friendships that were established during the years of wartime work.

At least three-quarters of the Women's Land Army members, (at the point of demobilisation) expressed a view that they wanted to continue working on the land. Within a week of the actual demobilisation of the Women's Land Army, 4000 women had joined.

Importantly, statements appeared whilst the organisation was still in existence that clearly and genuinely intended to accurately preserve the history and contribution to the war effort made by these women. Records were due to be collated and a definitive history penned.[20]

In a letter dated the 27th October 1917 from the Imperial War Museum, (Secretary of the Women's Section) to Mrs Carey Evans, 10 Downing Street, London, mention is made of the Hon. Lady Haig who had made it known that she planned to organise a collection which would be made up of personal information, photographs and objects that showed to the public what women had contributed to the war effort. The focus would be on their deeds of bravery, the medals and awards they had gained and a memorial to those who had died whilst serving their country. This would remain in the Imperial War Museum's archive.[21]

It is clear that the many acts of bravery shown by women during the Great War had made an impact on the Prime Minister.

This record became the Women's War Work Collection, (Imperial War Museum). Very little transpired long-term that fully realised the many other well-intentioned objectives, (proposed at the time) and as a result, the importance and legacy of the Women's Land Army of the Great War remains largely unknown about today.

A report that appeared just a few years later in April 1925 referred to Land Girls as wearing the breeches and smocks of the now, largely forgotten about Women's Land Army.[22]

Many women still clearly loved the land and felt both determined and able to secure an income and a profit from their work. It appears that despite the odds, many continued to thrive in a new and very different decade.

The Land Girl 'VC' Distinguished Service Bars

The Distinguished Service Bar was only awarded to women where exceptional acts of courage or unselfish devotion had been shown whilst in the service of others or where a special skill(s) had been demonstrated during their service.

The favoured figure is of 55 of these medals being awarded, (although the figures of 56 and as many as 59 were also mentioned in reports from the time). The Tractor Section of the Women's Land Army alone received 10 Distinguished Service Bars amongst its 20,000 workers.

56 recipients are remembered here.

Although earnt bravely and honestly, any subsequent bad behaviour would see the award swiftly retracted either temporarily or permanently.

During the Farewell Rally at Draper's Hall, Throgmorton Street in London on the 30th November 1919, details were read out of the circumstances that led to each woman being awarded the prestigious and revered Distinguished Service Bar.

At the time, these acts of bravery and devotion to duty were fresh in the minds of those in attendance but the subsequent passing of a century has meant that these individual, courageous acts have been all but forgotten.

Some names may differ slightly in their spelling due to the fact that they appeared in various newspaper reports. The county that each recipient worked in has also been added where possible. Where any details have been found, (regarding the circumstances that earnt them the honour) they have been included under each name. The names of the recipients appear in alphabetical order.

This chapter honours those women who were deservedly recognised just before demobilisation for their outstanding service in the Women's Land Army. The information that accompanies each name is quoted from The Landswoman magazine unless otherwise stated.

Recipients of the Distinguished Service Bar

Miss Ascanio

Miss Ascanio was presented with her decoration by Princess Mary. She also received the RSPCA medal at the same time.

Miss Jessie Barr
Hertfordshire Women's Land Army

Miss Barr saved a number of pigs from drowning. They had run onto a pond which was covered with a thin layer of ice during frosty weather and they all went into the water. Jessie hung onto a fence with one hand holding the pigs ears by the other, managing to pull the animals to safety. Another report said that she had climbed a tree overhanging the pond and supported herself from one of the boughs and was therefore able to pull the pigs out by their tails.

Miss M. Battersby
Lancashire Women's Land Army

Miss Battersby was decorated for exceptional courage. On an occasion when a horse had got out of control, Miss Battersby stopped the animal and showed great presence of mind by closing the gate after the accident occurred, undoubtedly preventing serious injury to some schoolchildren, who were playing nearby.

Miss M. Bevis
Devon Women's Land Army

Miss Bevis was decorated for exceptional courage and presence of mind when in charge of a cow, which, after calving, had become savage and dangerous. The cow tried to gore all who went near her but Miss Bevis with great courage approached the cow, (who was familiar with her) who, in turn, allowed her to comfort and pick up the calf.

Miss Annie Bohills and Miss Margaret Harrison
Northumberland Women's Land Army

Miss Annie Bohills, of Glebe Road, Bedlington and Miss Margaret Harrison of Franklin Street, Jarrow were working together on a farm when, following a heavy fall of snow, the byre roof suddenly collapsed during the night burying 16 head of cattle. The girls assisted the farmer, (at considerable risk) to extricate the cattle, with the exception of two beasts, which had to be killed to put them out of pain and three heifers, which were fastened in by the debris. Subsequently the two girls crept in under the fallen beams and milked the heifers.

Miss Kitty Botting
Nottinghamshire Women's Land Army

Miss Botting, from Loughborough was decorated for exceptional courage by the Hon. Mrs Lyttleton, Deputy Director of the Women's Branch of the Board of Agriculture at the Nottingham Exchange on Wednesday, 19th March 1919. Kitty had been employed at Stanford Hall, Loughborough by Major Peacock since August 1917 and she rescued a fellow Land Girl, Miss N. Burnell in June 1918 who was being attacked by a savage boar. At great personal risk, she bravely held the boar down with a pitchfork while the other girl escaped despite having sustained two serious tear-wounds in her leg from the boar's teeth that required medical attention for six weeks. Miss Burnell undoubtedly owes her life to Kitty's presence of mind and courage.

Miss Frances Evelyn Bridgeman
Lancashire Women's Land Army

Over a period of 16 months, Frances, who was from Lichfield had worked steadily and arduously. She had a weekly tractor average of double that of her fellow male workers and had been employed as a tractor driver by the Food Production Department in the Lancashire area.

Frances had been working on Moss House Farm, Boothstown, near Manchester for a few months. She could have been awarded the Distinguished Service Bar for her achievements with the tractor alone but another incident occurred which meant that she was even more worthy of receiving one of these esteemed awards.

Frances risked her own life by trying to steer a tractor away from some schoolchildren who were playing in the road at the bottom of a hill. Its brakes had failed on the steep and dangerous hill called Smithy Brow. Instead of taking the easy option of jumping off the tractor, (which she could easily have done) she hung on grimly, attempting to steer it until it had reached the bottom. Due to Frances' quick-thinking and calm state of mind, miraculously, nobody was hurt and the tractor remained undamaged.[1]

Miss F. Brook
Lincolnshire Women's Land Army

Miss Alice Brown
Devon Women's Land Army

Miss Brown was put forward for a decoration by way of notification to the Board of Agriculture. She was employed on a farm in Devon and jumped into the water and rescued seventeen pigs from drowning.

Miss C. Capper
Essex Women's Land Army

For exceptional devotion to duty in very trying circumstances.

Miss G. Chapman
Essex Women's Land Army

As a result of an accident, she broke a bone in her foot and injured her rib. In spite of this, she insisted upon doing her milk round as usual as no other worker was available at the time. On another occasion, when in charge of a hay wagon, a horse took fright, reared and bolted. Miss Chapman held on to its head throughout and finally brought the animal to a standstill.

Miss Florrie Dobson
Border Country Women's Land Army

Miss Dobson was decorated for exceptional bravery and devotion during the influenza epidemic. A moving letter was sent to The Landswoman magazine, (it appeared on 'Our Club Page' in the January 1919 edition) describing Florrie's selflessness and pluck.

> "I should like to mention a case of unselfish bravery in a Land Girl. In a farmhouse in the Bootle Union, the little farm servant died suddenly from 'flu' before she had been there a week. So great

was the fear of infection that not a woman would come near her to perform the last duties of the dead. The poor little corpse lay alone and untended for the whole of Sunday 24th. At last a Land Army girl, (name - Florrie Dobson) from the next farm heard of the case and at once came and did that which the village women and the owners of the farm were too cowardly to do."

Miss A. Fisher
Norfolk Women's Land Army

Miss Fisher was decorated for exceptional duty during a fire at her employer's house. She worked indefatigably and showed great courage in attempting to extinguish the flames.

Miss Laura May 'Peggy' Fisher
East Sussex Women's Land Army

A cowman who was about to chain up a bull, (which was loose in the stall) was knocked down by the animal. It promptly proceeded to gore him. On hearing his cries, Miss Fisher rushed in and jumping the barrier, attacked the bull by kicking its nose. The bull backed up and the man was able to get out. But for Peggy's pluck he would have been seriously injured and probably killed. This brave Land Girl not only saved the life of the unfortunate cowman but she also won herself a husband with her instinctive, gallant deed! Miss Peggy Fisher is now Mrs Marshall - the wife of the saved cowman!

Miss Mary Garnett and Miss Winifred Worthington
East Kent Women's Land Army

Miss Garnett and Miss Worthington were presented with their decoration by Miss Meriel Talbot. Both women were decorated for splendid records in ploughing. Miss Garnett and Miss Worthington both broke the Kent county record for using motor tractors for ploughing. They both ploughed more acres with the use of less petrol than any man similarly employed. This particular work required perfect physical fitness and endurance.

Mrs A. Gray
Middlesex Women's Land Army

Mrs Gray showed exceptional courage and devotion to duty when at various times she was left by her employer in sole charge of the farm and stock. On one particular occasion, she discovered that part of the roof of the cowshed had collapsed much to the distress of the animals. She managed to quieten the animals but furthermore at great risk to herself she removed them from a precarious situation.

Mrs Hallam
Cornwall Women's Land Army

Mrs Hallam was a shepherdess in Portlooe, Cornwall early in 1917 on a large farm where she was in charge of 200 pedigree South Devon sheep. Mrs Hallam had carried out all her shepherding duties and operations entirely alone. She camped in an empty cottage and cooked using a frying pan and a haybox. Conditions were tough and she lived like a hermit for two months. During her second lambing season, the number of lambs born surpassed all previous records and her employer said that, "She could throw a sheep better than any man he knew."

Miss Lily Harrison
Hampshire Women's Land Army

Miss Harrison was a new recruit and quite unused to horses but she rescued a young pony that was being viciously attacked and bitten by a hunter that had broken loose in the stable. Lily heard the horse crying pitifully and ran to the stable. The foreman was brought to the scene but did not think it was safe to go near but Lily managed to squeeze past and separated the animals.

Miss Frances E. Henley
Staffordshire Women's Land Army

A frightened cow was stranded on a small piece of dry land in the middle of the swift and wide River Trent, unable to reach either bank on account of the soft, slimy mud surrounding her. The cow was at risk of drowning but one of the Land Girls who witnessed this alarming spectacle, Miss Henley, took off her overall, boots and stockings and swam across the river, roped the cow midstream and drove it before her to the bank.

Mrs Hockin
Devon Women's Land Army

Mrs Hockin of Bridestowe was decorated for pioneering good work, skill and devotion shown during the course of her employment. She was the first member of the Women's Land Army in Devon to receive the honour. Miss Hockin had done much to arouse enthusiasm for the Women's Land Army and had managed to get 100 new recruits to join up in Devon. She has done yeoman service on the land, practically throughout the duration of the war.

Miss E. Johnson and Miss O. Johnson
Border Country, Women's Land Army

Miss D. Jones
Denbighshire Women's Land Army

Miss Jones was decorated for exceptional skill and devotion to duty. As a shepherdess, Miss Jones stuck to her post and rendered great service in one of the most inaccessible parts of the country.

Miss Nora Kenny

On two occasions, when the farmer was away, Nora attended, (unaided) to the cows when they were calving and by giving one calf special care and attention, saved its life. When all the girls were down with influenza and the welfare officer for the same reason was unable to attend to them, Nora, (who has had some knowledge of nursing) visited them every morning and evening and nursed them until they were well, in addition to doing her usual day of heavy work.

Miss May Kisielowski
Miss Marjorie Smith
Miss Jane S. Thompson
Berkshire Women's Land Army

Their decorations were given owing to exceptional courage and skill in the course of their employment as tractor drivers. They offered to plough a difficult and dangerous piece of sloping ground and they carried out the work successfully. This ground was situated at Wittenham, near Dorchester.

Miss Daisy Lardner
Northamptonshire Women's Land Army

Miss Lardner was from Ibstock in Leicestershire. A distressing event occurred on the 1st October 1919 on a farm in Finedon, Northamptonshire, (where she was working at the time) owned by Mr Knight. This event subsequently saw her awarded the Distinguished Service Bar. Before joining the Women's Land Army, Daisy had worked in munitions and prior to that she had been in the WAAC, (Women's Army Auxiliary Corps) for eight months. She had been a Land Girl for a year when the incident happened. Two thoroughbred horses had broken loose and galloped off at great speed. One had injured itself as a result and was bleeding badly from its leg, its reins still dangling down. Without any thought for her own safety, Daisy ran after the horses and eventually managed to restrain them both. Boot manufacturer, Mr A. Parker saw the whole incident unfold and decided to bring Daisy's bravery to the attention of the Women's Land Army.[2]

Miss E. M. Le Mar
East Kent Women's Land Army

Miss Le Mar was decorated in recognition of great courage and presence of mind when there had been a serious accident. She saved the life of a little boy. The boy was sitting on a stile in charge of a gun which slipped and practically blew his arm off. Miss Le Mar rushed to the child and carried him to the house where she bound his arm tightly with towels and attended to him until help arrived. The doctor said that without Miss Le Mar's prompt action, the child would almost certainly have lost his life.

Miss M. E. Leonard
Wiltshire Women's Land Army

Decorated for showing exceptional skill and devotional service in the Tractor Section. She won the county championship and broke several records. During the last harvest, she cut over 120 acres of wheat in one week.

Miss R. Leversuch
Worcestershire Women's Land Army

Despite considerable personal risk to herself, Miss Leversuch tended a cow that was suffering from a contagious disease. The veterinary surgeon said that her good nursing and scrupulous cleanliness helped enormously with the cow's recovery.

Miss Elsie Lewis
Flintshire Women's Land Army

Mrs Ellis was with her friend when they passed a motor tractor that was stationary at a crossroads. She, knowing the pony was restive, got out of the trap to lead him past the tractor, telling her friend to hold the reins. The friend, however, let go of the reins and got out of the trap. When they passed the tractor Mrs Ellis was unable to hold the pony and he bolted. Miss Lewis jumped off the tractor, ran after the pony, sprang into the trap, got hold of the reins, and, after great difficulty, succeeded in pulling up the pony, so preventing what certainly would have been a bad accident.

Miss Kate Lindsay
East Kent Women's Land Army

Miss Lindsay was presented with her decoration by Miss Meriel Talbot for exceptional courage and presence of mind at the time of a serious accident with a threshing machine. The machine turned completely over when being brought out of a muddy farmyard and one old man got pinned under the machine. Miss Lindsey, with the help of another man, managed to draw the victim from under the machine and by remaining calm and being firm she prevented panic amongst the other girls in the gang.

Miss Vera Mather
Berkshire Women's Land Army

Miss Mather's efforts were recognised in the first instance by a veterinary surgeon who recommended that she be put forward for the Distinguished Service Bar. Her efforts were brought to the notice of the Women's Branch, Board of Agriculture. The veterinary surgeon, Mr William Allen, MRCVS of Wokingham spoke highly of Vera's dedication to her work. Whilst working at her placement at Mrs Weston's, Holme Grange, Wokingham, some animals fell ill, one of which was a Jersey cow who, after calving had developed milk fever, (which affects the brain). Vera contacted the vet in the dead of night to ask him to try and save the cow, which was near death with multiple, severe symptoms.

Vera, although relatively inexperienced held the cow's head steady by its horns in an attempt to stop it from hurting itself as it was very distressed and thrashing about. The only other assistance she had had was from an elderly man. Vera undoubtedly saved the life of the cow with her meticulous and unremitting care over two days and nights.

There was also another incident that saw Vera care for a pregnant sow. It had developed septicaemia due to all of its piglets dying. The grim task saw Vera risk her own health, (blood poisoning could have resulted) as she took the little pigs away but this did not deter her. Instead, she nursed the sow over the course of five days and nights and enticed her patiently with a tablespoon of whisky and milk in an attempt to save her life. Mr Allen couldn't praise Vera's actions enough as he wondered how she had not fainted whilst carrying out such an awful procedure.

The final incident that saw a well-deserved Distinguished Service Bar being awarded was when Vera nursed the same Jersey cow round the clock that had previously been ill with milk fever. Unfortunately, Vera became ill during her time spent caring for this animal. Thankfully both Vera and the cow recovered![3]

Miss Kathleen May
Somerset Women's Land Army

Decorated for her exceptional devotion to duty. Miss May stuck to her work for a considerable time both as a tractor driver and shepherdess in an exceedingly lonely and inaccessible part of Exmoor.

Miss D. C. McCrae
Cumberland Women's Land Army

Miss McCrae was decorated for ploughing land in Cumberland which some male workers had refused to touch. She was so proficient and skilled as a tractor driver that she was given entire charge of a tractor department in a big firm of contracting engineers in the north. It is in recognition of this work that the President of the Board of Agriculture, Lord Lee sent her a message of special appreciation.

Miss E. Moore and Miss M. Moore
Warwickshire Women's Land Army

These two women from Berkswell were decorated for their exceptional devotion to duty and courage. These girls ran their brother's farm entirely by themselves whilst he was away on active service. Also, at 2am one morning they heard a commotion in a field and on seeing the cause of it, they pluckily separated a herd of bullocks from their own bull.

Miss M. Morley
Surrey Women's Land Army

Miss Morley saved a cow that was choking on a turnip. A man had refused to help her try and save the cow.

Miss E. Morris
Denbighshire Women's Land Army

Miss Morris was decorated for exceptional skill and devotion to duty. She was the champion horse ploughwoman for Wales and gained several prizes, besides doing excellent work in connection with ploughing on her father's farm.

Miss Ethel Nicholas

Eighteen year old volunteer, Miss Nicholas was the first L.A.A.S Land Girl to be awarded the Distinguished Service Bar for meritorious conduct. She was in charge of a cutting machine drawn by two horses when the leg of her employer was caught by the knife. Stopping the horses immediately, the girl put the machine out of gear and with her handkerchief and belt, skilfully tied up the wound. Next she secured the help of a neighbouring farmer and subsequently assisted the doctor to operate. The doctor reports that but for Ethel's clear presence of mind, her employer would have run a serious risk of losing his life from the bleeding and would almost certainly have lost his leg.

Miss K. Pitman
Wiltshire Women's Land Army

Miss Pitman worked as a shepherdess on a very exposed aerodrome for a whole winter. She lived in a shepherd's hut during the lambing season. She was decorated for exceptional skill and devotion to duty.

Miss Doris Raper

Miss Raper was employed on Major Behren's estate from September 1917 and looked after Shorthorn bulls. She performed difficult duties most efficiently and showed great courage and zealousness in the way she handled bulls - work which very few women would have had the courage to undertake and still fewer have been able to carry out so well. She had almost sole charge of some of the bulls and led several of them into the ring on occasion of the private sale last July. Before joining the Women's Land Army, Doris had worked in the ribbon department of a Birmingham store.

Miss K. Sherlock
Warwickshire Women's Land Army

Miss Sherlock was decorated for showing exceptional courage in averting a dangerous accident. Miss Sherlock stopped a runaway colt and hung onto it until help came.

Miss Laura Shipp
West Kent Women's Land Army

Miss Shipp from Dartford was decorated for exceptional courage. A soldier was ploughing when the horses took fright and the plough, which was a balance one, overturned, pinning the soldier between the horses and the machine. Laura, who was driving a tractor plough in the same field, ran and stopped the frightened horses and but for her plucky action the soldier would most probably have lost his life.

Miss Marjorie Spiking
Yorkshire Women's Land Army

Miss Spiking from the Dewsbury Road area of Leeds was only 20 years of age when she joined the Women's Land Army. Marjorie eventually worked as a horsewoman and went to work for Mr Beillby at Wothersome Farm, Boston Spa in 1917 where she remained for two years. Marjorie also received the award in part for her work during the influenza epidemic when she looked after 12 horses single-handedly.

Marjorie was in charge of a reaping machine when the two horses harnessed to it bolted. She stuck to her seat and the reins and drove the runaway horses through traffic for a mile until at last she brought them to a standstill.

Mrs Spurrin

Mrs Spurrin was decorated in recognition of exceptional skills and devotion in the care of horses, sheep and livestock during 3½ years of service.

Miss Margaret Starkey
Buckinghamshire Women's Land Army

Apparently Miss Starkey had a 'magnetic influence' over bulls! She was in charge of a valuable herd of Friesian cows on a farm at Horton, Leighton Buzzard. Margaret had a favourite young bull that followed her around like a pet lamb!

Miss Eileen Talmage
Breconshire Women's Land Army

Miss Talmage joined the Women's Land Army in May 1917 and worked on Captain Evans' estate at Ffrwdgrech until the end of November 1919.

Eileen was one of two women selected by the County Organising Secretary to represent Breconshire at the Farewell Rally held at Draper's Hall in London on November 27th 1919. Each of the landworkers, (to the number of about 400) received a photograph of the Princess. Eileen was one of a lucky few to receive a signed photograph of Her Royal Highness.

Miss C. Taylor
Kent Women's Land Army

Miss Taylor showed exceptional courage at great personal risk when she saved a fellow worker from burning. With presence of mind, she fetched water and threw it over an old man who was working with the threshing machine whose apron had caught fire. Miss Taylor's hair, hands and ears were burnt but if she had not come to the rescue, the man would certainly have lost his life.

Miss Ethel Thomas
Wiltshire Women's Land Army

Miss Thomas was decorated for exceptional courage and presence of mind when a fire was caused by accident. When Ethel started the engine on a machine it backfired and some petrol and oil which had spilt caught fire. She immediately turned off the engine and smothered the flames. Her prompt action saved what certainly could have turned into a big fire as the engine was in the barn when the accident occurred.

Miss Winifred Thoroughgood
West Suffolk Women's Land Army

Miss Thoroughgood came from Dunstall Green, Ousden in Suffolk. She was the second Suffolk Land Girl to receive the Distinguished Service Bar. It was awarded to her in recognition of her unselfish devotion to duty in attending to the child of Mr Hayward, Manor Farm, Hopton, who was suffering from a dangerous and infectious illness. A nurse was impossible to obtain at the time. Despite running the grave risk of infection, Winifred stuck to her post until the child was out of danger. Winifred joined the Women's Land Army in the summer of 1917 and did good work on various farms. After being demobilised, Winifred was employed at the Angel Hotel.

Miss W. Walder
Yorkshire Women's Land Army

Miss Walder rescued a valuable mare which she had found astride a length of barbed wire. She immediately loosened the stakes and let the wire down. This prompt action undoubtedly saved the mare from going lame.

Miss Elizabeth Walker
West Suffolk Women's Land Army

Miss Walker appears to have hailed from Culford, Suffolk and was the first Land Girl from West Suffolk to be awarded the Distinguished Service Bar. Elizabeth rescued a man who had been pinned against a wall by a bull, undoubtedly saving him from severe injury. She was also decorated for her special skill and devotion to duty in taking charge of animals who were suffering from inflammation of the udder, and, who, owing to Elizabeth's care and attention, were completely cured.

Recognition of long and exemplary service

Many women had served in land organisations for some considerable time before the Women's Land Army was established and their long, loyal and exemplary service was also acknowledged. An example of this was on the 16th March 1918 when 275 members of the Northumberland Guild of War Agricultural Helpers were presented with proficiency badges by their President, the Duke of Northumberland on Castle Square, Alnwick.

Miss M. Skeats and Miss G. Tyler were mentioned in December 1919 as having been specially invited to the farewell rally at Draper's Hall, Throgmorton Street in London on the 27th November 1919 in recognition of their long service and good record. They stayed for the supper and the concert which followed the presentations.

Miss Tuckfield and Miss Henderson of Devon Women's Land Army, Mrs Mildmay and Mrs Calmady-Hamlyn also had their long service acknowledged. Land Girl Jessie Petter in early 1919 received an award for the longest span of service with an employer in Midhurst, West Sussex.

A 'one-off' Good Service Badge was awarded to a Mrs S. E. Fry, a member of the Women's Land Army in Oxfordshire. Land Girls had all contributed money to buy a small gold brooch with the Land Army colours on it as a token of their appreciation.

The invaluable work of village women should also be remembered. They worked tirelessly alongside the Land Girl 'apprentices' throughout the war. It is therefore imperative that the contribution made by <u>all</u> landswomen is remembered.

The Legacies of the Land Lassies

For those women that had willingly and proudly served their country throughout the Great War, it was only right that their individual contribution to the war effort was acknowledged and honoured just before the organisation was demobilised; not just by their peers and county representatives but by members of the British Royal Family <u>and</u> a grateful nation.

Aside from the Farewell Rally that took place at Draper's Hall in London on the 27th November 1919 and a certificate that recognised their service in the Women's Land Army, presented to them at the time, very few memorials recognise the work of the women that served in the fields, forage depots and forests during the First World War.

The Women's War Collection of photographs, collated by the Imperial War Museum, The Five Sisters Window in York Minster, the 1513 names of women who died whilst serving their country during the Great War, inscribed on oak screens, (that make up the Women of The Empire - WW1 Screen in York Minster) went some way to preserving their legacy in the years immediately following demobilisation.

Memories however fade and interest inevitably waned as the decades stretched further on in time.

After a sustained campaign, the contribution made by women who had served in the Women's Land Army during the Second World War was officially recognised by the British Government in December 2007. Surviving Land Girls were issued with a special Veteran's Badge awarded from Defra, (Department for Environment, Food and Rural Affairs) and a certificate, signed by Gordon Brown in July 2008.

A memorial created by sculptor Denise Dutton was unveiled on the 21st October 2014 by Her Royal Highness, The Countess of Wessex at the National Memorial Arboretum in Alrewas, Staffordshire. It commemorates the members of the Women's Land Army from both wars. Two bronze figures, one depicting a Land Girl and the other a Lumber Jill are both from the Second World War. There is no bronze representation of a Great War Land Girl.

Today, recognition of their collective effort has largely slipped from public consciousness. On the rare occasions that Land Girls of the Great War do appear on television, only a fleeting glimpse is caught of them on a black and white clip!

And yet, despite this, their short but critical existence saw them leave behind such an indelible mark.

Chapter 16

Self-sacrificing service: The Land Girl Roll of Honour.

Consciousness of the Great War itself rarely, (if ever) extends to or even mentions the fatalities of women who worked during the Great War years in the Women's Land Army or Forage Corps. The number of deaths is admittedly tiny when compared to the staggering figures of dead and wounded men that occurred on the battlefields but for each woman that chose to serve her country who lost her life, (whether through accident or illness) she deserves to have her story told and remembered in perpetuity too.

Sacrifice didn't always mean losing your life in the name of service. Sacrifice meant forfeiting your life as you knew it for as long as the war determined. Family life, friendships, relationships, study, ambitions and careers were all simultaneously put on hold. Separation was commonplace for nearly every family in the land but now it was the turn of women of all ages and backgrounds to switch to a new life, completely at odds with the one they were living.

Tolerance and patience was now required from every recruit that began to train and work alongside each other for the first time. Classes from either end of the social spectrum were now meeting in the fields of agriculture, forage and forestry! It was abundantly clear that every woman needed to exercise restraint and forbearance in the months that lay ahead.

Appreciation expressed by the nation in 1918 was of little consolation to the many thousands of women who, long before, had answered the call of their country.

For many women, their health had steadily deteriorated. Anaemia and exhaustion became a common health problem as a direct result of the exacting demands of working on a daily basis with hazardous chemicals in the munitions factories all over the country.

They had no alternative but to leave the factories and when the time was right, perhaps consider continuing their national service on the land, which would at least, over time, aid their recovery.

This option was often recommended by doctors on the assurance that the majority of women would, in time, steadily regain some degree of health under medical supervision in the new Women's Land Army Probationary Training Centres set up to, in effect rehabilitate ailing munitionettes. Initially, the women were given light work to do outside, in order to build strength and improve their bluey/grey complexions. Nourishing food also aided their internal recovery.

The Landswoman's Editor, Miss Meriel Talbot piloted an experiment in her own garden, taking four such women under her wing each month. They were billeted in a little cottage and worked in a vegetable garden until their health problems improved, (which was as quick as a matter of weeks for some). It was a real boon for the Women's Land Army to in effect 'capture' extra women in this way.

Once nurtured back to fitness, they moved onto the Women's Land Army Training Centres proper where further, more specialised training was provided. This concept showed that the Women's Land Army was an inventive, progressive organisation. Meriel appeared immensely proud to be able to capitalize on this particular reconstructive rather than destructive element of women's war service.

> "Our work was always constructive, building up, helping to make things grow."[1]

The mental and physical health of many women frequently suffered as a result of poor working conditions, inadequate accommodation, lack of interaction with other Land Girls or the absence of any intervention or support from the realms of officialdom. Many women encountered bullying and saw their work belittled and undermined at every opportunity. Narrow-mindedness and venomous attitudes saw unreasonable expectations placed upon Land Girls which pushed them beyond what they were actually physically capable of resulting in a total breakdown in their health due to overwork.

An idea for a nationwide Roll of Honour was put forward in December 1915; one that acknowledged women's vital work on the land. The report records details of a conference between representatives of County Committees and Lord Selborne, (President of the Board of Agriculture). It was recommended that a Roll of Honour should be created in every village recording the names of women who were working on the land just as there was one for the men who were fighting. The take-up had been slow, with only one county having actually put the idea into practice at the time of the conference.[2]

Exactly which county was being referred to was not made known. It is however apparent that this proposal failed to materialise let alone exist in every village. Hence, the well-meant intention to remember the women's contribution at the time and for the future in perpetuity never actually came to fruition.

There was almost a sense of inevitability that this optimistic, rather overambitious idea would stall right from the start. Even in late 1915, many people would not have wanted to focus on anything that was connected to war service or that reminded them of any personal loss or perhaps friends or neighbours' losses. This may have been one of the reasons why no sense of urgency was shown to seize the moment to record what had already been achieved by so many landworkers. Instead of being recorded on a Roll of Honour, two unnamed Land Girls that died of influenza were merely mentioned at a meeting of the Nottinghamshire War Agricultural Committee in November 1918.

The words, 'Roll of Honour' are synonymous with male loss on a huge scale but also record men and occasionally women that served and survived service too. The formation of the Women's Land Army was still officially 14 months distant from the time Lord Selbourne made his impassioned request and although his idea was forward-looking at the time, the inclusion of names of any Land Girls on Rolls of Honour or war memorials were the exception - not the rule.

Had these Rolls of Honour been created, they would have acknowledged and provided a more accurate picture and record of the contribution made by those that served and those that had paid the ultimate sacrifice, along with details of awards and honours gained and perhaps even how they were gained. Wherever these records were located they would have seen more names added

Self-sacrificing service: The Land Girl Roll of Honour.

to them during the war and may have inspired others who saw them at the time to come forward to serve their nation from villages all over Britain. The opportunity to create an important record for future generations to learn about and reflect upon years later was missed.

By having a permanent visible reminder and by reading the names of each woman aloud every Remembrance Day, (as is the recognised tradition today at war memorials and churches up and down the land) it would have ensured that what they had worked so hard to achieve for their country continued to be rightfully honoured as the years passed. That it was deemed so important to be mentioned by Lord Selbourne as early as 1915 speaks volumes for the impact that women were already making and would continue to make in the following few years.

Rather movingly, bereaved parents, husbands and loved ones of the women who had lost their lives carrying out war work were contacted by the Women's War Work Sub-Committee. A request was made for a cabinet photo, (a photograph mounted on a stiff piece of cardboard) of the woman herself which would eventually be placed in a permanent collection at the Imperial War Museum, (which was officially opened in June 1920).

The Women's Section then collated these photographs of the women with the idea of forming a memorial which would eventually be viewed by the public. The Women's War Shrine opened at Whitechapel Art Gallery on October 7th 1918. It was free to visit and during the six weeks it was open, 82,000 people visited it! The Imperial War Museum also had galleries at Crystal Palace from 1920-1924. Above the entrance were the following words:

"They lost their lovely youth facing the rough cloud of war."

The women who died whilst serving their country during the Great War are commemorated at York Minster on the Five Sisters Window and the Women of The Empire - WW1 Screen which was dedicated on the 24th June 1925. 1,513 women's names are recorded on 12 oak panels, situated to the north side of St Nicholas' Chapel. Among the names are those that gave their life whilst serving in the Women's Land Army and Forage Corps. It is the only memorial in the country that is dedicated entirely to such women. These screens were created with the excess money raised for the restoration of the Five Sisters Window. This memorial was not part of the original plan.

Deaths were as a result of accident, health problems or illness. 18 Forage Corps workers are commemorated on the screen with 10 members of the Women's Land Army. Inevitably, many more women would have died during their service but are not commemorated in any official way. Their names have quite literally disappeared and been consigned to history. This chapter honours the landswomen who died whilst serving their country.

The information that accompanies each name is quoted from The Landswoman magazine unless otherwise stated.

In grateful remembrance.

Women who died whilst serving their country in the Women's Land Army.

Miss Mary Adamson
Born 1895, died 9th May 1919

24 year old Mary was a member of the Women's Land Army under the government scheme and had been employed at Gotterstone Farm, Broughty Ferry, Fife for about six months when the accident happened. Mary was killed in the courtyard of the farm. A new horse had recently been purchased and its erratic behaviour had already caused some concern. As it was released from the milk van that had just arrived from Dundee, it became agitated and reared up on its hind legs. Two men attempted to regain control of the animal by grabbing a rein each but the horse violently kicked back and Miss Adamson was struck with the full force of the horseshoe on her face and forehead. She sustained severe injuries as a result. A motor ambulance was immediately called for and arrived a short time afterwards but it was futile. Miss Adamson's young life was unable to be saved. Her fellow workers at Gotterstone were in a state of shock at what they had witnessed.[3]

News of Mary's harrowing death was sent by telegram to her sister. The official cause of death stated that Mary had died from a fractured skull. The force of the kick had shattered her frontal bone and eye socket leaving part of the brain exposed.[4]

Miss K. Bex
Died 3rd September 1919

Miss Bex was a tractor driver in the Women's Land Army and was remembered for her courage and devotion to her work. Her small obituary appeared in The Landswoman magazine. Miss Bex was:

> "One of the most skilled and reliable workers in the county and she was a well-known figure in the neighbourhood of Wye. She was one of those to whom we owe the splendid success of the Women's Land Army."[5]

She passed away at her home at Hamsey Green, Surrey on September 3rd 1919. She rests in the peaceful churchyard at Sanderstead.

Mrs Chapman

Mrs Chapman is commemorated on a panel on the Women of The Empire – WW1 Screen in York Minster.

Lily Davey
Born 1896, died 11th June 1919

Lily died as a result of the injuries sustained in a tragic accident on the farm of Mr Jackson, Little Marston Farm, West Camel. She passed away at Yeovil Hospital. A coroner's enquiry was held which saw her mother Elizabeth, Lily's employer and a Women's Land Army representative attend. Lily had been in the Women's Land Army for about a year. Her service had seen her placed in the Yeovil area, although she had no connection with the locality itself.

It appears that the family lived in the Tiverton area. Lily was one of a family of 16! Lily was not the only child the family had lost. Mr and Mrs Davey had already lost another son in the war.

A little boy, James Moger was riding with Lily on the wagon, (sitting inside it with seven churns) at the time of the accident and another witness, local boy Harry Slade, (also employed by Mr Jackson) recalled seeing Lily approximately two minutes before the accident occurred.

She was driving a horse which was pulling a small wagon carrying churns of milk bound for a factory at Little Marston. As Lily passed Harry's house, he saw her sitting at the head of the wagon with her feet on the shafts. A couple of minutes later when the wagon had turned the corner out of sight, James ran back to inform Slade about the accident. Lily had somehow slipped off the shafts of the wagon and both wheels had run over her.

Harry saw Lily sitting on the bank and held her hand, asking her if she had been hurt. Lily replied that she had been hurt as the wheels had run right over her. She told Harry that she thought she was going to die.[6]

The little boy when questioned said that Lily had struck the horse and that this was the reason she had slipped. It was noted too that there was no actual seat in the wagon so Lily was in fact sitting on the front board.

It did not appear that the horse was to blame. Harry was sent for a trap to get Lily to a doctor. This arrived within 7-8 minutes. Having seen a doctor at Queen Camel, Lily was taken to Yeovil Hospital. After initially rallying, her condition worsened and an operation was deemed necessary. The wagon had caused internal injury but little bruising to her body, (only her hands). Lily's abdomen had been perforated in the upper part of the small intestine. A repair using stitches was made but sadly, Lily only lived for a short time afterwards. The court confirmed that Lily died as a result of her fall from the wagon and also of the injuries sustained by the wheels which went over her.[7]

Blanche Elizabeth Garman
Born 25th March 1898, died 30th June 1919

Blanche's name appears on Martham War Memorial in Norfolk rather touchingly inscribed below the name of her brother Harry, who was killed in Flanders in 1915. This was not typical practice at the time.

Blanche's story is one that shows her spirited determination to serve despite suffering from a debilitating health condition which contributed to her early death. Blanche was born on the 25th March 1898 in Holt. She was one of 6 children born to William and Elizabeth Garman. Her father moved the family to Martham for work as a resident gatehouse/crossing keeper on the railways. Blanche is recorded in the school log at Martham as attending from the 8th July 1901 until the 3rd May 1912.[8]

Blanche suffered from chlorosis or 'green sickness' as it was then known, which is a severe type of anaemia. It can give the skin of those afflicted a greenish tinge and those that suffer from it may also experience a broad range of debilitating symptoms such as lack of appetite, fatigue, menstrual problems and pica, (a disorder where people want to eat things that aren't food such as plaster or clay).

Land Girls had to pass a medical before they could be accepted officially into the organisation so it is rather puzzling how Blanche got through hers. It seems nigh on impossible that she would have been granted any special dispensation if her condition had been made known to the doctor or indeed that she would have lied about her condition either in order to be accepted.

One possible explanation is that perhaps Blanche's health condition had been disclosed to the Women's Land Army and after careful consideration, she was accepted - but only on the basis that she performed light duties; ones that didn't strain her physically hence she drove a tractor. This work would have been viewed as restorative.

For young women like Blanche, it must have seemed like an incredibly exciting opportunity to learn about the machinery she would go on to operate. Whilst Blanche was driving a tractor, it caught fire and the shock of witnessing it caused a fatal heart attack, (her heart had been weakened by the chlorosis). She died on the 30th June 1919 and was buried in Martham Churchyard. She was just 21 years of age. Rather poignantly, the following words are inscribed on her headstone.

BLANCHE ELIZABETH
The beloved daughter of William and Elizabeth Garman.
Died June 30th 1919, aged 21 years.
Life's short journey o'er,
Duty nobly done,
Passing to the other shore,
Victory's crown is won.

Martham dedicated its War Memorial in July 1920. The names of 39 men and one young woman who made the supreme sacrifice were read out by Archdeacon Carr, Vicar of Great Yarmouth who also gave a touching address. It is worth remembering that commemorating Land Girls was not common practice. Blanche is indeed a rare example of a woman recorded in perpetuity alongside men as a casualty of war in her own right on her village war memorial. Not only must the local people have felt and shared the grief of the Garman family, they must have respected them a great deal too in order for this to have come to fruition.

Maude Winter Gibbins
Born c1879, died 8th May 1919.

Maude was born in Brighton and passed away aged 40 in Sussex, England. She is buried in Brighton Extra-Mural Cemetery. She had six siblings. Maude is the only female to be commemorated on the brass Roll of Honour located in the foyer of Hove Library. Her name is inscribed along with the names of 631 other men.

Mrs S. F. A. Hammond

Accidently killed whilst serving in the Women's Land Army. Mrs Hammond lived at 33 Benhall Green, Saxmundham, Suffolk at the time.

Marjorie Ellen Keye
Born 1900, died January 14th 1919

Marjorie was one of nine children and was employed by Mr Giles Randall of Moulsoe Park Buildings. Her weekly wage averaged 11s and 3d and she only worked in fine weather from 9am to 5pm. She was in charge of a horse which was drawing a load of fodder when an accident occurred. The Deputy Coroner, Mr Hobourn held an inquiry at The Rectory, Moulsoe.

Against her employer's wishes, Marjorie was riding on a horse and was thrown off. This resulted in her falling under the wheels of a wagon. The wagon passed over her chest causing instantaneous death. What was especially distressing was the fact that she had just passed her brother Baden who was in a milk float. He had shouted, "Hullo Mudge" to his sister. Soon after that the horse started to bolt.

The driver of the milk float said that they had given Marjorie plenty of room to pass and he could not understand what had made the horse gallop. Mr Randall stated that he had previously warned the girl against riding on the horse when on the highway as he knew it was a dangerous thing to do. Marjorie's brother Baden was one of the people who gave evidence.

A verdict of "accidental death" was entered by the coroner.

Marjorie's father George went on to apply, (unsuccessfully) for £150 compensation under the Workmen's Compensation Act against Randall Brothers, (farmers) and the case was heard at Newport County Court on Tuesday, 15th July 1919. George had worked as a groom for 29 years and he informed the court that it was not unusual for men to get on the back of a horse when wagons returned without loads.[9]

Marjorie had been told not to do this when she had started working for Mr Randall by the horsekeeper.

Baden vividly recounted the details of her final moments. His sister was not in fact wearing her Land Girl uniform and was riding side-saddle when the accident happened. After passing her, he heard the horse gallop and on looking round saw his sister lying in the road. He clearly felt that the way Marjorie rode the horse was as safe as if she had been leading it. He had seen other girls riding like it.

Barrister, Mr Shakespeare asked whether riding on the horse was an authorised act and secondly whether it was an improper way of doing an authorised act. He pointed out that the manner that Marjorie had ridden the horse was forbidden by the defendant.

Costs were waived on the understanding that the case was not taken any further.

Vivien Isabelle Knapton

Vivien's life is commemorated on Harrogate's War Memorial. This memorial more unusually records the full names of the women who died alongside those of the men. Vivien was one of the first to volunteer to become a Land Girl and moved through the ranks to the position of instructress. Prior to her becoming a Land Girl, she organised concerts for wounded soldiers in hospital.

Vivien contracted influenza but actually died of heart failure even though she appeared to be recovering. She is buried at Harlow Hill Cemetery, Harrogate in a grave with her sister.

Miss E. Le Vie

Miss Le Vie died of influenza-induced pneumonia. She was a forewoman in the Women's Land Army and served at Toddington. During her residence for a year, she had become well known in the county and was highly regarded. She had a genial disposition and was an indefatigable worker who did much to secure help for the farmers in the district. Her home was in London.

Mary L. Nicholls
Died April 16th 1917

Mary was accidentally killed whilst on duty.

Louisa Nutburne
Born c1900, died 1919

Louisa was working with a horse and cart in the fields collecting waste straw with another pupil named Elizabeth Thornby. The Superintendent of the County Council scheme, Dorothy Bull saw them at 11 o clock on the morning of the accident. At the inquest into Louisa's death, Dorothy told the deputy coroner that she had seen Louisa climb up into the cart and had told her not to until she could hold the horse's head. Despite being told not to do this, Louisa still got up and the animal bolted off.

Prior to this, the animal had always been quiet and placid. This was reiterated by the owner of the horse so the sudden change of behaviour was unexpected. Elizabeth found Louisa lying unconscious in the field. She had taken a fall which had resulted in a brain haemorrhage from which she died 2 hours later.

Mrs Petter

Mrs Petter is commemorated on a panel on the Women of The Empire - WW1 Screen in York Minster.

Annie Popplewell
Died October 5th 1918

Annie served in the Women's Land Army. She died as a result of a ploughing accident. The address that appears on the letter written by her brother was: Manor Farm, Nether Poppleton, Yorkshire.

Elizabeth 'Ellie' Porter
Born c1899, died February 4th 1918

Ellie was the eldest daughter of Mr James Dawson Porter and Mrs Annie Catherine Porter, (Sub-Postmaster at Eskdale) born in Eskdale, Cumbria. Ellie was killed in a tragic accident at Henhull Hall Training Farm, (the County Council Training School) Nantwich, Cheshire on the 4th February 1918 aged just 19 whilst serving in the Women's Land Army. She had arrived at the training centre on the 7th January and had almost completed her training. Ellie appears to have been an impeccable student in every way; a competent girl who was strong and healthy.

Mr and Mrs Porter were not present at the inquest as they were travelling to Nantwich.

The accident happened whilst Ellie and another girl were leading a horse and cart that was carrying mangolds. As they all passed through a gate, Ellie cut the corner and was crushed between the gatepost and the shaft of the cart. Whilst learning to drive carts, she had been told how to safely approach gates.

The other girl did not witness the accident happen but heard Ellie groan and on turning around, saw her on the ground. She also noticed that the end of the shaft had not come through the gate. The behaviour of the horse did not appear to be a contributing factor.

Ellie was carried immediately back to the farm where she remained unconscious for half an hour. She regained consciousness briefly and was able to say what had happened but was clearly not going to survive her injuries. The cart shaft had jammed her against the gatepost causing enormous pressure on her back which resulted in internal ruptures and severe haemorrhage. A doctor was sent for and he arrived just after 5pm. Sadly, Ellie died at about 5.20pm that afternoon.

Ellie's coffin was covered with a Union Jack and placed on a lorry. It was drawn to the railway station by one of the farm horses. The lorry was then followed by her parents, Mr Bolderstone, (the Farm Manager) and fellow Land Girl students. Her parents brought her body home on the last train to Ravenglass on the 6th February, arriving at midnight. On the 7th February, Ellie's funeral took place at St Catherine's

Church in Boot. Her coffin was brought to the church on a cart and her family followed in a car. Two Land Army girls from Santon Bridge also attended, along with some schoolchildren and their teachers from the local school. One of Eskdale's daughters was being given a fitting farewell.[10]

Ellie was finally laid to rest at St Catherine's Church. Her gravestone boldly and proudly states that she had served in the Women's land Army during the Great War. It is rare to see a private gravestone that mentions such service.

Ellie is also commemorated on the war memorial at Eskdale. The memorial was first dedicated on the 16th May 1920. Ellie's father attended the second dedication and unveiling of the War Memorial on the 10th April 1949. He was the oldest person in the dale to have lost a daughter during the Great War.

Some letters survive, written by Ellie's father regarding the request for a photograph, (which was to be part of the Women's War Work Collection).

A letter dated the 12th November 1918, was written to the Hon. Secretary, Women's Work Sub-Committee which explained the intentions of Ellie's father James. Mr Porter stated that no photograph had in fact been taken of Ellie wearing her Women's Land Army uniform. Instead, only photographs of her as a young child or in a family group existed. It was intended that a portrait was to be painted of Ellie by a family friend. Rather poignantly, Ellie's sister was going to sit for the painting. The portrait was not being started until the New Year. On its completion, Mr Porter said that he would send a photograph of the painting in order that it could be added to the collection.[11]

A further letter, dated the 4th December 1919, written by Ellie's father James included the long-awaited photograph of the painting of Ellie by family friend and artist, Mrs Fowler. Mr Porter had also enclosed a newspaper cutting which included all the details of Ellie's death and funeral. The letter is heartrending as he says how much of a likeness to Ellie the artist has managed to capture in the painting. Clearly, it had been difficult to get the painting completed as the artist lived some distance away hence the delay in sending the photograph.

The sheer pride and determination to have Ellie included in the collection is palpable in the letters he wrote.[12]

Violet Mabel Randall

Violet was only 18 years old when she died. She had been working in a harvest field at Coales, near Peterborough. She was driving a farm cart past a motor car when the horse became startled and she was thrown to the ground. The cart passed over her and she died shortly afterwards.

Miss Winifred Sims
Wiltshire Women's Land Army

Winifred trained at Patney and worked on farms at Coulston and Erlestoke. She died of influenza. Her funeral was at Steeple Ashton and several of Winifred's Land Army friends and other landworkers formed a poignant yet fitting guard of honour outside the church.

In grateful remembrance.

Women who died whilst serving their country in the Women's Forage Corps, (RASC).

Baling hands

May Victoria Bishop

May's next of kin was her mother, Mrs Bishop, Pike Fish Farm, Yalding, Kent.

Daisy Kate Clarke

Daisy's next of kin was recorded as Mrs Sarbutt, 17 Sandringham Road, Lowestoft.

Gertrude Coles

Gertrude's next of kin was recorded as Mrs Stephenson, 5 Francis Place, St James, The Barton, Bristol.

Bessie B. George

Bessie died of meningitis. Her next of kin were her parents, Mr and Mrs George, 21 Albion Hill, Brighton.

Annie Howe

Annie's next of kin was recorded as Mrs Potts, Chapel House Farm Cottages, Scotswood-on-Tyne.

Lilian L. Kane

Lilian died of influenza. Her next of kin was recorded as Mrs Kane, 20 Arthur Street, Hove.

Margaret Amelia Johncock
Born 1897, died 1918

Margaret died of influenza contracted on duty aged just 22 whilst serving in the Forage Corps at West Ashford, Kent. She was born at Thanet, Kent. Margaret's next of kin was recorded as Mr Johncock, 6 Church Square, Broadstairs.

Ethel Rosetta Smith

Ethel's mother was recorded as her next of kin at 26 Melbourne Road, West Bridgeford, Nottingham. On a corrective record, stamp-dated 5th/6th September 1919: Nominal Roll for Issue of Memorial Scroll and Plaque, her Regimental Number is listed as simply Y.5.

Elsie E. Williams

Elsie's mother was recorded as her next of kin at 7 Cyrils Place, Blana Road, Abertillery.

Elsie E. Wiltshire

Elsie's next of kin was her mother, Mrs Wiltshire, 24 London Road, Swindon. The formal letterhead shows the address of the Women's Work Sub-Committee, Imperial War Museum, Queen Anne's Gate, Westminster, SW1.

This standard letter starts with Sir or Madam. The words "Sir or" have been crossed out in this instance as the intended recipient is Elsie's mother. There is a blank space into which is handwritten the name of the bereaved parent, husband or loved one. It is very impersonal and the lack of sensitivity must surely have been noticed by those that sadly received it.

Store Hands

Julia Winifred Knight

Julia died of pneumonia contracted whilst serving in the Forage Corps. Julia's next of kin was her mother, Mrs Knight, 54 Lamport Street, (off Warwick Street) Liverpool. On a corrective record stamp-dated 5th/6th September 1919: Nominal Roll for Issue of Memorial Scroll and Plaque, her Regimental Number is listed as H.6126.

Another rather curious letter survives, written by Julia's mother Alice. Although Alice is clearly able to write, she is not able to express herself competently. Alice appears to refer to an occasion where a legal representative informed her about a will connected to her late daughter Julia. She had heard nothing since and she was writing to enquire if any assistance could be provided on the matter.[13]

The reply that came from the Hon. Secretary Women's Work Committee, dated 8th October 1919 was unable to assist Alice with her enquiry but instead provided an address whereby she might be able to gain further assistance.

Mary Ann Whaley

Mary Ann died of influenza. Her next of kin was her father, Mr Thomas Whaley, 10 East Terrace, Cardiff.

HT Driver
Kathleen Mary Clayton Smith

Kathleen's next of kin were recorded as Mr and Mrs Clayton Smith, 42 Brentford Road, Romford, Essex.

Quarter Mistress
Edith Bettis
Born 1893, died 1918

Edith was born in Southend, Essex. Her next of kin was recorded as Mrs Bettis, 31 Colchester Road, Prittlewell, Rochford, Southend-on-Sea.

Corporal
Ada A. Palmer

Ada's next of kin was recorded as Mrs England, 5 Horsepond, Friarn Street, Bridgwater.

Assistant Forwarding Supervisor
Clara Mildred Hancock

Clara died of influenza, contracted whilst on duty. Her next of kin was her father, Hancock Esq, Roodport, Transvaal, South Africa.

Forwarding Supervisor
Eva E. Gates
Died 28th June 1919

Eva had appendicitis and died after an operation. Her next of kin was recorded as S. Sergeant Gates, c/o DPOS Beds. 24 Rothsay Road, Bedford. Eva appeared to have also served in the Women's Land Army at some point too.

Area Inspector of Women
Ellen Ingrey Green
Died 4th November 1918

Ellen died of influenza after a short illness whilst serving in Exeter, Devon. Her husband Frank S. Green was recorded as her next of kin and their address was Archery Road Hostel, Eltham, SE9.

Ellen's husband was the former manager of the Prince's Theatre, Park Row in Bristol. Her father George was the conductor of the orchestra at the theatre. Ellen's brother, (also called George) succeeded his father in the same post! Theatre was clearly in Ellen's blood but she answered the call to work during the Great War in the Forage Corps.

No deaths are recorded for women who served in the Forestry or Timber cutting sections on the Women of The Empire - WW1 Screen at York Minster.

For those women that time has forgotten......

In grateful remembrance.

Women who died whilst serving their country in the Forestry and Timber cutting sections.

Chapter 17

Demobbed and beyond: Carry on. Hold on. Look on.

As demobilisation loomed on the horizon, there were many avenues that a competent and aspirational Land Girl could consider. The pull of adventure saw emigration appeal to many, setting up a smallholding was another option and marriage beckoned for others.

In early 1919, it was suggested that 5% of Land Girls wanted to emigrate and set up poultry or livestock farms in countries like Canada and Australia. Some women had relatives or family overseas so there was an added incentive to try and carve a life out somewhere else. The thought of returning to a life of domesticity or their old pre-war life in whatever form that took, (having gained many new skills and enjoyed a fulfilling experience) filled many women with dread.

Emigration was potentially financially lucrative but it initially required some personal financial capital to be invested by each woman. Women could potentially earn £3-£4 a week in Canada and Australia but additional training had to be completed first. That role was taken on by the Women's National Land Service Corps. To prepare women for what lay ahead would take between three to six months.

A specific training centre was established for would be emigrants under the supervision of a woman who had first-hand experience of working on farms in different countries. A model farm was set up and run along the same lines, (apart from the climate) to enable the prospective farmers to become accustomed to what lay ahead.

In the spring of 1919, an amusing story appeared about how demobbed female war workers had created a surge in demand for daintier underwear.[1]

Their national service had clearly deprived them of the necessity to wear pretty undergarments, so when demobilisation came, the immediate sense of release felt by the women caused a surge in sales. High-end department stores in the West End of London filled their shop windows with displays of expensive silk in various delicate colours to attract customers.[2]

How welcome it would have been for these women of all ages to finally shrug off the rather drab colours and shapeless fits of the war uniforms and enjoy the feel of silk again, (if they could afford it).

Protocol had been followed throughout the war in order to achieve common goals. Rules and regulations were adhered to in order for the multitude of jobs to be carried out seamlessly. One of the characters in a contemporary novel written by Berta Ruck made the point that during times of war, it was necessary to forfeit the luxuries that one might have got used to. It was now time to dress accordingly, in order to be able to efficiently carry out the manual work that needed to be done.[3]

Whatever path was decided upon, the implications would be far-reaching. Families, friends and sweethearts would all have been affected. The lure of 'what could be' combined with the inevitable pull back to 'what had been' would be strong in equal measure. It was therefore courageous to move beyond demobilisation and walk on yet another untrodden path. Many felt that they were living in and moving through a period of immense change and yet it was a time that also brought about great opportunity. Everyone had pulled-together to save their nation and the varied uniforms of the land organisations stood proudly alongside the military khaki; colours that were an outward display of the unified efforts of a country doing everything in its power to secure freedom and see an end to the war.[4]

It is clear that their national contribution was held in high esteem, respected and admired by a grateful country and it was soon recognised that their skills and expertise needed to be harnessed and propelled forwards in a unified way after the official demobilisation date.

The National Association of Landswomen was therefore established to do just that. By fostering the professionalism and garnering it collectively into a worthwhile organisation, it would be viewed as current, progressive and forward thinking.

There was a need to seize the moment and maintain momentum in order to 'catch' women who might, given too much time, just turn their back on agriculture altogether, forever.

The spirit of friendship, camaraderie and the cross-class nature of the Women's Land Army saw bonds formed that for some, continued long after the war had ceased. The friendships that women made had shown to the public the wider rationale behind such a crucial organisation; a rationale that needed to continue to foster such varied assets in a positive way and keep women interested in the very things they had felt the need to leave their old lives to do in the first instance.

The demobilisation of the Women's Land Army was felt very deeply both by individuals and by the nation who had grown to respect and enjoy the revitalising presence of Land Girls in the countryside. It was therefore important to provide a smooth transition into the National Association of Landswomen for those that expressed interest.

By February 1919, 5421 members of the Women's Land Army had indicated that they wanted to remain in agriculture and 3278 had declined. Clearly, there was still a lot more that needed to be done to either persuade them to remain or retrain.

The first woman from East Kent that emigrated overseas was an L.A.A.S girl, (Land Army Agricultural Service) called Miss Longman. She sailed for Canada on September 17th 1919 in order to continue working in farming with her family.

The genuine feeling of loss felt by the nation was also reflected in the warm, respectful and personal eulogical articles written by the President of the Board of Agriculture and Fisheries and the Right Honorable, The Lord Ernle.

"The Land Army may be justly proud of its service. It has proved its grit."[5]

Begrudging praise, but praise nonetheless from farmers perhaps veiled the extent of the true admiration and respect they now had for the women who had stepped forward to lessen one of the nation's biggest wartime problems.

Any woman that had joined a land organisation or the Women's Land Army broke free of the last remnants of Edwardian society with its strict class boundaries and stifling conventions. Women frequently defied the wishes of their family and societal expectations in order to serve; shocked parents were often helpless to stop their daughter from joining what was then an 'unknown' army. As time progressed however, even the most sceptical of parents saw just how important the work was and the positive changes that such work brought to the physical and mental wellbeing of those women of all ages that bravely joined up.

The nation was grateful indeed. More than it could ever have realised.

Epilogue

Land Girls worked for little reward, often in very remote parts of the country. They carried out their work tirelessly, for a small wage without ceremony. Many people witnessed them hard at work and admired them for their diligent nature and devotion to service. Some felt compelled to write to newspapers to share their feeling of pride having seen the efforts being quietly made by these women all over the land.[1]

For the vast majority of women that volunteered to do National Service, they withstood challenges with enthusiasm and bore countless difficulties with a quiet dignity. Years of war had moulded them into completely different individuals from those that had gone about their business during peacetime. Prolonged conflict and the necessity to 'do your bit' for your country saw most women blossom into competent members of any organisations they joined.

Despite the unattractive wage, (when compared to other women's auxiliary services) if women joined the Women's Land Army, they were organised well but were worked hard.[2]

The forbearance shown by Land Girls from the earliest origins of the various landworker organisations helped stay the country during years of great instability and turmoil.

Living in a country at war meant that many unexpected and sudden changes simply had to be absorbed and worked through. Women of all ages showed an immediate willingness to alter their priorities in life, putting on hold successful careers or taking a leap into the unknown. They did so with unflinching energy, a zest for life and a 'do or die' attitude.

They had a natural ability to make the best of any bad situation and what they did remains relevant more than a century on. These women are worthy role models. With their effervescent spirit, sound principles and values, they have endured by leaving behind a mettlesome legacy.

Their attitude and approach to challenging tasks saw them sing, tease and rib each other as they worked. The outdoor life, although hard to tolerate at times was also invigorating and character-building. Land Girls' spirits generally remained high, weak muscles soon became strong and any joints that were stiff or limbs that were sore eventually became supple over time. There simply wasn't time to moan or be petty. A grumble 'on the quiet' may have been allowed – but it was crucial to stick at the task in hand no matter what![3]

It wasn't just those that observed these women that saw the need to be grateful for their efforts. The need to record and remember what they had accomplished was at the forefront of many a Land Girl's mind too, especially after demobilisation. One Land Girl intended to frame a letter received from Miss Meriel Talbot along with her armlet and badges for posterity. This official acknowledgement of service was obviously treasured. Recognition of any kind was important, welcomed and valued.

Land Girls had not sought reward(s) for their war service but recognition, (at the very least) for their efforts. Whatever form it manifested itself in, it was always appreciated. It was immaterial which land organisation a woman had been part of or had gone on to join, it was the fact that the nation was now aware of some of the individual sacrifices each woman had made in order to serve in such mould-breaking organisations.[4]

The individual stories of Great War Land Girls have travelled by-and-large unobtrusively through the intervening decades without fuss or ceremony.

Their mission was indeed a quiet one.

Bibliography

Adie, Kate, Fighting on the Home Front. The legacy of women in World War One (Hodder and Stoughton, 2013).

Butler, Simon, Land Girl Suffragette. The extraordinary story of Olive Hockin (Halstar, 2016).

Chapman, Terry, The First World War on the Home Front (André Deutsch, 2014).

Greaves, Simon, The Country House at War: Fighting the Great War at home and in the trenches (The National Trust, 2014).

Judd, D. A, Living in the country: Life in rural Northamptonshire from before the First World War (Judd Publishing, 1991).

Lawley, Eric, A Year on the Farm (Chedham's Yard 2014).

Martin, Brian P, Tales of the old countrywomen (David and Charles PLC, 1997).

Marwick, Arthur, Women at War 1914-1918 (Fontana Paperbacks, 1977).

Sawford, Philip, Northampton. Remembering 1914-18. Great War Britain (The History Press, 2015).

Shewell-Cooper, W. E, Land Girl. A manual for volunteers in the Women's Land Army 1941 (Amberley, 1941, 2011).

Storey, Neil R, Housego, Molly, Women in The First World War (Shire, 2010).

Storey, Neil R, Housego, Molly, The Women's Land Army (Shire, 2012).

The National Roll of The Great War 1914-1918, Section XII. Bedford and Northampton.

Thomas, Maurice, Do you remember what Granny told you about the Women's Land Army? (Percy Gilkes Printers, Banbury).

Twinch, Carole, Women on the land (The Lutterworth Press, 1990).

Van Emden, Richard & Humphries, Steve, All Quiet on the Home Front. An oral history of life in Britain during the First World War (headline, 2003).

White, Bonnie, The Women's Land Army in First World War Britain (Palgrave Macmillan, 2014).

Sources: Articles, journals, magazines and newspapers

East Midlands History and Heritage, Issue 8, January 2019, p22-p25.

Hilary, M. K, The Women's Land Army: Gender, Identity and Landscapes, (West Michigan University, 2014).

The Landswoman magazine - various months during 1918, 1919 and 1920, (Successor rightsholder unknown).
The Northampton Independent, 9 March 1918, p10 and p11.
Weedon Deanery Parish Magazine, September 1916.

British Library, London

British Library interview: Florrie Dundee, (Southampton resident interviewed by Jean Berry) 1983-09-09.

Imperial War Museum, London

Private diary written by Miss Beatrice Bennett containing details of her service with the Women's Land Army, accommodation, training and duties on a farm at Tonbridge, Kent and also her work with the Women's Timber Corps at Chilgrove Camp. Documents 2762. Undated but possibly written between December 1917 - February 1918.

Two letters written by the father of Elizabeth 'Ellie' Porter, Mr James Porter to the Hon. Secretary Women's Work Sub-Committee. Imperial War Museum archive reference: EN1/3/DEA/019/15 and EN1/3/DEA/019/17.

Northamptonshire Archives

Northamptonshire Record Office. Board of Agriculture and Fisheries. Report of a Conference between Representatives of County Committees and The Right Hon. The Earl of Selborne, KG, GCMG, President of the Board of Agriculture and Fisheries on: "Women's Labour on the Land." Friday, 31st December 1915, p6 and p13. (Box 4209, Document 13).

Northamptonshire Records Office: Sources booklet online, WW1 pdf. Box X3672, Box 4209.

St Hilda's College, Oxford archive

The documents used and photographs published in this book from this archive are by kind permission of the Principal and Fellows' of St Hilda's College, Oxford.

Grateful thanks to the Archivist of St Hilda's College, Oxford, Mr Oliver Mahony for his assistance with sourcing and providing relevant material from this archive for use in my book.

Group photograph showing the principal and students of St Hilda's, 1916. [Reference: 26/2: Box 1a]

Interview with Eleanor Marguerite Verini. Interview date, 10th November 1986. [SA 1 A9 A&B]

Letter dated the 6th of April 1952 from Lorna Howell, [St Hilda's 1914] to the former Principal of St Hilda's, Miss Burrows. [Reference: 26/4: Box 8b]

Photograph album belonging to St Hilda's Hall student Lorna Howell.

Vacation work on a Northamptonshire farm. Farming party: M Shufeldt, K Gibberd, L Howell, R Woodthorpe, S Macey, G Jones [and K Kempthorne]. [Reference 26/5: Box 8d]

Poem called 'Farming Song' written in 1916 by one of the students from St Hilda's Hall who worked on the land during their summer vacation at Brockhall, Northamptonshire. [Reference: 26/4: Box 8b]

St Hilda's Hall Students' War Work. List of students and their war work, October 1916. [BURR 029/20]

The St Hilda's Hall Oxford Report 1915-1916, p11, [PUB 001/18]

Online sources

blogs.loc.gov (search Women's Land Army of America).
www.britishnewspaperarchive.co.uk
www.hertsmemories.org.uk (search Women, Food and Farming in WW1 by Jennifer Ayto).
history.blog.gov.uk ("A Call to the Women of Great Britain" Pre-Women's Land Army: Women Land Workers, 1915-1916).
www.iwm.org.uk (Imperial War Museum).
www.marthamnorfolk.co.uk (search Blanche Garman).
www.smithsonianmag.com (search farmerettes).
www.womenslandarmy.co.uk
ww1centenary.oucs.ox.ac.uk (search The Land Girls of the First World War).
yorkminster.org (Five Sisters Window).

Notes

Introduction: Mud, filth and clouds!

1. E. S. Wilkinson, Blackwood's Magazine, (originally called Edinburgh Monthly Magazine) 'Our Land Days. II. The Call Of The Land' (January 1919), p71.

Chapter 1: Adequate replacements

1. E. S. Wilkinson, Blackwood's Magazine, 'Our Land Days. XIV. Looking Back' (March 1919), p366.
2. Newcastle Journal, 7 May 1917, p3.
3. Women's Land Army L.A.A.S Handbook, July 1919, p24.
4. John Bull, 8 November 1919, p2.
5. Ibid.
6. Cambridge Independent Press, 3 August 1917, p6.
7. The Landswoman, 1 October 1919, p242.
8. Globe, 24 October 1916, p7.
9. Nottingham Journal, 15 January 1919, p3.
10. Private Papers of Miss B Bennett - IWM Catalogue number: Documents. 2762.
11. Cambridge Daily News, 5 January 1918, p3.
12. The Landswoman, 1 September 1918, p196.
13. The Landswoman, 1 September 1918, p194.
14. Northampton Chronicle and Echo, 6 June 1916, p2.
15. Northampton Chronicle and Echo, 16 June 1916, p4.

Chapter 2: The awakened women

1. Dundee People's Journal, 17 June 1916, p1.
2. The Graphic, 22 July 1916, p120.

3. The Landswoman, 1 May 1918, p106
4. Worthing Gazette, 8 May 1918, p6.
5. The Graphic, 22 July 1916, p120.
6. The Landswoman, 1 May 1918, p106.
7. The Landswoman, 1 January 1919, p7.
8. Western Chronicle, 7 December 1917, p4.
9. The Landswoman, 1 January 1919, p19.
10. Ibid.
11. Ibid.

Chapter 3: Pluck and patriotism

1. Staffordshire Advertiser, 2 February 1918, p4.
2. Western Daily Press, 17 November 1917, p7.
3. E. S. Wilkinson, Blackwood's Magazine, 'Our Land Days. XII. The Crux Of The Year' (February 1919), p227.
4. The Landswoman, 1 March 1918, p46.
5. Sheffield Daily Telegraph, 9 May 1918, p3.
6. Surrey Mirror, 20 June 1919, p7.
7. Wiltshire Times and Trowbridge Advertiser, 3 November 1917, p5.
8. The Landswoman, 1 March 1919, p51.
9. E. S. Wilkinson, Blackwood's Magazine, 'Our Land Days. XIV. Looking Back' (March 1919), p363.
10 Leeds Mercury, 12 February 1919, p9.
11. Sheffield Daily Telegraph, 4 October 1919, p7.
12. Western Times, 19 April 1918, p3.
13. Sheffield Independent, 29 January 1919, p7.
14. Globe, 12 January 1918, p7.
15. Sheffield Independent, 29 January 1919, p7.
16. Evening Mail, 3 July 1916, p8.
17. The Sphere, 13 October 1917, p36.
18. Ibid.
19. Sheffield Independent, 29 January 1919, p7.
20. Vote, 14 February 1919, p6.
21. E. S. Wilkinson, Blackwood's Magazine, 'Our Land Days. XII The Crux Of The Year' (February 1919) p225.

22. Dundee Courier, 28 February 1917, p2.
23. Sussex Daily News, 28 February 1917, p6.
24. Daily News, 13 September 1918, p7.

Chapter 4: Strength in unity

1. The Sketch, 7 April 1915, p11.
2. Common Cause, 13 August 1915, p1.
3. West Sussex Gazette, 26 October 1916, p3.
4. The Sketch, 29 January 1919, p132.
5. E. S. Wilkinson, Blackwood's Magazine, 'Our Land Days. VI Fresh Fields' (January 1919) p77.
6. Dundee People's Journal, 20 November 1915, p7.
7. Western Chronicle, 5 July 1918, p3.

Chapter 5: Infra dig!

1. Yorkshire Post and Leeds Intelligencer, 15 June 1916, p4.
2. St Hilda's Hall, Oxford Report 1915-1916, PUB001/18.
3. Illustrated War News, 11 October 1916, p36.
4. Bromyard News and Record, 21 September 1916, p4.
5. Ibid.
6. Illustrated War News, 11 October 1916, p36.
7. Weedon Deanery Parish Magazine, September 1916, p3.
8. The full six verses of the poem are reproduced by kind permission of the Principal and Fellows of St Hilda's College, Oxford.
9. The Scotsman, 17 April 1916, p7.

Chapter 6: The picturesque garb

1. Maidstone Telegraph, 2 September 1916, p8.
2. The Daily Mirror, 31 August 1916, p2.
3. Gloucester Journal, 20 October 1917, p8.
4. Illustrated War News, 23 August 1916, p34.
   Lincolnshire Echo, 17 April 1916, p2.
5. E. S. Wilkinson, Blackwood's Magazine, 'Our Land Days. III The Beginning Of It' (January 1919) p73.
6. Nottingham Journal, 5 September 1919, p4.

7. Daily Mirror, 17 March 1919, p5.
8. Northampton Mercury, 31 March 1916, p2.
9. The Sketch, 14 February 1917, p150.
10. E. S. Wilkinson, Blackwood's Magazine, 'Our Land Days. III The Beginning Of It' (January 1919) p73.
11. Daily Mirror, 11 January 1917, p7.
12. John Bull, 20 July 1918, p4.
13. Ibid.
14. Western Daily Press, 17 November 1917, p7.
15. Yorkshire Evening Post, 31 January 1919, p6.

Chapter 7: Billets from hell

1. Northampton Mercury, 12 April 1918, p6.
2. Gentlewoman, 1 June 1918, p2.
3. The Essex Newsman, 17 June 1916, p1.
4. Ibid.
5. Globe, 20 April 1916, p3.
6. The Landswoman, 1 February 1920, p45.
7. Sheffield Daily Telegraph, 9 May 1918, p3.
8. Evening Mail, 2 June 1916, p8.
9. The Landswoman, 1 October 1919, p241.
10. Western Daily Press, 17 November 1917, p7.
11. Ibid.
12. Evening Mail, 3 July 1916, p8.
13. Ibid.
14. Ibid.
15. Oxford Chronicle and Reading Gazette, 27 October 1916, p4.
16. John Bull, February 1919, p7.
17. Ibid.
18. Aberdeen Press and Journal, 30 September 1918, p5.
19. Bournemouth Guardian, 4 May 1918, p8.
20. Illustrated Sporting and Dramatic News, 8 April 1916, p158.
21. The Penrith Observer, 20 August 1918, p3.
22. The Landswoman, 1 November 1918, p240.
23. The Penrith Observer, 20 August 1918, p3.

24. Illustrated War News, 16 May 1917, p34.
25. Ibid.
26. Women's Land Army L.A.A.S Handbook in the, 'Copy of the New Terms and Conditions of Service' section, p10.
27. The Landswoman, 1 February 1919, p47.
28. The Landswoman, 1 January 1919, p7.

Chapter 8: Wasp stings and weary heads!

1. The Landswoman, 1 August 1918, p13
2. Wiltshire Times and Trowbridge Advertiser, 24 November 1917, p9.
3. Western Daily Press, 17 November 1917, p7.
4. E. S. Wilkinson, Blackwood's Magazine, 'Our Land Days.' X. Chiefly Concerning Sam' (January 1919), p85.
5. E. S. Wilkinson, Blackwood's Magazine, 'Our Land Days. XIV. Looking Back' (March 1919), p364.
6. Ibid.
7. Western Daily Press, 30 January 1918, p2.
8. Ibid.
9. E. S. Wilkinson, Blackwood's Magazine, 'Our Land Days. VII – Winter's Jobs' (January 1919), p80.
10. Western Daily Press, 30 January 1918, p2.
11. E. S. Wilkinson, Blackwood's Magazine, 'Our Land Days. VII – Winter's Jobs' (January 1919), p80.
12. Western Daily Press, 30 January 1918, p2.
13. E. S. Wilkinson, Blackwood's Magazine, 'Our Land Days. VIII – Spring Sowing' (January 1919), p82.
14. Leeds Mercury, 1 November 1918, p6.
15. Globe, 20 April 1916, p3.
16. Sussex Agricultural Express, 13 June 1919, p7.
17. Coventry Herald, 22 December 1917, p6.
18. Western Daily Press, 17 November 1917, p7.
19. The Leeds Mercury, 17 December 1917, p5.
20. Illustrated War News, 8 August 1917, p34.
21. Western Daily Press, 17 November 1917, p7.

22. Ibid.
23. Ibid.
24. Western Daily Press, 30 January 1918, p2.
25. Western Daily Press, 30 January 1918, p7.
26. L.A.A.S Handbook, p9.
27. Letter from Edith Lyttelton, Deputy Director, Women's Branch, Board of Agriculture and Fisheries, Food Production Department to Lady Exeter. 21 November 1918. Box: X3672A, ref: YZ9619. Northampton Records Office.
28. Sussex Agricultural Express, 13 June 1919, p7.

Chapter 9: Quirks, oddities and curiosities!

1. The Landswoman, 1 May 1918, p106.
2. E. S. Wilkinson, Blackwood's Magazine, 'Our Land Days. II The Call Of The Land' (January 1919), p72.
3. The Landswoman, 1 January 1919, p7.
4. The Landswoman, 1 February 1919, p27.
5. The Landswoman, 1 March 1918, p45.
6. Ibid.
7. Ibid.
8. Western Daily Press, 30 January 1918, p2.
9. The Landswoman, 1 May 1918, p96.
10. Illustrated London News, 8 November 1919, p33.
11. Yorkshire Evening Post, 20 September 1918, p4.
12. Western Daily Press, 30 January 1918, p2.
13. Liverpool Echo, 17 July 1917, p2.
14. The People, 24 March 1918, p5.
15. The Sketch, 20 December 1916, p250.
16. The Landswoman, 1 April 1919, p89.
17. The Landswoman, 1 March 1919, p26.
18. Essex Newsman, 17 June 1916, p1.
19. E. S. Wilkinson, Blackwood's Magazine, 'Our Land Days. XI Early Summer and Haytime' (February 1919) p225.

Chapter 10: Unshakeable camaraderie

1. L.A.A.S Handbook, p5.
2. Mid Sussex Times, 4 November 1919, p3.
3. Ibid.
4. Mid Sussex Times, 27 May 1919, p8.
5. The Globe, 27 November 1919, p6.
6. Mid Sussex Times, 27 May 1919, p8.
7. Evening Mail, 3 July 1916, p8.
8. The Globe, 12 January 1918, p7.
9. The Landswoman, 1 October 1919, p237.
10. The Landswoman, 1 October 1919, p241.
11. Ibid.
12. Nottingham Journal, 31 December 1918, p2.
13. Ibid.
14. Ibid.
15. Ibid.
16. Ibid.
17. Ibid.
18. Hampshire Telegraph, 6 September 1918, p2.
19. Daily Mirror, 9 February 1918, p2.
20. Northampton Mercury, 9 August 1918, p3.
21. Western Times, 23 November 1917, p5.
22. Hampshire Advertiser, 20 July 1918, p6.
23. The Landswoman, 1 December 1918, p50.
24. The Landswoman, 1 January 1918, p9.
25. Ibid.
26. The Landswoman, 1 December 1918, p50.
27. Western Daily Press, 17 November 1917, p7.
28. The Landswoman, 1 December 1918, p50.
29. Wells Journal, 9 June 1916, p3.
30. Common Cause, 7 June 1918, p90.
31. Ibid.
32. Daily News, (London) 30 July 1918, p5.
33. Illustrated War News, 18 April 1917, p34.

34. Buckingham Advertiser and Free Press, 18 March 1916, p6.
35. The Bioscope, 4 October 1917, p83.
36. Women's Land Army L.A.A.S Handbook, July 1919, p6.
37. Suffolk and Essex Free Press, 8 May 1918, p6.
38. The Landswoman, 1 November 1918, p18.
39. Stonehaven Journal, 22 March 1917, p4.
40. Women's Land Army L.A.A.S Handbook July 1919, p5.
41. The Landswoman, 1 September 1918, p197.
42. The Landswoman, 1 October 1918, p223.
43. The Landswoman, 1 May 1918, p96.
44. Shipley Times and Express, 22 February 1918, p7.
45. The Landswoman, 1 September 1918, p197.

Chapter 11: Farmerettes and friends

1. Illustrated War News, 17 October 1917, p34.
   Common Cause, 13 September 1918, p251.
2. The Landswoman, 1 February 1919, p26.
3. Birmingham Daily Gazette, 30 April 1919, p1.
4. Common Cause, 13 September 1918, p251.
5. The Landswoman, 1 February 1919, p27.
6. The Cornishman, 28 January 1915, p2.
7. Ibid.
8. Shipley Times and Express, 22 March 1918, p3.

Chapter 12: Royal approval

1. The Landswoman, 1 April 1918, p75.
2. Globe, 5 December 1918, p4.
3. Letter from the Board of Agriculture and Fisheries, Women's Branch, 27th May 1919. Letter from Lady Exeter to Miss Hirst Simpson, the Organising Secretary. Record held at Northampton Record Office.

Chapter 13: An epidemic of marriages!

1. Bromyard News, 23 October 1919, p3.
2. Daily Mirror, 24 August 1918, p2.
3. Sussex Agricultural Express, 14 November 1919, p5.

4. Ibid.
5. Leeds Mercury, 17 December 1917, p5.

Chapter 14: Misbehaving misses

1. Bexhill-on-Sea Observer, 25 August 1917, p7.
2. Women, Farming and Food in WW1: Hertfordshire Memories. Reference: HALS/AEC/7
3. Ibid.
4. Caernarvon and Denbigh Herald, 17 August 1917, p6.
5. Northampton Chronicle and Echo, 4 October 1918, p4.
6. Western Daily Press, 12 June 1918, p2.
7. Ibid.
8. Bromyard News, 23 January 1919, p4.
9. Tonbridge Free Press, 25 October 1918, p2.
10. Yorkshire Evening Post, 27 July 1918, p4.
11. Warwick and Warwick Advertiser, 9 November 1918, p2.
12. Taunton Courier and Western Advertiser, 6 August 1919, p2.
13. Ibid.
14. Ibid.
15. Yorkshire Evening Post, 30 August 1918, p5.
16. Ibid.
17. John Bull, 23 November 1918, p12.
18. Dover Express, 4 July 1919, p7.
19. Ibid.
20. Ibid.
21. Ibid.
22. Ibid.
23. Morpeth Herald, 13 December 1918, p6.
24. Ibid.
25. Tonbridge Free Press, 7 November 1919, p3.
26. Ibid.
27. West Sussex County Times, 18 May 1918, p4.
28. Ibid.

29. Evening Herald, (Dublin) 28 February 1918, p3.
30. Ibid.
31. Sheffield Daily Telegraph, 1 November 1919, p5.
32. Hampshire Advertiser, 6 September 1919, p6.

Chapter 15: Respect and recognition

1. The Landswoman, 1 May 1918, p96.
2. Ibid.
3. Sunday Mirror, 21 April 1918, p5.
4. The Sphere, 4 May 1918, p4.
5. Common Cause, 3 November 1916, p371.
6. Buckingham Advertiser and Free Press, 18 March 1916, p6.
7. Ibid.
8. Ibid.
9. Ibid.
10. Common Cause, 3 November 1916, p372.
11. Common Cause, 3 November 1916, p371.
12. Ibid.
13. E. S. Wilkinson, Blackwood's Magazine, 'Our Land Days. XIV Looking Back' (March 1919) p365.
14. E. S. Wilkinson, Blackwood's Magazine, 'Our Land Days. XIV Looking Back' (March 1919) p366.
15. Exeter and Plymouth Gazette, 1 February 1919, p4.
16. Lincolnshire Chronicle, 5 April 1919, p7.
17. Gloucestershire Echo, 27 November 1919, p5.
18. The Landswoman, 1 June 1918, p132.
19. Letter dated 27 May 1919 from the Food Production Department, Women's Branch. From: The Marchioness of Exeter to Miss Hirst Simpson, Organising Secretary. Document held at Northampton Records Office.
20. Vote, 19 December 1919, p434.
21. Letter dated 27 October 1917, (EN1/3/MED/003/1/26) from the IWM, (Secretary of the Women's Section) to Mrs Carey Evans, 10 Downing Street, London.
22. Belfast News-Letter, 14 April 1925, p3.

Recipients of the Distinguished Service Bar.

1. Lichfield Mercury, 28 November 1919, p2.
2. Northampton Mercury, 21 November 1919, p2.
3. Reading Standard, 22 November 1919, p12.

Chapter 16: Self-sacrificing service: The Land Girl Roll of Honour.

1. The Landswoman, 1 April 1919, p88.
2. 'Women's Labour on the Land.' Board of Agriculture and Fisheries. Report of a Conference between Representatives of County Committees, 31 December 1915.
3. The Dundee Courier, 10 May 1919, p7.
4. Dundee Evening Telegraph, 26 June 1919, p3.
5. The Landswoman, 1 October 1919, p242.
6. Western Chronicle, 20 June 1919, p5.
7. Ibid.
8. Information source from: marthamnorfolk.co.uk website.
9. Northampton Mercury, 18 July 1919, p4.
10. Mansergh, Whitehaven in the Great War, Pen and Sword (2015).
11. A letter dated 12 November 1918 to the Hon. Secretary Women's Work Sub-Committee. IWM: EN1/3/DEA/019/17.
12. A letter dated 4 December 1919 also written by Ellie's father James provides further information. IWM: EN1/3/DEA/019/15
13. A letter dated 5 October 1919 written by Mrs Alice Knight. IWM: EN1/3/DEA/019/19.

Chapter 17: Demobbed and beyond: Carry on. Hold on. Look on.

1. Leeds Mercury, 14 March 1919, p9.
2. Ibid.
3. Ibid.
4. Coventry Herald, 5 April 1919, p14.
5. The Landswoman, 1 December 1919, p270.

Epilogue

1. The Sunday Pictorial, 6 October 1918, p9.
2. Derbyshire Advertiser and Journal, 20 December 1919, p15.
3. Coventry Herald, 22 December 1917, p6.
4. Lincolnshire Chronicle, 5 April 1919, p7.